Trauma, Attachment and Family Permanence

DUNDEE

University Library

Trauma, Attachment and Family Permanence

Fear Can Stop You Loving

Edited by Caroline Archer and Alan Burnell for Family Futures

Foreword by Daniel A. Hughes

Jessica Kingsley Publishers
London and New York

First published in the United Kingdom in 2003
by Jessica Kingsley Publishers Ltd
116 Pentonville Road
London N1 9JB, England
and
29 West 35th Street, 10th fl.
New York, NY 10001-2299

www.jkp.com

Copyright © 2003 Jessica Kingsley Publishers

Library of Congress Cataloging in Publication Data

Trauma, attachment, and family permanence: fear can stop you loving/edited by Caroline Archer.
p. Cm
Includes bibliographical references and index
ISBN 1-84310-021-5
1. Psychic trauma in children. 2. Attachment behavior in children. 3. Family--Psychological aspects. I. Archer, Caroline, 1948-
RJ506.P66 T734 2003
618.92'8521--dc21

2002038949

British Library Cataloguing in Publication Data

A CIP catalogue record for this book is available from the British Library

ISBN 1 84810 021 5

Printed and Bound in Great Britain by
Athenaeum Press, Gateshead, Tyne and Wear

Contents

Part II State of the Art: Theory into Practice

Part III State, Community and Family: The Future

Foreword

Dr Daniel A. Hughes

Over the past 50 years, attachment theory has evolved into a primary, if not *the* primary, model of child development throughout the world. Over the past 20 years attachment theory has become an organising principle for development throughout adulthood. Research based on, or heavily influenced by, attachment theory has demonstrated its impact on neuropsychological, emotional, cognitive, and social development throughout the life span. The legacy of John Bowlby and Mary Ainsworth has become both international and multidisciplinary in scope. It continues to generate insights and questions about our human condition that are very clear as well as being profound.

It has only been more recently that practitioners in mental health and social work, education and health, have begun to make serious efforts to understand attachment theory and research and apply these findings to many of the real life problems of our time. Nowhere is the need to make these applications greater than in the areas of child maltreatment, foster care, and adoption. The majority of young children who have been maltreated by their parents manifest attachment disorganisation, a classification considered to be a definite risk factor for the development of psychopathology. A much smaller group is diagnosed with reactive attachment disorder, a disorder thought to arise from severe physical and emotional neglect and multiple caregivers. In both groups the developing child is left with significant deficits in his or her ability and/or readiness to trust and rely on his or her new caregivers. As a result, this child is often neither able to resolve the devastating effects of trauma, nor able to utilise the opportunity to have the attachment security that would facilitate his or her continuing development.

Caroline Archer and core members of the Family Futures Consortium have written a marvellous work that attempts to demonstrate how they have taken insights from attachment theory and research and spread them liberally over their very comprehensive and integrated programmes. This work presents both relevant statistics of maltreatment and adoption and also a detailed description of one unique adoptive family's journey. It discusses finding the right family as well as fully supporting the child and his or her new family. It presents details of psychotherapy unique to this population as well as the need for comprehensive assessments. It presents the psychobiology of both trauma and healing. Throughout these varied and very relevant chapters regarding trauma, attachment, and family permanence, the members of the Family Futures Consortium have been able to remain true to their basic assumption which states: 'A family is the most important resource the child has.' A securely attached individual is known to manifest a 'coherent autobiographical narrative'. Such coherence is difficult to achieve for children exposed to multiple traumas and caregivers, with little continuity from one relationship and experience to the next. The programmes at Family Futures, so well presented in this book, make valiant efforts to provide the comprehensive and integrated experiences and insights necessary for the child to develop coherence in his or her personal life story. I applaud their work, both in its day-to-day expression, and in this book.

Daniel A. Hughes PhD
Clinical Training Consultant to Family Futures
2002

Acknowledgements

We would like to acknowledge the courage of adoptive parents who in taking children into their families have acted in good faith. Despite the many challenges they faced, their commitment and perseverance has confirmed that adoption does provide the best possible opportunity for even the most troubled children. In sharing their experiences with us they have helped to identify weaknesses from the past and map the path of best practice for the future.

The courage of adoptive parents is surpassed only by the courage of the children who have had to leave behind their birth families and take the greatest leap of faith in joining new ones. We would like to acknowledge the hurts, the tragedies, the joys and triumphs over adversity they have sustained. In doing so they have challenged Philip Larkin's poetic admonishment (1996) to avoid handing on human misery by leaving home as early as possible and avoiding family life altogether. Their willingness to share some of 'the drama of adoption' with us offers, instead, great insights and hope for the future global community.

We would like to remember those vulnerable children who did not make it through, or who continue to suffer the long-lasting effects of their early traumatic lives. We remember, too, all the members of birth families who have suffered and lost so much. Let us not allow them to suffer in vain.

Finally, we would like to thank all the other players who have contributed to our therapeutic enterprise and this literary production – both on stage and off. Some, such as Dr Paul Holmes, may have taken some professional risks in supporting our challenges to traditional theory or practice, providing us with inspiration and integrity; some have introduced us to new and unexpected therapeutic horizons, which we have striven to integrate into our therapeutic approach. Meanwhile, our own family members have remained towers of hidden strength, as we felt our way cautiously towards understanding and coherence.

Introduction
A Tapestry of Colours
Caroline Archer

Opening Credits

We are very grateful to Daniel Hughes for agreeing to provide the foreword to our book. Dr Hughes, a renowned clinical psychologist, has himself written two powerful volumes (Hughes 1997, 1998), in which he explores the impact of early separations, losses and maltreatment on the capacities of children to form healthy attachments. In both Dan draws on his own extensive clinical practice, and his sound understanding of developmental attachments, to suggest a framework for effective, therapeutic interventions. In parallel with sustaining his outstanding clinical practice, Dan has taken an active role on the International Board of the Association for Teaching and Training in the Attachment of Children (ATTACh). He is a much sought after trainer of therapists and social workers across the United States, and more recently within Europe, and maintains ongoing consultation with a number of pioneering child care services. Dan became clinical training consultant to Family Futures Consortium in November 2000 and is committed to providing continuing in-service training programmes to child psychotherapists and child care professionals within the United Kingdom, in association with Family Futures.

Square Pegs and Round Holes

This book, like most things of true value, is the product of inspiration, blood, tears and perspiration (though not necessarily in that order). It is not the outcome of a single, analytical mind working in isolation but rather the coming together of a number of creative ones. Such is often the case with enterprises that challenge conventional wisdom: in this case refusing to fit 'square' children, who have experienced early traumatic separations and losses, neglect, abuse, instability or unpredictability, into the 'round' holes of 'normal' families and 'normal' therapies, where they are expected to 'talk the talk' when in developmental terms they have not learned to 'walk the walk'. Instead, a small number of flexible minds from diverse backgrounds, providing each other with vital encouragement and support, set out to explore radical, alternative therapeutic options. These included devising 'square hole' services for 'square' children: embracing adoptive parents as part of the therapeutic team and removing from them the persistent shadow of blame for their children's lack of 'goodness of fit' within their essentially 'round' families (see Chapter 2).

The diverse provenance of the Family Futures team has infused the enterprise with unique vitality but has simultaneously created a dilemma in achieving a concise title for this, our first volume. In order to draw more closely together several distinct strands of theory and practice, we wished to address a broad readership, drawn from disciplines which have traditionally been seen as quite discrete. Since an essential part of our solution to the 'square pegs and round holes' challenge has been to create a multi-faceted 'team solution' it was imperative that we also created a multi-faceted title – yet one which was succinct and did not extend over half the title page! We hope that our integrated approach is reflected in the eventual choice: *Trauma, Attachment and Family Permanence*, which represents a biopsychosocial exploration of the needs of children in permanent substitute families.

Within the text we maintain two 'round hole' devices, for convenience only: electing to refer to children throughout as 'he', to encompass both female and male youngsters, and employing the term 'adoptive families' to indicate 'permanence', including enduring foster placements and those designated 'with a view to adoption'. We make few apologies for the interchangeable use of 'mother' and 'primary caregiver', for if we consider the infant's needs, the mother's primacy is self-evident from the moment of conception. We are, however, aware that there are differences in social caregiving patterns across time, class, culture and geography. Moreover, we acknowledge that the challenges and complexities of creating a single, coherent volume of reasonable proportions mean that, inevitably, there will be many omissions. In particular we have chosen not to address issues of race and culture directly, although we recognise that they are highly relevant to adoption and fostering today. In no way do we wish to minimise the importance of these issues: on the contrary we feel we would be unable to do them justice here. Where we may appear 'ethnicity-blind' we are, in fact, attempting to remain 'ethnicity-neutral', reflecting fundamental and universal patterns of child development, attachment and trauma.

'Fear Can Stop You Loving'

Our subtitle, 'Fear Can Stop You Loving', is taken from the track *Fear and Love*, sung by Morcheeba. We are grateful to songwriters Godfrey and Edwards, Chrysalis Records and Music Sales Ltd for permission to reprint some of the song's lyrics in our book, including the refrain:

> Fear can stop you loving
> Love can stop your fear
> Fear can stop you loving
> But it's not always that clear.

Here the lyricist has intuitively grasped a central aspect of trauma which 'grabs the gut', connecting with something deep, timeless and incontrovertible in our lives: that fear can be so all-engulfing that it obliterates essential interpersonal connections and leaves children feeling hopelessly isolated in an impenetrable world. It is evident that it takes more than inexhaustible patience and endless love for the 'clouds of dust' to settle in the lines 'Got no map to find my way/ Amongst these clouds of dust' and for a child to redraw workable 'route maps of the world'. This is a theme to which I will return in my chapter *Weft and Warp: Developmental Impact of Trauma and Implications for Healing.* However, as we will hear repeatedly from contributors throughout this volume, these ingredients of 'time and love' are undoubtedly essential; without them no therapeutic interventions could hope to succeed.

Through many years of living and working with children in adoptive families I have witnessed the frustrations associated with achieving the seemingly reasonable expectation that even the most traumatised children will engage eventually in healthy family relationships, given sufficient unconditional time and love within a stable family environment. That this expectation is an oversimplification has been explored in some depth by groundbreaking clinicians in the United States, such as Cline (1992), Hughes (1997, 1998), and Levy and Orlans (1998, 2000), over the past twenty years. At home, recent studies by David Howe and associates (Howe 1998; Howe *et al.* 1999) have more than confirmed the profound and long-lasting difficulties of a small but significant minority of children placed in adoptive families. Much has been made of the distorted patterns of attachment that such youngsters display (Fearnley and Howe 1999; Gordon 1999). This issue will be discussed in further depth by several contributors, including Alan Burnell with Caroline Archer in *Setting Up the Loom: Attachment Theory Revisited* and Elsie Price in *The 'Coherent Narrative': Realism, Resources and Responsibility in Family Permanence*. Indeed, the concept of distorted and disorganised attachments has been very helpful in extending our understanding of the inner worlds and the overt behaviours of distressed children – and in effecting appropriate healing interventions.

Recent advances in the field of developmental neurobiology have allowed us to incorporate into this burgeoning sphere of knowledge an awareness of the fundamental biologically-driven systems which underpin our psychological and socio-emotional behaviour. I explore this area in greater detail in *Weft and Warp*, since I believe that it is crucial to the evolution of sophisticated therapeutic interventions for traumatised children and, more vitally, to our children's lasting well being. Here we can begin to make intellectual sense of our 'gut feelings' and find confirmation that neurobiological responses to fear, as with other intense negative affects such as shame, can seriously inhibit a child's capacity to feel safe, secure and nurtured, in very real ways. If a child is persistently being thrown back, from a low base-line of fear (Perry 1995), into the 'fight, flight or freeze' alarm states of his distressed early childhood, he will be unlikely to recognise, or benefit from, the caring and comforting environment into which he is transplanted. Instead he will continue to view the world through 'clouds of dust', lacking the appropriate 'world maps' to find reassurance and security.

From a slightly different perspective, Jaak Panksepp (1998) proposes that there are a number of basic behavioural systems common to all mammals. Citing extensive animal studies, he argues that some of these systems may be mutually exclusive. For example, from observations of the laboratory behaviour of rats, Panksepp demonstrates that the mere odour of cat is enough to inhibit normal rat play and proposes that the affective 'FEAR' circuit (his capitals) will inhibit simultaneous access to the animal's

'PLAY' circuitry. According to Schore (1994), play and playfulness form an integral part of 'primary intersubjectivity' (Trevarthen 1979), that intensely attuned, reciprocal mother-infant relationship from which healthy attachments develop. It therefore makes sense that, where the infant's fear responses are repeatedly being triggered during this critical developmental period, playfulness will be inhibited. As a consequence the child's sense of being loved or loveable will be seriously compromised. The state dependent nature of human learning (Perry *et al.* 1995, Perry 1999) will reinforce this deficit state – and where 'fear can stop you feeling loved' it will certainly stop the loving in return. This knowledge, and its extension to other intense negative affect states, such as grief, anger and shame, forms the basis for much of the innovative work being pioneered by the Family Futures team.

Evolution of the Family Futures' Approach

I first met Alan Burnell, one of the three founders and co-directors of Family Futures Consortium, in the early 1990s, when my four adopted children were still relatively young. My husband and I were seeking additional help for the quite complex long-term difficulties we were experiencing as an adoptive family. Having exhausted our local social work and child and family therapy services, we approached the Post Adoption Centre (PAC) in London (then the only one of its kind in the United Kingdom) with a good deal of trepidation, since we had been hurt, and made to feel culpable for our children's ongoing struggles, on many previous occasions. We were intensely vulnerable, expecting rejection and further hurts. As I was to learn subsequently, this scenario accurately mirrors the traumatised child's early experiences of family life and reflects his expectations of further abandonment and maltreatment within his new adoptive family. I was reminded by Alan only recently of one of my very first questions to him once he had introduced himself as our new post adoption counsellor: 'Are *you* going to kick me in the teeth too?' Instead of dashing our dentures with his lower extremities, this conscientious, self-effacing man opened up a new world to us: a world within which we had choices over the help we received for our family and where what we, as parents, thought and felt was truly valued. This 'radical' perspective has continued to have a profound influence on my life to date.

Several years later, as I continued to grow in confidence and became an increasingly active member of the Adoption UK (then PPIAS) team, I began to explore issues of attachment and post adoption support in greater depth. Simultaneously I became aware that Alan Burnell, now director at the Post Adoption Centre, was seeking to establish a pilot 'parent training' programme for adoptive and permanent foster parents of children with serious attachment difficulties. With the collaboration of PPIAS, I introduced Alan to Christine Gordon, who had been so instrumental in creating and producing our first book of parenting strategies, *'the hedgehog book.'* Together we undertook our first training programme on adoption and attachment. This proved so successful that we ended our six, monthly sessions with more parent participants than when we began! Subsequently, Christine was able to expand the parenting programme for PAC, in collaboration with a small number of social workers from the social work agencies for whom she was providing the training.

Building the Team

More or less concurrently, members of the PAC team, under Alan Burnell's leadership, were exploring sources of funding in order to establish an intensive, therapeutic attachment programme for children in adoptive families. They eventually received financial support for a two-year therapeutic pilot project from the Department of Health. In seeking an expressive, rather than a word-bound, psychotherapist with extensive experience of working with young people and loss, they were extremely fortunate to identify Jay Vaughan, whose original training was in dramatherapy. They were also lucky to obtain the backing of a child psychiatrist, Dr Paul Holmes, who had a background in psychodrama and a strong interest in attachment issues in adoptees. Dr Holmes has maintained his commitment to developing effective services for adoptive families in East Sussex and was pivotal in obtaining Government funding to establish the multidisciplinary Attachment Project in the Brighton and Hove area. He continued to provide vital, ongoing consultation to the Family Futures programme during our first three years.

To complete the original 'attachment team', Alan again invited Christine Gordon and me to provide the experience, understanding and much needed parent support elements to the distressed adoptive parents of children referred to the attachment programme. Whilst family, work commitments and geography precluded me from continuing to take an active part in the project, Christine's presence has proved to be both invaluable and enduring.

The original team of Alan, Jay and Christine eventually went on to found the Family Futures enterprise, once the original funding for the pilot project at PAC had ceased. In time I have been able to rejoin the expanding 'core team' at Family Futures, providing the parent support strand of their therapeutic interventions to families living in Wales.

Since its inception in 1995 the Family Futures team has gradually grown, and its knowledge base and expertise extended, as it continues to be fertilised by new strands of thinking and new challenges from traumatised children and their adoptive families. Griselda Kellie-Smith, with her background in special needs education and integrative arts psychotherapy, and Elsie Price, bringing with her expertise from residential and family placement work, and both make valuable contributions to this book, represent just two of our growing number of core members.

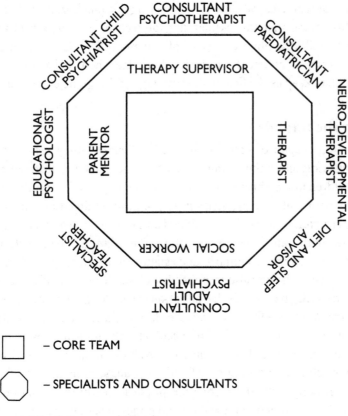

Figure 1.1 Family Futures multidisciplinary team structure

Surrounding the core team there are a number of consultants from health and education to whom we are able to turn for advice and support. These include: Jeanne Magagna, consultant child, adolescent and family psychotherapist at Great Ormond Street Hospital; Dr Deborah Hodes, paediatrician; Dr Ghazala Afzal, consultant adolescent psychiatrist; Dr Maurice Greenberg, adult psychiatrist; Dr Richard Lansdown, educational psychologist, and Dr Daniel Hughes, clinical psychologist and training consultant.

Like Fahlberg's *Residential Treatment: A Tapestry of Many Therapies,* echoing Carole King's hauntingly tuneful lyrics, this blending of textures and shades of thinking provides a colourful, vibrant synthesis, where the whole is greater than the sum of the parts. This is a tapestry in which expertise derived from a wealth of personal, child and family experiences has been interwoven with observation, theory and practice in child and family interventions, combining strands from quite diffuse areas of knowledge to form an intricate and creative backcloth deserving of a much wider audience. It is for this reason that this exhilarating project, of turning a primarily experiential, multidisciplinary voyage of metamorphic discovery into a watertight vessel of coherent words, has been launched. It has been my daunting task to keep us all afloat in the first stage of this grand endeavour.

Weaving the Strands

In the opening chapter of Part I, (*State of Play: Current Theory and Practice*), Adrian Briggs discusses the changing needs of permanently fostered and adopted children in substitute families and the challenges to local authorities and independent child care agencies in responding to alterations in social and family structures. Adrian has combined an extensive career in child care social work with innovative work, alongside Alan Burnell, fostering collaboration between voluntary and statutory services providers in Brighton and Hove; he was also responsible for establishing Family Futures' charitable arm. Adrian contends that adoption can no longer be viewed as an infant placement service for white, middle class, childless couples: a system bound up in secrecy and with the filing cabinet well and truly closed, once the adoption order had been granted. Now we have a multicultural population of children needing new families: youngsters mainly of school age, often bringing with them complex physical, learning or emotional difficulties. The assessment, preparation and ongoing support requirements of the families they join are also being recognised as far more complex. The process of meeting these needs is evolving more slowly, as emphasis and resources begin to shift from preparation, to placement, to permanence and integrated, multi-agency provision, towards planning over the life-span. This theme is continued in *The 'Coherent Narrative'* (Chapter 2), by Elsie Price, now an integral member of the Family Futures team. Elsie explores the value of new approaches to assessing, preparing and supporting 'good enough' families, using attachment-based criteria, and examines models of working that could more effectively meet the challenges of today's children and families.

In *Setting up the Loom* (Chapter 3), Alan Burnell, with Caroline Archer, draws together major strands from attachment theory, developmental psychology and family placement practice to devise a framework for effective interventions. Together they explore how current scientific research validates the intuitive theories of early prominent thinkers like Bowlby and can guide us to 'joined up thinking' and hence influence 'joined up practice'. My individual contribution, in Chapter 4, *Weft and Warp*, is the seriously technical piece – read it slowly but please do read it! Here I take the established theories of attachment and development and interweave them with 'state of the art' knowledge concerning the neurobiology of trauma, its long-term impact on children, and the sophisticated, integrated parenting and therapeutic strategies which are needed to improve the well being of traumatised children. In doing so I attempt to integrate personal and professional experience with good practice and left-brained 'logical' thinking with right-brained 'gut feelings' and intuitive, holistic thought.

Building Bridges

The two concluding chapters in Part I form bridges between the work of the Family Futures' core team and the broader community. First, Jeanne Magagna, currently head of child and adolescent psychotherapy services at Great Ormond Street Hospital and supervisory consultant to Family Futures, constructs a theoretical bridge between traditional psychotherapeutic concepts and the conceptualisations, understanding and practice we are evolving at Family Futures. Thus, in Chapter 5, *Clinical Concepts and Caregiving Contexts*, Jeanne discusses three forms of primitive identification, drawn from psychoanalytic psychotherapy, that are of particular relevance to traumatised children and their substitute families. Finally, Lucy Greenmile's moving account of 'one day in the life of' her adoptive family forms a highly appropriate 'affect bridge' between theory and lived experience. Lucy, who has assumed a pen name to protect the anonymity of her children, paints the only too real picture of chaos, confusion and misunderstandings that characterise life with adopted, traumatised children. It would be tempting to view her story, *A Hard Day's Night*, as extreme but unusual. Sadly it is all too typical of the distressing stories of adoptive and foster families across the United Kingdom that form the basis of the composite family history outlined below.

Setting the Stage

Part II, (*State of the Art: Theory into Practice*), begins with Jay Vaughan's brief outline of Jenny and Marty's Story. Here she sketches the framework for a fictionalised family, representative of many of the families who approach Family Futures for help. Jenny, Marty and their adoptive parents, Mr and Mrs Saunders, are the subjects of the vignettes from which all our contributors draw practical examples in this therapeutic practice section. Readers will build up a more coherent narrative surrounding the Saunders family throughout Part II: it would therefore be advisable to read each chapter in sequence.

Alan Burnell picks up the threads in Chapter 7, *Assessment*, as he addresses the practicalities of obtaining comprehensive and coherent assessments of the child and family's needs. In particular he considers the seven elements of the Family Futures' unique assessment process. These include exploring the child's early history; patterns of attachment and current behavioural difficulties; the adoptive parents' relationships, expectations and current responses to the child; and existing community support networks. This is followed in Chapter 8 by Jay Vaughan and Alan Burnell's *Rationale for the Intensive Programme*, in which they provide convincing arguments for the Family Futures' approach. In *The Drama of Adoption* (Chapter 9), Jay Vaughan outlines some of the dramatic therapeutic interventions she has evolved to work with traumatised children and their adoptive families during the Intensive Programme. She continues this theme in Chapter 10, *The Drama Unfolds*, where she explores the principles and practice of the vital Follow Up Programme for children and families developed by the Family Futures team.

Family Matters

Alan Burnell's final contribution, *Contact as Therapy* (Chapter 11), is a discussion of the potential therapeutic value of contact with birth family members. Drawing on best practice in the mediation of separation, divorce and contact, Alan recognises the need to introduce qualitative considerations, beyond the traditional, quantitative ones (such as 'how often' and 'for how long') into decision making processes for children and families. Alan describes how non-litigious problem solving and effectively mediated 'leave taking' are in children's best interests, enabling adopted and fostered youngsters to 'move on' and really 'join' their new families. Relinquishing families are also seen to benefit from this sympathetic, therapeutic process as they move towards closure of some extremely painful issues.

An integral and integrated part of the Family Futures' approach is the value placed on providing ongoing support and mentoring services for beleaguered parents of traumatised children. In Chapter 12, *Holding the Fort*, Christine Gordon, an experienced adoptive parent and co-director of Family Futures, describes the parent support programme that she has developed within the Family Futures team. Christine discusses its underlying philosophy, that adoptive parents are the single and most valuable therapeutic resource available to traumatised children and that to empower parents to do their job effectively we must first 'nurture the nurturers'. She also considers why traditional behavioural approaches for these children and young people are unlikely to be effective, illustrating this with numerous examples of creative child management strategies that do work and that, simultaneously, encourage healthier attachment relationships within families. In *Hands on Help* (Chapter 13) Christine extends these themes as she describes how the team sustains this vital family support role within the family home, throughout the Follow Up Programme and beyond.

Joined Up Working

Many children with attachment difficulties have accompanying development difficulties. In Chapter 14 Griselda Kellie-Smith considers whether such children have 'difficulty with learning' or are reacting to adversity by 'learning to be difficult'. At Family Futures we have identified typical patterns of learning dysfunction, including dyslexia, dyspraxia, sensory integration problems, poor attention, weak concentration and impulsiveness, that are traceable to the child's early experiences of unpredictability, abuse and neglect. Combining her background in education and her work with dyslexic children and integrative arts psychotherapy, Griselda weaves an additional, vital strand of understanding into this area of concern and explores how networking in the educational field can enhance outcomes for traumatised children. In doing so, she exemplifies the benefits of multi-disciplinary collaboration and the integrated approach to mind and body that are essential if we are to provide such youngsters with real opportunities to learn, both formally at school and informally at home.

A Work in Progress

In Part III (*State, Community and Family: The Future*), Chapter 15 (*Weaving the Threads*), I attempt to draw together many of the strands explored by individual contributors, make new connections and explore new directions. It is this process of bringing together different, but contiguous, areas of expertise that stands out as one of the main strengths of *Trauma, Attachment and Family Permanence*. It is a living process that continues to grow and expand as research and theoretical concepts develop and we learn more from our greatest teachers: the children and families with whom we work. I trust that readers will draw strength and inspiration from our work that, in its turn, will extend their own thinking and creativity in these complex areas of child and family practice.

Whilst we have examined a small and well-defined area of need, our multidisciplinary, attachment and developmentally-based approach has major implications for many services to children and families. Moving away from a 'pathological parenting' model towards a 'pro-parent' relationship model allows caregivers to connect with service providers, relinquish their defensive stance and identify both their weaknesses and their strengths. The process leads to enhanced self-confidence, increased self-efficacy and improved relationships within families. Such a therapeutic approach would be particularly well suited to addressing issues in step-families, other situations where attachments have been interrupted, as through illness and death and, for example, dealing with the protracted and very distressing difficulties faced by families of youngsters with eating disorders. In essence what is being proposed is a 'holding environment' for parents: providing the adult caregivers with a 'secure enough base' from which they can safely explore new ways of interacting with, and relating to, their family environment. What Bowlby believed to be true for young children is equally valid for individuals of all ages, on both the psychosocial and neurobiological levels: that establishing durable, trusted connections with others confers resilience and facilitates flexibility. This highly adaptive process lends itself to meeting the needs of even the most dysfunctional individuals and families, to the greater benefit of themselves and of communities in general.

It is clear from clinical research (Fonagy 2002; Liotti 1995, 1999; Schore 1994, 2001b) that failure to address trauma-related attachment disorganisation leads to serious, enduring mental health problems. We have only to consider the Government's ongoing concerns about 'untreatable' adults with severe personality disorders to recognise the enormous personal, political and economic implications of these distressing, early forming disorders. Dr Bob Johnson (2001), drawing on his innovative psychiatric work with violent offenders, provides 'grounds for optimism' in treating adults with serious personality disorders, exploring the relevant issues in greater depth in *Emotional Health* (2002b). However, as yet, treatment programmes like the one he proposes are neither widely recognised nor understood; it could be many years before effective, appropriate services are generally available for the adult population.

If we are to improve the mental health prospects of traumatised children currently being raised in substitute families, keep them out of residential and secure accommodation during childhood, and out of mental health facilities and the criminal justice system as they approach and move through adulthood, we must acknowledge, identify and work with them as early as possible. This is borne out by cost benefit analyses undertaken by After Adoption, Adoption Forum and Adoption UK as part of their briefing to the House of Lords (2002) and by Knapp, Scott and Davies (1999), in relation to children with anti-social behaviour patterns. The Department of Health also plans to investigate the value of early interventions with parents through the National Institute for Clinical Excellence (Carvel 2002). In advocating early intervention we are able to utilise the period during which youngsters' brains and nervous systems demonstrate greatest plasticity and when opportunities to benefit from 'good enough' attachment relationships are maximised. Although our integrated approach may be costly in terms of initial therapeutic resources and supports, we believe that it will prove to be highly cost-effective, both to individuals and communities over a lifetime: providing families with real and realistic futures.

The connection between physical holding and the 'holding environment' is obvious. Nevertheless, I would like to explore this phenomenon in more detail, in relation to the highly-charged, negative-affect states common to traumatised children (see Chapter 4). It should be self-evident that a body-oriented approach, such as holding, can keep dissociative children 'in their bodies', by providing essential somatic feedback. Fight, flight, freeze and shame responses all demonstrate powerful dissociative qualities, experienced as profound and extreme behavioural states, with unique, state-dependent self-representations, internal working models and metacognitions (Fonagy 2002; Liotti 1999; Putnam 1997). Poor self-regulatory capacities, including the capacity to make transitions from state to state (Putnam 1997; Shirar 1996) render traumatised children highly vulnerable. Even apparently benign circumstances can trigger entry into these extreme states (Perry 1999; van der Kolk 1996c, 1999).

Regular family cradling with committed and attuned adoptive parents provides the child with a 'second chance' to acquire the fundamental physiological regulation which underpins self-awareness and reflective capacities (Archer 1999a, 1999b; Hughes 2002; Levy and Orlans 1998). The child experiencing terror, expressed through active 'fight or flight', is provided with a holding environment within which he can learn to lower his raised blood pressure, heart rate and respiratory rate in attunement with his caregiver. In addition, the rage-filled child can experience the luxury of containment in the hands of a more powerful yet secure and trustworthy adult. He learns that he is not all-powerfully destructive as he fears, nor vulnerable to the hostile behaviours of a 'frightening' adult (see chapters 3, 4 and 5). Conversely, the child who habitually freezes or enters low-arousal shame states, is exposed to the higher, balanced autonomic functioning of his caregiver as he is held close to her heart.

Being held 'in arms' (Levy and Orlans 1998) also provides optimal opportunities for the eye contact that is so vital to attachment (Schore 1994) and to the development of shared mindreading (Baron-Cohen 1999). For the child who manifests shame, the re-energising touch of the caregiver (Schore 1994) is also potentiated by close physical proximity. In addition, I would suggest that the 'frozen' or shame-filled child benefits from the relative invisibility conferred by 'burying himself in his mother's body'. Thus he is able to escape the mortifying 'gaze of the world' (Schore 1994), experience himself truly in his body, and begin to reflect on his emotions (see also Chapter 5). Creating healthier attachment relationships and enhancing self-regulatory, integrative functions can also allow parents and children to approach difficult issues more safely, since the child feels sufficiently contained. Using sensitive attunement, often employing non-verbal cues only possible through the intimacy of touch, it can become possible to explore distressing issues that would otherwise be intolerable to consider, without the youngster becoming psychically overwhelmed, or resorting to somatic dissociation.

The current emphasis on child protection issues places social work practitioners in the invidious position of having to consider the child's best interests, whilst prescribing certain actions of caregivers and proscribing others. Thus advice to adopters of children with challenging behaviours is to avoid physical restraint, instead using the physical separation of 'time out' to allow the child time to calm down and reflect. Ignoring 'bad behaviour' is also frequently advocated. However, traumatised children lack basic self-regulatory and reflective capacities and are therefore unlikely to benefit from these conventional parenting strategies. Instead they are likely to continue to escalate their high arousal, leading to self-harm or destruction of personal property. The isolated child feels out of control and abandoned, replicating the abusive, dysfunctional patterns within his birth family. He is forced, once more, to resort to maladaptive controlling behaviours, including inappropriate self-soothing through emotional or somatic dissociation. Conventional parenting techniques are potentially very abusive for previously maltreated children.

'High risk children' (Cline 1992) demand unconventional, even high risk, solutions. It is a central tenet of the healing arts that the healer should 'do no harm' and take the least intrusive route to recovery. In advocating that parents use 'holding time' (Welch 1988) to provide the additional security and containment their child needs we are advocating 'heart surgery without the knife'. In reparenting traumatised children, parents need to employ patterns of interaction normally associated with much younger children; 'thinking toddler' (Archer 2001) is essential. By safely containing 'toddler tantrums' and practising early mother and child 'good baby experiences', distressed adoptive families can keep going and start to establish healthier attachment relationships, allowing children to 'redraw their inner road maps' (see Chapter 4).

Living with a traumatised child can feel like living in a war zone. Elective holding can enable adopters to stay in control safely, rather than losing control under duress, with the obvious potential for abusive interactions.

Without safe management strategies for out-of-control children, parents can feel frustrated and helpess, or hostile and resentful. They are then likely to respond punitively, with physical or verbal aggression: unwittingly mirroring the hostile interactions in birth families and confirming the child's internal representations of caregivers as malign. In a similar way, the perceived abandonment of being sent to his room can be extremely retraumatising for a previously maltreated child, reinforcing his disorganised representations of relationships and potentiating his maladaptive survival strategies.

Adoptive parents need effective 'battle strategies' as part of 'the war on trauma'. As the traumatised child grows, so the risks grow. Adopters may find themselves in the unhappy position of having to choose to continue living in the 'war zone' or agreeing to their youngster being moved to residential or even secure accommodation, with high economic, social and personal cost implications. Family cradling, as part of the developmental reparenting process, can provide essential opportunities for providing children with safe containment and 'rewiring' the disorganised neuro-biological substrate that, according to Spangler and Grossman (1999), underpins attachment disorganisation. Since the organisation of the brain and nervous system is 'experience dependent' (Perry 1999; Schore 1994), neural reorganisation also demands repeated, reparative, state-dependent experiences. We believe that family cradling offers unique opportunities in this respect, has high healing potential, is 'growth promoting' (Schore 1994, 2002) and non-abusive.

Part I

State of Play

Current Theory and Practice

CHAPTER 1

Adoption and Permanence Today
A Discussion
Adrian Briggs

Introduction

This chapter considers adoption and permanence today in order to set a social policy context for subsequent chapters examining 'the Family Futures' way'. It is divided into sections that will briefly discuss:

- how adoption has changed (and continues to change) because the needs of children requiring permanence are changing

- the many problems and issues currently confronting adoption and permanence services, whilst viewing adoption as an effective option on a continuum of permanence

- ways forward: new approaches to meet the needs of today's children.

Unfortunately, the scope of this book and space do not allow discussion of the key needs of, and issues regarding, birth parents and adopted adults; in no way does this minimise their importance.

Adoption has Changed, is Changing

Research and various Government and Social Service Inspectorate (SSI) reports have confirmed that adoption has changed radically and continues to change (Department of Health [DoH] 2000; Performance Innovation Unit [PIU] 2000; SSI 1996, 2000a). The number of adoptions has reduced dramatically, from its peak of 22,502 in 1974, to around 4000 in 1999/2000 (Ivaldi 2000). The increased availability of contraception, abortion and acceptance of single parenthood has resulted in fewer babies being available for adoption, whereas the number of children adopted from care (around 2000) has remained fairly consistent (SSI 2000a). However, the decline in the number of children looked after by local authorities over the last thirty years, to the current figure of under 60,000, has resulted in a relative increase in the percentage of children adopted from care, from 1.5 per cent to around 4 per cent (SSI 2000a).

Older children (predominantly from the looked after care population) with complex care histories and a range of attachment and developmental difficulties now form a large proportion of children being adopted or placed permanently. The SSI has found that 80 per cent of children referred to adoption services were already in the care system; of these half were aged six years or older (SSI 1996). Of the 2200 adopted from care in 1999, 9 per cent were under one year old (not accounting for babies voluntarily relinquished), 57 per cent were one to four years old, 26 per cent were five to nine years old and 7 per cent were ten years and over (Ivaldi 2000). The largest group, one to four year olds, can be viewed as 'early placements'. However, the increase in placement moves a significant number of these children have suffered, and the levels of the original abuse or neglect, renders this distinction immaterial. It should also be borne in mind that *all* adopted children are potentially vulnerable and may experience low self-esteem; a significant number will have difficulties developing a coherent sense of self (Archer 1999a, 1999b; Watson 1997).

As the majority of children now being adopted are older, it could be too easy to ignore the particular needs of children adopted as babies or infants. Verrier (1993) pointed out that adoption represents a dramatic emotional trauma for the child and mother, which resonates throughout their lives and must be addressed for healthy adjustment to occur. Too often social workers have assumed such children are 'easy to place'. The myth of unproblematic early placement ignores pre-birth traumas, perinatal difficulties and evidence that young children may have suffered neglect and abuse from their birth parents at the pre-verbal stage which could lead to particular difficulties processing their traumas verbally (Archer 1999a, 1999b; van der Kolk 1996b). Currently there are increasing numbers of placements of children removed at birth or shortly after and placed for adoption against the wishes of their parents. In all cases the 'explaining' task continues to pose difficult challenges for adoptive parents and their children. Whilst these difficulties are not insuperable, the basic foundation of disadvantage, reinforced by the complexities of contemporary adoption, has to be taken into account in the provision of support services for adoptive and relinquishing birth families.

In the recent past, multiple placement moves and insufficient post placement support have exacerbated risks of disruption. Sadly, some of the damaging moves children suffer have resulted from a too strict interpretation of the Children Act 1989, with an increase in the number of additional late placements caused by 'failed rehabilitations' increasing the age of children at time of (eventual) permanent placement. Although earlier placement should be advocated and unnecessary delay avoided, the provision of effective support services would help to reduce risk to all placements. Whilst the numbers of children involved appear low, when disruption of permanent placements occurs it has a disproportionate impact on the families and agencies, especially if the crisis is dealt with by social workers inexperienced in adoption. The human and financial costs of adoption disruption are immense to the child, their adoptive family, birth family, social workers and agency and in the negative ripple effect it has on other child care agencies and the community. For example, disruptions involving older children may force social services departments to purchase alternative specialist agency placements, often very distant from children's roots. Significantly, a major part of these agencies' fees are earmarked to fund post adoption support services which they view as integral to maintaining 'hard to place' children in permanent placements.

The Prime Minister's Review of Adoption recognises that children now being adopted from care are more challenging, and have experienced more placement moves, than previously (PIU 2000). As with social work with looked after children, an increasingly important part of adoption work is concerned with negotiating and maintaining contact arrangements over the lifetime of the placement. At least 70 per cent of adopted children now have some form of contact with their birth families. This further increases pressures and demands on adoptive families and staff (PIU 2000).

The incoming Labour Government of 1997 increased the sense of urgency about reforming services for looked after children, especially in the area of adoption and permanence. These concerns also helped to bring about the influential circular, *Adoption – Achieving the Right Balance* (DoH 1998a), which focused 'attention on adoption as an important and beneficial option in the care of children and…intended to bring adoption back into the mainstream of children's services' (p.1).

The groundbreaking *Quality Protects* programme followed later that year, injecting substantial funding to local authorities to boost services to looked after children, with a particular emphasis on improving adoption services. These initiatives paved the way for *The Prime Minister's Review of Adoption* in 2000, which in turn carried out significant groundwork for the Government's *White Paper* culminating in the *Adoption and Children* Bill and the *National Adoption Standards* in 2001.

Historically, the secrecy associated with adoption suggested that adoptive families should be treated similarly to biological families and consequently specific services should not, or did not need to be provided after an adoption order. This perspective needed to be challenged and a culture shift had to occur. Essentially a 'post adoption perspective' was required which would recognise that adoption differs from other family situations and that social workers and other professionals need to work *with* adoptive and birth families and adopted persons and make flexible lifetime supports available (Burnell and Briggs 1995).

Major pressure for change came from service users and their organisations, especially Parent to Parent Information on Adoption Services (now Adoption UK), the Natural Parents Network (NPN) and the National Organisation for the Counselling of Adoptees and their Parents (NORCAP). With a number of progressive voluntary organisations, such as British Association for Adoption and Fostering (BAAF), the post adoption centres and Parents for Children, they campaigned to raise awareness about the changing nature of adoption. These groups maintained that children being placed were more damaged than many professionals recognised and that adoption was a lifetime project, needing lifelong support. Adoptive parents had to suffer (and still suffer, to a lessening extent) not being taken seriously by professionals or being made to feel that they and their family dynamics were at fault. Members of Adoption UK were particularly tenacious in the face of professional and political indifference: under their influence the DoH and social services gradually began to recognise that many adopted children were experiencing attachment difficulties which were having a huge impact on adopters and their families. Adoption UK's journal, *Adoption Today*, has played an influential role in enabling struggling parents to gain a national voice and in giving them the confidence to campaign for reform.

Current Problems and Issues

Despite these changes, there are many issues remaining which cause unnecessary distress to children, adopters, birth families, adopted adults and professionals. The Government's *White Paper* (2000) crystallised the concerns of service users, professionals, and the general public about delay, insufficient and inconsistent use of adoption, inadequate recruitment of adopters and the need to make adoption safer and more attractive to potential adopters, particularly by the provision of proper post placement/post adoption support (DoH 2000). The *White Paper* confirmed what many adopters and enlightened professionals had said for years, that 'There is very little support available for adopters once a child has been placed for adoption' (DoH 2000, p.17).

Proposed Government reforms include:

- investing £70m over three years in adoption services

- setting a target of increasing by 40 per cent, by 2004–05, the number of looked after children being adopted

- legislating to reform the legal framework for adoption, including a national adoption register, the right to an assessment for post placement support and aligning the Adoption Act 1976 with the Children Act 1989

- establishing national adoption standards

- developing innovative approaches

- exploring a range of powers against councils which consistently fail to provide a reasonable level of service

- reforming the court service to reduce legal delays (DoH 2000).

The application of the Children Act 1989 effectively marginalised adoption services. Raising the profile of rehabilitation considerably meant this option was often pursued beyond its usefulness to children and their families. Fortunately, political and professional changes have begun to shift ground and the perspectives of many senior managers in social services have been transformed. Stereotypical thinking does, however, remain in some quarters, putting obstacles in the way of providing essential services to children and families. It is vital to recognise that for children who are unable to return to their birth parents or relatives, adoption provides unique legal and psychological security and permanence. No other long-term placement option can provide this. Whilst for a variety of good reasons, some older children may have to remain in long-term foster care and will benefit from it, it would be misleading to say that this gives true permanence and lifetime family commitment (BAAF 1996). Although many problems remain to be overcome, adoption continues to be a positive, effective option on a continuum of permanence for children unable to return to their birth family or kinship network.

Currently, as a result of Government directives, the value of adoption is being recognised more consistently by social services' senior management and, as it moves into the mainstream of child care services planning, it should provide a model for other aspects of child care. There continues to be a dynamic interface between adoption and the looked after care system, since adoption removes children from the formal system and, if consistent, adequate support is provided, the costly re-entry of vulnerable children with complex needs into the public care system could also be reduced. With the development of countrywide adoption support services the number of looked after children could dramatically decrease, in particular where more long-term foster carers are encouraged to adopt the children for whom they currently care.

Contemporary adoption of older children demands a different approach from the 'closed' practices of the past and 'open' adoption, with a range of contact arrangements, is becoming increasingly accepted. Adolescence may be a stressful time for many young people and their parents but is magnified for children separated from their birth parents (Archer 1999b). Again, adoption can play a more positive role than other care options (BAAF 1996), particularly if families are given appropriate preparation and support (Howe 1998).

From DoH statistics it is clear that adoption is an under used permanence option for many children, especially older children with specific difficulties and disabilities. A significant number of these children drift in 'short' and long-term care and do not return to their birth families. Expanding the use of adoption for older children and children with special needs unable to return to their birth families or kinship networks would create a less expensive permanency option than existing alternatives. Supporting adoption of 'hard to place' children over their lifetimes would still result in considerable economies for local authorities, making further funding available for the development of additional adoption support and child care services.

Residential placements in England and Wales cost on average £78,247 per year and foster placements £11,734, rising to £31,587 for an independent fostering agency placement (IPFA 2001). Although reliable figures are not available for the cost of adoption allowances in England and Wales, they are small compared to the huge costs of residential and foster care. Even with a significant additional allocation for post adoption support, adoption remains a cheaper permanence option. Given more prominence and credibility by the provision of consistent support services, more social workers would consider encouraging long-term foster carers to become adoptive parents and many foster carers would become more receptive to change of legal status if they believed they would have access to ongoing support. Clearly this should only be proposed where it was in the interests of the child and carers felt comfortable with the changes. The *White Paper* itself encourages this trend, proposing that assessment of foster carers should be fast tracked (DoH 2000). If followed through, this would have a significant impact in every local authority area, leading to a reduction in the numbers of looked after children. In the longer term, additional services could help to reduce the adoption disruption rate, since a number of studies of foster placements that have become permanent conclude that the disruption rate is lower in this group (Sellick and Thoburn 1996).

Although the statutory requirement to provide post placement/post adoption services will be underlined by new legislation, the nature of such service delivery should not be bureaucratic nor so bound by review and regulation. Post order adoption placements do not require statutory visits and reviews, thus would not demand the expensive quantity of professional and administrative time involved in supervising looked after children. Following an adoption order a more equal relationship between adoptive families and professionals should be developed. Adoption service users are themselves expressing the desire for a more accessible service, involving multidisciplinary co-ordinated inputs (Archer and Swanton 2000). Properly supported adoption would considerably reduce the risk of disruption and the huge human and financial costs involved. Risk obviously cannot be eliminated altogether but the rate of distress involved could be lowered to a more acceptable level, which would simultaneously be cost effective. Many voluntary adoption agencies are already providing post adoption support as an integral part of their services to children and families and have low disruption rates (Irving 1997).

The wider social and economic benefits of promoting open adoption, with appropriate support and contact arrangements, would also be manifest in the over representation of young care leavers amongst offenders and the homeless. This is frequently the result of lack of positive experiences of family life, or lifelong support of parents and family at this critical stage in their lives (Audit Commission 1994). Older adopted children and their families are also over represented in referrals to child and adolescent mental health services (Healy 1992). This is a clear indication of great need. It also raises the question of whether consistent provision of post placement/ adoption services would have helped to prevent such high referral rates and reduce the cost of relatively late therapeutic interventions. For example, Stephen Scott recently highlighted the additional ongoing costs to society of failing to meet the needs of young children (who display anti-social behaviour) effectively at an early stage (Knapp, Scott and Davies 1999).

Finally, although adoption is the major permanence option for children unable to return to their birth families, other permanence options do exist, including long-term foster care, residence orders and kinship care. Where a child retains strong links with their birth family and indicates they do not wish to be adopted (and is of an appropriate age), it makes sense to pursue a non-adoption permanence option. Some minority ethnic communities also have religious and cultural difficulties with current adoption law. These could be overcome by the proposed new legal option of 'special guardianship' (House of Commons 2001).

What is to be Done? – A New Approach

Whilst the present Government's commitment to transforming adoption services should be welcomed, there should be continuing opportunities for constructive critical engagement within this reforming process. Adoption UK and others have already discussed some of the pitfalls of the reforms, which could vitiate progress if not properly addressed:

- Although undoubtedly adoption should be expanded, the proposal to increase the rate by 40 per cent, without ensuring a sufficient infrastructure is in place to support the expansion, could be dangerous and cause disenchantment. Targets must be realistic, taking account of the complexities of the adoption process and ensuring good quality outcomes for children and adoptive parents, as well as 'getting children off the books'.

- The *Quality Protects* programme had already funded improvements in adoption services and begun to increase the number of children adopted from care (DoH 2000). It is proposed that new monies would be channelled to local authorities primarily through *Quality Protects* grants. Hence there are anxieties that the adoption reform programme would not be supported by new money, as this is already being spent on existing programmes. However, there does appear to have been a genuine increase in funding for social work training (DoH 2000).

- Policy makers, resource controllers, professionals and the community may continue to hold outmoded views about adoption (as closed and marginal to mainstream services), which would remain a real barrier to change. Similarly, there is a need to educate the general public since it takes a community to raise a child (Clinton 1997).

- Establishing adoptive parents' rights to an assessment of post placement needs is to be welcomed. However, without subsequent legislation requiring local authorities to provide, or to enable the provision of, services deemed as necessary, this would be frustrating for all concerned.

Service user groups, voluntary organisations, independent providers and many enlightened local authority professionals have pointed out that social services need not necessarily be the sole providers of post adoption services. Already hard-pressed family placement teams would be relieved to share these responsibilities, although social services do have a key role as enablers and facilitators. An independent dimension is required to balance local authority power and to enable partnerships to develop (Burnell and Briggs 1995). Helping agencies to work together – in Government parlance 'joined up thinking' – would not only be cost effective but could also be of particular value in adoption, where health and education issues predominate. Close interagency co-operation is crucial to sustaining and achieving permanence.

It has been argued for many years that adoption services should be more accessible to black and minority ethnic communities (Sawbridge 1988). There has been some progress in addressing cultural/heritage issues regarding the placement of children, but it remains unclear whether services have become sufficiently accessible, especially in light of the insights of the Stephen Lawrence inquiry (Home Office 1999). In this context, the SSI's new national standards for working with black and minority ethnic communities are to be welcomed (SSI 2000b).

Children's Needs

Recent Government reports on adoption rightly insist that we must 'put the needs and rights of children at the centre of the adoption process' (PIU 2000, p.5). Many children are inadequately prepared for their placements, yet working with children *prior* to placement should be an integral part of their ongoing/through placement support (Lowe *et al.* 1999). This should include access to full, clear and accessible information on their birth families, life before placement and their new families. The importance of such information cannot be over stressed. It is therefore essential that it is made available in ways appropriate to the child, including allowing him to process powerful feelings without becoming retraumatised. Children and their parents should be made aware of the national telephone help-line TALKadoption and Adoption UK's advice and support service.

The Government's espousal of multidisciplinary assessment (DoH 2000) is a huge step forward but needs to be strengthened by new services providing assessment of children's attachment patterns *before* placement. The therapeutic support process should also begin at the point of identification of a child's difficulties, to include health, education and family support. It is encouraging that the development of concurrent planning projects since 1997 has aimed to limit considerably unnecessary and damaging placement moves prior to permanency (Monck 2001).

Adoptive Parents, Permanent Carers and Their Families

Adopters are often inadequately prepared for permanence (Lowe *et al.* 1999). There is, therefore, a need for 'reframing' concepts of preparation and support:

> There is a need for agencies to acknowledge that preparation is essentially an educative task...encouraging and facilitating the learning of the particular, and sometimes very demanding, social competences associated with parenting older children who have usually lived disturbingly turbulent times. (Lowe *et al.* 1999, p.12)

Sadly, adopters do not consistently receive full information on their children before or after placement, despite strong guidance from Government (DoH 1998). This should include sensitive exploration of the placement's meaning for the child: what it has done *for* the child rather than merely what was done *to* him, therefore making it real (Howes 1997). For example, caregivers may gain a fuller, more human picture from reading 'softer' information contained in case files. Reading the specific details about the neglect or abuse of a child may help to bring home the distressing realities to adopters, which may not come across in edited reports. This can assist the parents' claiming process and strengthen their initial commitments or clarify that the placement should not proceed. If implemented consistently in all placing agencies this policy would help prevent disruptions, reduce distress, save adoptive parents and professionals time and energy and facilitate better use of scarce resources.

It is imperative that the provision of essential information is viewed as a shared task to be provided by professionals having an understanding of the key details and their implications. This needs to include opportunities for sympathetic dialogue within which feelings and concerns may be exchanged sensitively. The current situation (with notable exceptions in a number of local authorities and voluntary organisations), in which the provision of information to adopters is limited and arbitrarily administered on the grounds of confidentiality and pressure of work, is unacceptable. Any perceived loss of professional power would be outweighed by clear benefits to children and their new parents and the greater levels of trust achieved. Knowledge is indeed powerful and liberating. The use of the word *partnership* in childcare work has been in vogue for some years but has seldom been realised. To put children at the centre of the permanence process parents, professionals and all other agencies need to work together as part of a team which validates the contribution and expertise of each. Clearly this does not mean agreeing with each other all the time or the avoidance of honesty.

The new national standards relating to *assessment* rightly state: 'The assessment and approval process will be comprehensive, thorough and fair' (DoH 2001). Whilst assessing, social workers must also endeavour to work in partnership with prospective adopters; it is necessary for both parties to be clear that a risk assessment is being carried out when a home visit is occurring. There are tensions between Governmental pressure for faster, easier adoption; 'reframing' preparation for adoption towards an educative process; continuing political and professional concerns about child protection; and increasing attention to 'competences' in parenting. Adopters and social workers caught between these competing forces can only hope to manage them by establishing mutual trust.

Although it looks as if the legislative case for post placement/adoption support will largely be won in parliament, to ensure its implementation the arguments for life long and varied support services will need to be examined repeatedly both to overcome inevitable inertia and as new needs become apparent.

Social services departments, with society's acquiescence, still endeavour to 'transplant' damaged children from insecure family situations to insufficiently supported adoptive families, frequently leaving them alone to sink or swim, then express surprise when such placements falter or fail. In similar circumstances would a gardener transplant a delicate plant or tree from one garden to another, then no longer tend and water it?

Adoptive parents and families have additional post placement needs that should be addressed for the placement to remain secure and satisfying. If they have biological and other adopted children (and other relatives) living with them, they too have needs which, if not attended to, can contribute to disruption (Sellick and Thoburn 1996). The positive therapeutic model evolved by Family Futures of including parents as peer educators within their multidisciplinary team should be given serious consideration in planning of all post placement support services. The inclusion of 'parent practitioners' demonstrates true partnership in action, and offers uniquely valuable insights and inspiration to adoptive parents, who see that one of the team has been through difficulties similar to theirs and survived. Similarly, Adoption UK's training and support programme ('It's A Piece of Cake?'), run by and for adopters, is a highly significant development. Encouragingly, since its launch in 2000, it has generated interest and programme purchases from many local authorities and independent organisations, giving Adoption UK even greater confidence to press for user inspired support services.

What Future Adoption Support Services Would Look Like

'Current family placement practice over-emphasises recruitment, training and matching, whilst underestimating preparation and post placement support. Paradoxically, post placement and post adoption family support should begin before a placement is actually made' (Family Futures 2000, p.2). This concurs with the views of Lowe *et al.* (1999) that adoption services need 'reframing'. At present, there are a growing number of examples of positive local authority post adoption initiatives. However, they are the exception rather than the rule, with the voluntary and independent agencies tending to provide more consistent, specialised post adoption services.

Universally, what is required is a supportive, flexible, cost effective service provided by agencies with credibility and expertise, in collaboration with service users and their organisations, to complete the adoption circle. This would provide, in conjunction with other statutory agencies, such as health, education, housing and the new Connexions service, a comprehensive lifetime service to all those involved in adoption and permanence. A major role for social service agencies would be to act as co-ordinators and facilitators of services within a geographical area, rather than being the sole provider. Aspects of a successful co-ordinated service derived from current best practice would include:

- thorough preparation of all children and their prospective adoptive parents or carers prior to placement
- systematic multidisciplinary assessment of needs before placement, for all children, to identify developmental and attachment needs
- appropriate multidisciplinary therapeutic input for children with developmental attachment difficulties
- support for adoptive and birth families from specialist social workers pre and post adoption order
- readily accessible, specialist respite care schemes for children with emotional disabilities as well as physical and learning difficulties
- adequate and universal adoption allowances
- counselling for birth parents from their own, specialist social worker
- access to effective independent advice, information and counselling for service users and staff about all aspects of the adoption life cycle

- specific, regular training/development activities for various user groups, involving trained service users as facilitators

- Section 51 counselling for adult adoptees

- access to mediation and contact services

- culturally sensitive provision for black and minority ethnic communities

- support groups run in conjunction with users

- 'buddy buddy' schemes in which trained, experienced service users act as mentors

- information, publicity and public education systems involving user networks, local media, public libraries and statutory agencies, and utilising information technology

- regular training and consciousness raising for family placement and fieldwork social workers and managers

- consultation with and involvement of users and their organisations in planning and development of services

- active encouragement of users to join appropriate user organisations, such as Adoption UK, NPN, PNPIC (UK) (Parents Network for the Post Institutionalised Child) and NORCAP

- independent evaluation to verify services are achieving desired outcomes.

Summary

Adoption has changed, and is changing, primarily because the needs of children are changing. A major positive force for change has come from service users, which in turn has helped to generate a sea change in Government and official attitudes, with a dramatic culture shift away from closed adoption towards greater openness and a wider concern with permanence. Many significant problems and issues remain, particularly regarding delay, insufficient and inconsistent use of adoption and uneven post adoption services. Nevertheless, for children unable to return to their birth families or kinship care networks, adoption continues to be a positive option on a continuum of permanence. The unique legal and psychological security it confers upon children should be unashamedly proclaimed, and its cost effectiveness and social and economic benefits receive greater recognition.

A new approach is needed. The Government's commitment to transforming adoption services should be welcomed and critically supported. Service users and professionals must continue to campaign to ensure these new rights to assessment of post placement needs are translated into comprehensive, multidisciplinary services for and with all participants in the adoption cycle, and that they put children genuinely at the heart of the adoption and permanence process.

CHAPTER 2

The 'Coherent Narrative'
Realism, Resources and Responsibility in Family Permanence

Elsie Price

Introduction

Social workers charged with the onerous task of finding good enough, permanent substitute families for today's population of children are increasingly articulating questions which, in the past, may have gone unvoiced. With the growing challenges posed by this group of children it has become ever more vital that social work practice adopts coherent, universal practice guidelines both in relation to potential adopters and foster carers and to these very vulnerable youngsters themselves. Historically, the emphasis has been on identifying the adults most suited to the task of substitute parenthood. Currently, greater attention is being paid to identifying the complex dynamics affecting children seeking families. I intend to discuss these issues briefly, and in parallel: to embrace the assessment, preparation and support needs of both the major parties as they embark on the lifelong 'drama of adoption'.

The 'Coherent Narrative', Attachment and Family Permanence

Transparency, integrity and coherence of function are essential both in the way individual agencies approach family placement and across the board nationally. The 'coherent narrative', a term increasingly employed within attachment-based research, is often regarded as meeting these important criteria. The introduction of the Adult Attachment Interview (AAI), which explores the coherence of autobiographical narratives, as an assessment tool by placing agencies, is being encouraged (see below). The concept can also be used in relation to the adopted child who needs to understand his past, in order to make sense of his present and grow into his future. It was this concept which was instrumental in the development of 'life-story work' by social work practitioners helping children settle into permanent substitute families (see also chapters 7 and 11). However, the way the child's narrative was constructed was often formulaic, lending itself to over-positive interpretations of the child's life experiences. Consequently, the therapeutic value of the process has been questioned by Treacher (2001), who suggests that its primary function may be in helping practitioners to deal with the implications, for their profession, raised in approaching a child's 'unspeakable' distress.

The vast majority of children requiring preparation for permanent family placement have traumatic backgrounds that put them at high risk of developing disorganised attachment patterns (see chapters 3 and 4). These are children who, because of early attachment experiences perceived as frightened/frightening (Main and Hesse 1990) or hostile/helpless (Lyons-Ruth, Bronfman and Atwood 1999), were unable to develop coherent strategies for relating to their primary caregivers. Lyons-Ruth *et al.* state that:

> Disorganised infants appear to be unable to maintain the strategic adjustments in attachment behaviour represented by organised avoidant or ambivalent attachment strategies, with the result that both behavioural and physiological dysregulation occurs. (p.33)

They go on to suggest that:

> In addition to this central construct of contradictory tendencies governing the infants' attachment behaviours, discontinuity or dissociation of mental contents occurs at the level of mental representation among parents of disorganised infants. This discontinuity appears as a lapse in the monitoring of reason or discourse in the Adult Attachment Interview... Thus across the lifespan, the disorganised attachment category is characterised by contradictory behavioural strategies and unintegrated mental contents. (p.34)

Over time, according to Solomon and George (1999a), 'disorganised' children develop apparently coherent, controlling strategies, in an attempt to make the caregiver's behaviour more bearable and manageable. These are children who are at greatest risk of psychological disturbance throughout the life cycle (Fonagy 2002; Liotti 1999; Lyons-Ruth *et al.* 1999).

There are, as yet, few attachment-based studies focusing specifically on adopted or fostered children and their caregivers, or exploring the dynamic relationship between factors relevant to each. Those that do exist are in their early stages. I therefore intend to discuss pertinent studies in some detail.

The Adult Attachment Interview

The Adult Attachment Interview (AAI), developed by George, Kaplan and Main (1985), is a standardised assessment tool developed to explore adult attachment patterns. It is the corollary of the 'strange situation', originally developed by Ainsworth and colleagues (Ainsworth *et al.* 1978) to assess the attachment patterns of very young children (see also Chapter 3). The AAI is designed to explore the interviewee's capacity to give a coherent narrative account of early parental/caregiving relationships and experiences. AAIs with expectant mothers are said to be up to 80 per cent accurate in predicting the subsequent attachment patterns of their babies. Thus Main and Hesse (1990) propose that the child develops a particular attachment style as a result of their dyadic relationship experiences with primary caregivers.

Currently there is growing interest in research studies exploring the attachment styles, or 'states of mind in relation to attachment relationships' of adoptive and foster parents. This could provide an important, and potentially groundbreaking, first step towards standardisation and rationalisation of assessment procedures, in line with recent Government recommendations. Practitioners advocating the use of the AAI as a tool in the assessment of prospective adoptive and foster parents suggest that it could:

- reduce the amount of time spent on home studies
- provide a more evidence-based approach
- be an effective tool to predict support needs
- minimise individual practitioner idiosyncrasies
- assist in the matching process

- more readily predict adults at risk of re-enacting their early abuse
- provide objective criteria to justify non-acceptance of would-be applicants on appeal.

However, the AAI takes well over an hour to administer and several hours to score. Moreover, training in the accurate use of this research tool has high resource implications, in both human and financial terms. Prospective applicants might also be disconcerted to learn that the intention of the AAI is 'to surprise the unconscious' (George *et al*. 1985).

Antonia Bifulco, in conjunction with Parents for Children, London, is currently researching ways of adapting the ASI to aid assessment in adoption and fostering procedures. She has developed the Attachment Style Interview (ASI) to offer a more 'user friendly' process for social workers. According to Bifulco (personal communication), the ASI is a standardised, semi-structured assessment of adult attachment style, based on self report of attitudes and behaviour in accessing and utilising support from close others. It takes just one hour to administer. This approach offers applicants a more transparent method of assessment then the AAI. The profiles generated, covering marital relationships, social support, attachment, parenting and self-esteem, are claimed to have good inter-rater reliability and to be appropriate to the field of adoption and fostering. Bifulco, Director of the Lifespan Research Group at Royal Holloway, University of London, is currently using the ASI retrospectively, to explore the attachment styles of adopters who have already been accepted as adopters by Parents for Children (personal communication).

Miriam Steele and colleagues (1999) have conducted research into adoptive placements, identified by Thomas Coram Adoption Service, London, as 'successful', using the AAI. Here success indicates that the placement had not disrupted and that children were 'observed to be moving along developmental milestones within the range of their potential'. Children in the study were all described as having developmental disabilities; some demonstrated extremely challenging behaviour; most displayed 'moderate' levels of difficulty. The results of Steele's study were not typical of the general population, where approximately 70 per cent are normally classified as 'autonomous' (secure), 20 per cent are categorised as 'dismissing', (insecure-avoidant) and 10 per cent identified as demonstrating 'preoccupied', or insecure-resistant patterns. In Steele's study, a high proportion of adults classified as 'dismissing' (52%) met the 'successful' criteria and a smaller than expected number were assigned the autonomous classification (32%). The study did not identify adults who in childhood would have been classified as 'disorganised'. Such adults are generally categorised as 'unresolved' and allocated a secondary secure or insecure classification.

'Autonomous' adults are able to give succinct, relevant and detailed verbal accounts of their experiences of being parented and place a high value on attachment relationships. Their reflections on self and others are comprehensive and coherent (Lyons-Ruth et al. 1999). 'Dismissing' and 'preoccupied' attachment patterns in adults are linked to lack of coherence, indicating some discontinuity or dissociation of mental contents. For example, the 'dismissing' adult may report normal or good childhood experiences but be unable to support this with appropriate memories. The 'preoccupied' adult's strategy during interview leads to evaluations accompanied by an overabundance of memories from child and adulthood. These frequently generate feelings of anger, or a sense of resignation that difficulties cannot be overcome, that intrude into the present (Steele et al. 1999).

In their discussion Steele and colleagues point out that many of the women in the study had previously worked within human services; the majority of the adults (80%) had sought specifically to adopt a child with special needs and 64 per cent had some prior personal experience of disability. Perhaps most notably, 96 per cent of the group reported having endured the loss of someone close during childhood or adulthood. Steele et al. interpreted this as an indicator of resilience, since only three of the interviewees showed signs of lack of resolution to the loss. According to Lyons-Ruth et al. (1999), it is not loss or trauma per se that is disorganising, rather it is failure to achieve resolution that is problematic. Individuals able to find resolution may indeed be strengthened by their traumatic experiences.

Steele and colleagues raise concerns, in their discussion, over the small, self-selected population studied and the relatively short-term nature of the study programme. These are valid aspects that, it would be hoped, will influence their continuing research. It is also important to consider how far data may be generalised from a sample of children with developmental disabilities to the traumatised child population with whom we work. Moreover, a major interpretation of the findings, that a majority of the 'successful' adopters were rated as 'dismissing', must still be approached with some circumspection, given Main and Hesse's (1990) original findings that older children placed with substitute caregivers retained 'disorganised' attachment patterns. According to Steele and colleagues a parental 'dismissive' stance towards close relationships may represent an 'optimistic' frame of mind that could be of tremendous benefit when dealing with the day-to-day care of a child with special needs. However, Bates and Dozier (2000) suggest that although a dismissive parenting stance may be protective for the parent, they have found significant associations between 'dismissing' foster caregiving and disorganised attachments in their children.

Furthermore, it is noteworthy that Thomas Coram Adoption Service, as with Parents for Children, has led the way in developing preparation programmes for prospective adopters for children with special needs. They provide good levels of long-term support to their families once children are placed. This could go some way to providing the 'holding environment' for the family that we believe is essential if adoptive families are to survive. With their support a good number of these families would also have obtained significant adoption allowances in respect of their children, including special enhancements. This could serve to reinforce parents' views that they are performing a valuable 'job', simultaneously enhancing parental confidence and supporting their more detached approach to their children.

Parents' and Children's Attachment Patterns

Exploring the attachment patterns of substitute parents without assessing the attachment patterns of the children to be placed provides us with an incomplete, and potentially distorted, perspective: not least because attachment itself is defined as a reciprocal, dyadic process. Research projects examining both adults and fostered and adopted children in context are beginning to emerge, both in the United Kingdom and in the United States. In the main these examine attachment relationships soon after placement. Assessing a child's attachment patterns on or prior to placement provides vital information on aspects of children's relational and emotional status at that time. However, it is essential that assessments integrate many related areas of concern, to provide coherent representations of this population's needs over the short and long term. Currently, children's developmental, physical, socio-emotional, educational and health needs are neither well understood nor integrated into placement practice. The extent of maltreatment in families of origin is not adequately recognised and understanding of its implications for family preparation and support not yet widespread. The complex relationship between trauma, attachment and development demands exploration from a holistic, multidisciplinary perspective; long-term outcome studies are essential.

Steele, Hodges and associates (1999) are currently conducting a research project to evaluate the attachment patterns both of substitute parents, using the AAI, and children awaiting placement, using story stems. The story stem assessment, developed by Hodges, is carried out on placement and repeated one and two years later, allowing exploration of modifications to children's mental representations of attachment relationships within more benign family environments. According to Hodges (personal communication) children demonstrated the ability to create newer, healthier attachment representations in parallel with their original, distorted ones. This supports observations at Family Futures that traumatised children create multiple, internal, attachment models; under stress, they appear to revert to the 'roadmaps' relating to their original caregivers. Hopefully, continuing research will improve understanding in this field, enhance the capacity to 'match' parents to children's specific needs and inform child and family support services.

Mary Dozier and colleagues at the University of Delaware are the leading American researchers into attachment patterns of infants and their substitute caregivers, primarily foster carers. Initial studies by Stovall and Dozier (1997, 2000) provide evidence for links between infant age at placement and capacity to benefit from the nurturing care of autonomous caregivers. However, a later study (Dozier et al. 2001), involving a larger group of foster caregivers, challenged these original findings. The authors continue to review the development of these children, in a longitudinal study, with the intention of determining whether youngsters who appear to have reorganised their attachment strategies within secure caregiving environments will continue to do as well, in middle childhood, as 'secure' children within intact biological dyads. This is an important area of future research, since experience at Family Futures indicates that a significant number of adopted children placed as infants demonstrate relationship and behavioural difficulties in their later years. It will also be essential to employ criteria that explore both overt attachment-related behavioural organisation and internal cognitive attachment representations, since according to Lyons-Ruth et al. (1999), the former may become more organised whilst the latter remain disorganised.

Dozier interprets findings from her earlier studies in terms of the tendency for foster caregivers, even those rated as autonomous, to mirror the rejecting or withdrawing behaviours of their infants. Tyrrell and Dozier (1999) argue that substitute caregivers cannot be expected to understand the attachment-related needs of their charges and should receive specific training to act in an effectively therapeutic role. This is supported by Archer (1999b) who contends that, without a clear understanding of the reasons underlying children's behaviour, adoptive parents are likely to mirror their children's distorted attachment patterns, as they strive to achieve attunement with them. Hence preparation and support should also include self-care skills, to enable parents to maintain, or regain, their own inner balance, so that they can provide a good enough self-regulatory model for their children and meet their fundamental needs for attachment security.

Dozier and colleagues have applied their research findings to the development of training and intervention programmes for substitute parents. They aim to support parents, irrespective of their own attachment rating, in recognising and interpreting the youngster's overt attachment behaviours in terms of his underlying attachment needs. They explore what factors may prevent caregivers from responding in nurturing ways. This enables parents, with ongoing support, to respond in ways that encourage children to develop more secure attachment styles. Whilst not utilising formal measures of attachment security, the developmental reparenting work in this country described by Archer (1999a, 1999b, 1999c), and Adoption UK's 'It's a Piece of Cake?' programme for adoptive parents, bear many similarities to this pioneering approach.

It is essential that research relating to the influence of age at placement on the development of attachment security should be extended to school age and adopted children who, from our experience at Family Futures, tend to continue to display fundamentally disorganised attachment patterns. Spangler and Grossman (1999) demonstrate that neurobiological dysregulation in neonates predicts attachment disorganisation in later infancy and is significantly associated with 'controlling' behaviours by school age. Moreover, in contrast to Main and Hesse's (1990) original assertions that attachment classification is dyad-specific, they found that 'disorganised' classification of youngsters in this group predicted 'disorganised' attachment patterns with other caregivers. It is therefore hardly surprising that older placed children frequently demonstrate continuing insecure attachment behaviours and that the influence of subsequent caregivers may appear limited.

Children's continuing difficulties within substitute families may also be understood in terms of Perry *et al.* (1995) 'state to trait' proposition that fight, flight or freeze neurobiological state responses, typically employed by traumatised children, become consolidated over time into characterological traits. Hence, the longer the child has to 'practise' these survival adaptations the more entrenched they will become. Bowlby (1988) emphasised the need to continue to explore internal and external influences on children's development; Parker (1999) confirms the multi-factorial nature of influences on adoptive placements. Clarke and Clarke's (2000) interpretation of early adversity as setting up a transactional, cumulative chain of consequences across time is also worthy of consideration here. Researchers should also distinguish between time-limited foster care placements and permanent adoptive and foster placements, given that Bates and Dozier (2000) emphasise the influence of caregivers' beliefs 'that they can make a difference' in promoting successful attachments. There may be fundamental differences between short- and long-term caregivers' perceptions and expectations, which affect their approach to attachment relationships with their children.

Approach-Avoidance Dynamics

In theoretical terms the approach-avoidance dynamic, so central to disturbed attachments (e.g. Lyons-Ruth *et al.* 1999), plays a major role in the viability of permanent placements. Parents with secure attachment styles make many more 'approaches' to their children, in attempts to engage them in healthy attachment interactions, than 'preoccupied' or 'dismissing' parents and more consistent, positive ones than parents classified as 'unresolved'. The internal representations of traumatised children, derived from their earliest experiences, represent caregivers along the 'hostile-versus-helpless' (Lyons-Ruth *et al.* 1999), or 'frightened/frightening' (Main and Hesse 1990), continua. Thus adopted children are unlikely to respond to positive parental approaches appropriately, even within new family settings. Instead they are likely to engage in bimodal 'avoidance' behaviours, including aggression and hyperactivity, or compliance, withdrawal and 'going off in a dream', typical of attachment disorganised, or dissociative, children. Although these originally adaptive behaviours will feel far safer than allowing intimacy, according to the child's distorted mental representations, their persistence must now be considered maladaptive. Where once they ensured the child's survival they now actively inhibit him from benefiting from a healthier familial environment and compromise his future well being.

The superficial 'match' of attachment patterns between 'dismissing' parents and traumatised children could perpetuate the intergenerational transmission of trauma, allowing the youngster's affect dysregulation and attachment disorganisation to continue. It seems highly unlikely that the traumatised child's fundamental neurobiological dysregulation (Spangler and Grossman 1999) and segregated attachment systems (Bowlby 1979; Liotti 1999) could become regulated and integrated without a healthy measure of intrusive intimacy and dyadic intersubjectivity. Egeland, Jacobvitz and Sroufe (1988) have shown that significant changes in the caregiving environment and relationships are essential to effect change in distressed children's attachment patterns. This, in turn, would be an essential prerequisite to children achieving the 'full potential', to which Steele *et al.* (1999) allude in their definition of 'successful' placements.

Without informed support, as advocated by Tyrrell and Dozier (1999), even the most 'autonomous' adoptive parents may ultimately feel overwhelmed by the rejecting, aggressive, ambivalent and controlling behaviours displayed by their distressed children. They then lose confidence in their capacity to be 'good enough' parents (Archer 1999b; Hughes 2002; Keck and Kupecky 2002). Archer (1999b) argues that the extent to which adoptive parents report subjective distress may be directly proportional to their capacity to become truly attuned to their child. These feelings of helpless inadequacy, or hostility, towards the child can be exacerbated by high self-expectations, or inappropriate criticism and interventions from professionals, friends and relatives. Hence placement disruptions in families with 'secure' parents, who express their concerns, may be more likely than for 'dismissing' caregivers. The latter, employing mental and behavioural strategies to avoid thinking about intimacy, may be able to keep the placement going at the cost to the child of vital, new relationship experiences and real change. The use of lack of disruption as the major criterion for placement success could therefore distort research findings significantly.

From his global analysis of adoption research, Parker (1999) also argues that disruptions are not necessarily the most sensitive indicators of outcomes. To illustrate this point he quotes from Thoburn's (1991) study:

> Some placements, which appeared to have broken down, could be seen, in light of the information we received about earlier severe problems and later progress and improvement in life chances, to have been successful. On the other hand, some of the placements, which did not actually break down before the young people reached the age of 18, did not provide them with a 'family for life'. (p.10)

A longer term quantitative *and* qualitative perspective is therefore vital. From my own experience, observing the quality of the family's intimate interactions, particularly on 'home ground', could be a more effective indicator of placement 'success' over the longer term.

Cultural and Group Narratives and Issues

Although adoptive parents and children are the central actors in the 'drama of adoption', it is also vital that we consider the narratives of integral 'offstage' players. Clearly we are all affected by our childhood experiences: a reality pertinent to us all, from policy makers to 'hands on' workers in every area of human services. Youngsters who have been traumatised and abused have known extreme hurt and isolation, for which they blame themselves; many demonstrate symptoms of post traumatic stress disorder (PTSD). Not infrequently their substitute parents come to feel equally hurt, isolated and blamed or self-blaming. As a result of attempting to respond sensitively to the feelings their child is generating, parents are at risk of becoming victims of secondary traumatic distress. Similarly, supporting practitioners, at every level, run the risk of developing tertiary, victim-related symptoms of PTSD (Cairns 1999).

Charged with the responsibility of supporting distressed children and their parents, professionals may in their turn feel isolated, inadequate and overwhelmed by the enormity of their responsibilities. Their ability to manage tasks may be heavily influenced by direct or indirect exposure to the high levels of hurt and distress carried by children and their adoptive parents, as well as by their personal histories. Socio-political influences and the working environment can compound these stresses. For example, practitioners based in local authority departments often have to contend with lack of adequate training and support, the disruption of frequent structural reorganisation and widespread under-resourcing, including chronic under-staffing. Furthermore, none of these personal, family or departmental issues occurs within a social vacuum. All the adults involved in the 'drama of adoption' will also have their views, understanding and expectations influenced by societal and cultural narratives about family life. These frequently include what we see and hear via 'the media', including dramatic portrayals in television 'soap operas'. As a result, families not linked by blood ties may feel marginalised and somewhat less valued than other families (Treacher 2001).

During the 80s and 90s, awareness of child sexual abuse was raised through the media: something those working in the field of child protection welcomed. As a result of the more sensational kind of coverage many people received messages that those children, particularly boys, who had been sexually abused would, in turn, become abusers in child or adulthood. Similarly, 'received knowledge' relates to the likelihood of other maltreated youngsters repeating cycles of abuse: re-enacting abusive relationships with their own children. While clearly there is some truth in these observations, the reality is much more complex and involves a variety of factors.

Adult attachment research demonstrates that the capacity to relate and to manage distress in the present is not compromised in adults able to give coherent, narrative accounts of adverse parenting experiences (Lyons-Ruth et al. 1999). Nevertheless, such 'urban myths' can continue to influence the perceptions and expectations of prospective applicants, so that they feel inhibited about revealing personal histories of maltreatment. Others may conclude that abused children will inevitably become abusers and may therefore elect not to apply to care for such children, or approach the process from an unrealistic desire to 'rescue' them. Thus allowing applicants opportunities to reflect on their own experiences in a safe environment, during the period of assessment and preparation, could enable them to make more sense of their own lives, beliefs and expectations of parenting and family life. It could also help them understand the healing process through which maltreated children will need to pass and realistically to recognise their potential for greater emotional health.

Individual social work practitioners, too, bring with them perceptions and expectations of the needs and difficulties of children requiring adoptive families, based on personal narratives. It is likely that a significant proportion of child care practitioners will have personal experience of childhood abuse, given the incidence of childhood maltreatment within the general population. This may, indeed, be a factor in drawing people towards working with vulnerable children, just as it may be for potential adopters. It may influence their attitudes towards potential applicants and the qualities they look for in substitute caregivers, some of which may be unrealistic and unnecessarily limiting. Moreover, there may be a tendency for practitioners to over-identify with the children for whom they are seeking families, which may adversely affect their capacity to empathise with the difficulties adoptive parents face. Images of social workers, both of themselves and in the eyes of the general public, may also be influenced by negative media coverage, since social workers tend to receive a high profile only when something goes seriously awry. Preparation and supervision for practitioners that embraces attachment theory and the exploration of coherent narratives could provide workers with greater insights and enhance personal and corporate confidence.

Best Practice in Preparation, Assessment and Support

Preparation, assessment and support must be entered into on the basis of real partnership. The process of assessing applicants' unique attributes and their individual support needs must be undertaken as a shared venture between parents and professionals. Applicants should be given clear and coherent information about the common difficulties of children needing families and more specific discussion of the individual child's issues at the preliminary 'matching' stage. The pressures on, and expectations of, parents taking traumatised children into their homes must also be explored in some detail. Failure to do so will leave adopters not only unable to make informed decisions about their own capabilities but also ill equipped for the arduous task they are undertaking. In turn this may reflect on their capacity to understand their children and adopt effective attachment-based reparenting approaches.

Comprehensive assessment and preparation, although initially costly in financial terms, could provide substantial long-term economies. Enabling less suitable candidates to withdraw on their own terms and allowing others to make informed decisions and preparations for their future families would clearly be cost effective. Informed counselling for prospective adopters on the pressures and challenges they are likely to face, alongside well-informed and well-resourced support services, would enhance the lives of many adoptive families and improve the life chances of a significant number of our most vulnerable children. As Clarke and Clarke (2000) point out, the human and social costs of failing to intervene effectively are immeasurable. These would include the suffering of future generations, through the continuing intergenerational transmission of unresolved distress (e.g. Lyons-Ruth *et al.* 1999).

The use of the AAI as part of this complex process is an attractive idea, although initial training for practitioners would be costly and its value in terms of facilitating adoptive placements remains to be demonstrated. Evidence of the benefits of identifying parents' strengths and weaknesses and family support needs is not yet available and there is a danger of jumping on the latest practice bandwagon prematurely. This could leave adopters continuing to shoulder most of the responsibility for difficulties within the placement and struggling with little meaningful, practical support. Best practice in social work has always drawn creatively from other disciplines and this is no exception. Rather than carrying out the AAI as a straightforward assessment tool, it could be better used to explore, in partnership with prospective parents, the foundations of good enough attachments and the influences of personal narratives on current family interactions. In particular, applicants would need to consider the impact of maltreatment on themselves and their children and be prepared for the ongoing influences of their past experiences on adoptive family life.

It is also essential to explore the attachment histories of all children being placed in detail and to re-evaluate expectations that adults with particular attachment patterns, secure or insecure, would best be able to integrate traumatised children into their families. The search for the 'perfect match' could go too far at the expense of the search for the best collaborative resource package. Rather than identifying the 'ideal' assessment tool to determine the 'perfect placement', practitioners should embrace the concept of 'good enough' parenting. With adequate preparation and support, good enough adopters could be empowered to meet the rigours of parenting children with disorganised attachment patterns and to provide the stable bedrock of attachment youngsters need if they are to heal (Hughes 2002). This would involve something of a shift of emphasis away from assessment *per se* towards an integrated, coherent preparation and post placement support service.

Lastly, we must not focus on the 'main actors' in the 'drama of adoption' to the exclusion of the 'supporting cast'. The adage that it takes a community to raise a child is particularly pertinent for 'transplanted' children. Creating newer, more coherent narratives for such children also requires that we each examine our own narratives and, as a society, provide a more coherent background of understanding and support for substitute caregivers. Clifford

(1999) discusses the realities, resources and responsibilities of organisations, departmental managers and individual social worker practitioners, the power dynamics involved and the implications this has for real 'partnership'. It is to be hoped that these concepts will be extended to embrace the wider community, in line with current Government philosophy.

Summary

Society's perceptions of the needs of vulnerable children and the part they can play in their healing are central to an effective adoption service. To a certain extent adopters are a self-selecting group, often appearing to 'get through the process' despite the many obstacles they face. Although this may be a powerful measure of their resolution and resilience it is likely to leave them feeling alienated from, rather than connected to, placing agencies. Increasing realistic awareness within the community, developing broader social responsibility, and providing this precious population of caregivers with more systematic and coherent information and resources would serve to enhance, both quantitatively and qualitatively, the Government's declared long-term goal of providing permanent substitute families for vulnerable children. Not only could this lead to more, increasingly well-prepared, adoptive parents, it would also according to Tyrrell and Dozier (1999) and Archer and Swanton (2000), greatly facilitate the creation of the 'growth promoting environment' (Schore 1994) such children demonstrably need.

Dan Hughes (1997) discusses the qualities he considers essential for 'facilitating developmental attachment' in therapeutic adoptive or foster homes, emphasising the need for a relaxed empathic, secure, predictable, sharing and fun atmosphere that can be sustained in the face of challenges from the child to recreate his familiar, familial environment. Such a 'holding environment' demands that 'the personal is political': that the 'bottom up' realities and responsibilities of individuals is mirrored in the realisation of 'top down' responsibilities and resources and the sharing of knowledge and understanding gained both from evidence-based sources and from personal experience. In this way we can create an increasingly coherent narrative for our most vulnerable children by ensuring that 'children are securely attached to caregivers capable of providing safe and effective care for the duration of childhood' (*Quality Protects* Programme 1998b).

Endnote

In the past two decades, issues of race, gender and sexuality have been debated at length with regard to adoption. However this chapter does not provide enough space to do justice to such large and important topics. Thus I have focused this chapter on specific issues relating to attachment.

CHAPTER 3

Setting up the Loom
Attachment Theory Revisited

Alan Burnell with Caroline Archer

Historical Framework

Until the 1970s, adoption in the United Kingdom was synonymous with baby placements (Cabinet Office 2000). The placement of babies for adoption appeared to require little theoretical rationale: it was rooted firmly in history, in morality and in common sense. The needs of babies for parents and the needs of infertile couples for babies were easy for most people to comprehend. For those babies and those parents to become family units and to grow together into the future was the prevailing dictum. However, with the advent of innovative adoption practices, such as those pioneered by Parents for Children in collaboration with PPIAS (now Adoption UK), older children and children with disabilities were gradually deemed 'adoptable': the image of adoption began to change. The placement of children previously regarded as 'hard to place' or 'having special needs' created a more complex picture: it confounded the traditional model of adoption and posed significant questions in terms of practice. The challenges and complexities of such relationships patently required post adoption support if adoptive families were to survive (Macaskill 1986). It was out of these experiences that the need for a designated post adoption service emerged, and the original Post Adoption Centre (PAC) was established in London in 1986.

Interestingly, in my role as counsellor at PAC during the late 1980s, what immediately stood out were the ongoing needs of families who had adopted infants. They sought advice and help in:

- 'telling' their adopted children about their families of origin

- finding ways of understanding and coping with what would become known as the 'adaptive grieving stage' of middle childhood (Brodzinsky 1990)

- counselling for adopters and their children during adolescence, when issues around identity come to the fore (Howe 1990)

- updating life storybooks

- dealing with issues of contact.

A small but significant minority of these adoptive parents also expressed concerns about the emotional, behavioural and relationship difficulties their children continued to display.

However, as time passed, parents who had adopted older children became more prevalent amongst service users at PAC. The problems presented by their children were often more complex, more challenging and more disturbing than for infant placements. Many of these parents had struggled for some years with their children's difficult behaviours and were presenting at the point of despair, often blaming themselves for their family's difficulties. As a counsellor faced with such distress, the traditional understanding of identity issues and adaptive grieving processes could not adequately explain the quantitative or qualitative disturbances that this generation of adoptees was displaying. Personally and professionally I felt that I was offering too little, too late. It became clear that in order to help these families, a new, and more profound, understanding of the impact of traumatic separations and the nature of attachments was required.

With the innovation of late-placement adoptions, permanency planning and open adoption by the early 1990s, it was American therapeutic practice that led the way, providing much-needed hope for families with 'high-risk children'. Clinicians such as Cline (1992) had been writing for some time about the attachment issues of adoptees; Cline and his colleagues had been developing some quite controversial intervention strategies; the American psychiatric community had succeeded in getting reactive attachment disorder recognised as a diagnosis in DSM IV. Underpinning their thinking was the recognition of the relevance of Bowlby's attachment theory (1969) and the subsequent research work of Mary Ainsworth (1978) and Main and Solomon (1990). The irony of our needing to turn to American practice, developed from Bowlby's fundamentally British model, is perhaps more apparent than real, since both Ainsworth and Main collaborated with Bowlby and his colleagues in Britain on theoretical developments. However, at the time, it felt as though we were bringing coals back to Newcastle since, hitherto, attachment theory had been given little credence in our understanding of the nature of the adoption experience.

Such an obvious and fundamental starting point as attachment theory had possibly been overlooked because the baby adoption tradition relied heavily on the innate 'naturalness' of placing a relinquished infant in his new mother's arms. Conversely, the evolution of feminist theories may have been instrumental in marginalising Bowlby's ethological and psychoanalytical perspective, since its 'biological essentialism', misinterpreted as promoting the return of women to home-making, post World War II, rendered it socio-politically unacceptable. Be that as it may, the contemporary adoption experience of placing older or disabled children, who may not have been relinquished voluntarily and whose biological parents had frequently caused them 'significant harm' through their neglectful or abusive parenting, demanded a re-exploration of attachment theory. The interweaving of the impact of early trauma, and the development of attachments within adoptive family dynamics (Archer 1999c) form the complex, yet inspiring, tapestry that is adoption today. I intend to consider these strands further within this chapter.

Attachment – The Fabric of Being

Klaus and Kennell (1976) propose a simple but succinct definition of attachment as: 'an affectionate bond between two individuals that endures through time and space and serves to join them emotionally'. This statement encapsulates the essential elements of attachment that we see in children with whom we work. Irrespective of their previous experiences there is always an 'affectionate bond' that persists, connecting children to their birth parents. There may be other 'bonds' but, even in extreme cases of neglect or abuse, there is an enduring loving and longing for the birth parent. This is consistent with literature on 'attachment to the perpetrator' outlined by Ross (1997). In our experience, these bonds not only endure 'through time and space', their tenacity can also appear irrational and is often strengthened, not extinguished, by absence. Moreover, these are bonds that 'join them emotionally' at a primal level, long before the maturation of verbal or reasoning capacities. The severance of these bonds begins at the visceral level (Porges 1998) and is indeed, in the words of Nancy Verrier (1993), a 'primal wound'. Viewed in this light, the magnitude of the task that children and their adoptive parents face in forming new attachment bonds becomes immediately apparent.

Bowlby (1973, 1988) said that, from a very early age, the child lays down representations of self and primary attachment figures as 'internal working models' (IWMs). Archer (see Chapter 4) refers to these as 'road maps' providing the child with an internal framework of his world which is 'experience-dependent' (Perry 1999) and which maps out the most suitable response-routes to familiar, and unfamiliar, challenges. IWMs reflect the child's view of, and confidence in, the attachment figures' capacity to provide a safe and caring environment. Moreover, these models, in turn, organise the child's thoughts, memories and feelings regarding attachment figures. Inevitably, they will also act as guides and predictors of future behaviour for the child and analogous attachment figures, such as adoptive parents. Internal working models are organisational constructs that are burned into the nervous system at the neurobiological level (Schore 1994). They are not only unconscious but, once established, are also highly resistant to change (Solomon and George 1999b), since they tend to assimilate change: we tend to expect and perceive 'more of the same', rather than to identify and accommodate to change (Siegel 1999; Waites 1993, 1997). As Dan Hughes frequently comments during training sessions, children see the world through 'the lens of attachment' and interpret what they see according to existing internal working models.

It is not uncommon for the children with whom we work to demonstrate a hierarchy of internal working models of attachment, relating to different time periods and attachment figures. For example, children may hold working models relating to their birth parents, separate ones relating to foster carers and separate models again relating to their adoptive parents. As one might expect, the earliest, and hence the most long-standing, patterns appear to be the most influential. During normal childhood development, internal working models of primary attachment figures are updated and modified as the child grows and develops. They provide 'felt security' (Bowlby 1969, 1988) and function as a 'psychological immune system' against future stressors. However, where there has been traumatic separation, loss or maltreatment, models can become fixed, often remaining fragmented and unintegrated (Fonagy 2002). Ideally, within normal development, working models are continually revised and become continuous, as changes to relationships are integrated into existing mental schemata. This can only be achieved if they are readily accessible to conscious awareness and a coherent narrative is developed that incorporates changes to primary relationships over time.

Bowlby (1979) observed that when children experience neglect or abuse their primary representation of themselves is one in which they feel 'unwanted and unloved'; the dominant representation of the attachment figure mirrors this, as one of someone who does not care, or who rejects. These models conflict with other more positive representations, real or imagined, of the self and others which children develop from birth. This led Bowlby (1979) to describe what he called 'segregated systems', or fragmented attachment patterns, which are repressed as they are too painful to hold in the conscious mind. These patterns are not forgotten but operate unconsciously and are activated by normal attachment cues. When reactivated they appear irrational, unpredictable, out of context and out of control. Recent observations by Solomon and George (1999a) supporting Bowlby's original segregated systems proposition include:

- pronounced absence of attachment behaviour where expected, for example when a child falls over but fails to cry or seek comfort from caregiver

- out of context and out of control attachment behaviour, such as excessive crying, or violent anger with no apparent trigger

- alternation of these two states.

Threads of Attachment

Mary Ainsworth developed Bowlby's ideas during the 1970s and began categorising children's attachment patterns as: Avoidant (Type A), Secure (Type B) or Ambivalent (Type C), using the 'strange situation' procedure (Ainsworth *et al.* 1978) with children aged between 14 and 20 months. Main and Solomon (1990) extended this classification to include the Disorganised-Disorientated category (Type D). The majority of children we see at Family Futures fall into this last category.

Disorganised Attachment

Disorganised attachments develop when attachment figures fail to inhibit strong, or chronic, activation of the attachment system (Maine and Hesse 1990), for example, failing to reduce discomfort, pain or anxiety. Often parents are not only unable to terminate their child's attachment-seeking behaviour appropriately, they may also be the cause of the original attachment-seeking behaviour. This could occur where, for example, parents are abusive or neglectful, or repeatedly generate distress through chronic instability or domestic violence. In such situations, familiar to many children entering the care system, it is not only the parents' inability to terminate their child's attachment-seeking behaviour that leads to disorganised attachment. The fact that, simultaneously, caregivers are perceived as the source of that distress is particularly problematic and potentially damaging (Main and Hesse 1990).

Solomon and George (1999b) also cite lack of reparative behaviour from the caregiver as a crucial interactive feature in establishing disorganised attachment patterns. This is consistent with Schore's (1994) shame hypothesis, in which the temporary breaking of attachment bonds during socialisation (see also Chapter 13) must immediately be repaired by the caregiver for the child, rendered temporarily abandoned, helpless and hopeless, to feel comforted, secure and autonomically revitalised. Failure to do so leads to overwhelming stress responses, expressed bimodally, either as 'cast-down' shame or aggressive 'shame-rage' (Schore 1994). Lyons-Ruth, Bronfman and Atwood (1999) contend that lack of interactive repair seriously inhibits the primary development of organised attachment patterns. They also found very significant correlations between contradictory, 'hostile-helpless' states of mind in parents and youngsters assigned the 'D' classification. This is consistent with Siegel's (1999) proposition that parents 'download' their mental contents into the infant's developing brain: the child organises his states of mind in accordance with his caregiver's. In the view of Lyons-Ruth et al. (1999) trauma and loss are significant only where they remain unresolved. This, too, they relate to poor parental caregiving capacities, elaborating Main and Hesse's (1990) 'frightened/frightening' dimension to embrace restricted affect, lack of responsiveness and repair, poor soothing and co-regulation within an unbalanced dyadic relationship.

Research has shown that 80 per cent of children with disorganised attachments have been maltreated (Carlson et al. 1989) and demonstrate a marked inability to utilise caregivers for soothing. Instead they attempt to co-regulate for the parent (Lyons-Ruth *et al.* 1999) and develop pathological methods for self-regulation (Schore 1994). However, Lyons-Ruth and colleagues' (1999) relational diathesis model supports Bowlby's earlier proposition that rejection, extended separation and loss are also implicated (Bowlby 1979). Whilst findings from Main and Hesse (1990) confirm trauma and loss in caregivers as significant, Lyons-Ruth *et al.* (1999) develop a more sophisticated model, taking into account parents' capacities for reflection and resolution of distress. Disorganised parents may suffer from depression, drug dependency, marital conflict or psychiatric problems and have been maltreated in childhood; the child himself may be the victim of sexual, physical or emotional abuse, or neglect (Solomon and George 1999a). The resultant insensitive, controlling or contradictory caregiving appears bimodal, reflecting the caregiver's bimodal, segregated mental self-representations (Lyons-Ruth *et al.* 1999). Further, significant characteristics that should be considered here include:

- genetic vulnerability in child (Lyons-Ruth *et al.* 1999)

- age of child at onset of maltreatment (including uterine distress) (Archer 2001b, 2002)

- quality of primary attachment relationships prior to maltreatment (van der Kolk 1996d)

- frequency of occurrence and characteristics of stressor (Lyons-Ruth *et al.* 1999)

- duration of period of maltreatment

- significant separations, losses, illnesses and moves in child's early life

- parents' own attachment history and organisational status (Main and Cassidy 1988; Lyons-Ruth *et al.* 1999)

- loss or other unresolved trauma in caregivers (Main and Hesse 1990; Lyons-Ruth *et al.* 1999).

It is essential to bear in mind that attachment patterns are not merely a function of the child, tending to evolve out of the dyadic relationship between child and caregiver. Where there is asymmetry of power in the relationship, the controlling behaviours associated with disorganised attachments ensue.

Dissociative Cross-Weave

Main's work suggests that parents of children rated as Disorganised appear frightened, frightening or disorientated in their communications with their children, whilst Lyons-Ruth *et al.* (1999) implicate relational dysfluency, derived from unintegrated parental states of mind. An infant whose alcohol-abusing mother might, from moment to moment, change from caring, to emotionally unavailable, would both witness and experience fear, and feel confusion and chaos, rather than containment and predictability. This has been shown to be particularly damaging during the first year of the child's life (Main 1990) when internal working models are being established. In such situations the attachment figure provides an inherently paradoxical stimulus, leaving the child's normal attachment-seeking behaviour unresolved and irresolvable. In effect the child is drawn to seek comfort from the source of his distress and is thus placed in an intolerable, 'Catch 22' situation. According to Main (1990) such parents are seen both as cause for alarm and the source of safety, observing that the child's inability to resolve this paradox leads to a 'collapse' of behavioural strategy and attention. From her observations, typical response behaviours were for the child to freeze, enter trance-like states, fall prone on the floor huddled up, or cling whilst crying hard and leaning away, with gaze averted. These types of behaviour can be described as approach-avoidant.

The most extreme feature of the disorganised attachment pattern is that of dissociation (Solomon and George 1999a). Liotti (1995) makes strong links between disorganised attachment patterns in children and personality disorders and serious dissociative disorders in adulthood. As Schore (1994) points out, failure to address such serious attachment-based difficulties in childhood leads to lifelong mental health problems, many of which are deemed 'untreatable' within contemporary British psychiatric medicine (Johnson 2002a).

Solomon and George (1999b) speak of the avoidant, anxious and ambivalent attachment patterns as being 'organised', in that patterns of relating are consistent and coherent. What clearly distinguishes disorganised attachment is its primary disorganisation. It should be noted that children classified as 'disorganised' may demonstrate more than one type of attachment behaviour towards the same attachment figure. Our experience at Family Futures is that traumatised children tend not only to show different attachment patterns to different people but also to demonstrate more than one IWM relating to a single individual. This seems the case particularly where chaotic and unpredictable parenting has been experienced. For example, the child may have several, parallel IWMs of attachment to 'Sad Mother', 'Angry Mother', 'Needy Mother', 'Caring Mother' and so on. This view is supported by Fonagy's (2002) development of Main's work on multiple metacognitions.

As they mature, children categorised as disorganised display typical features of disorganised attachment alongside other observable attachment behaviour patterns. This is consistent with Bowlby's 'segregated attachment systems' proposition (1979), and Liotti's (1999) 'multiple internal working models' hypothesis. According to Solomon and George (1999a), these youngsters adopt superficially more organised behavioural patterns whilst retaining mental representations of self and others that remain fundamentally disorganised. Hence Main and Solomon (1990) recommend that all disorganised infants be assigned 'closest fitting' sub-classifications A–C; current secondary classifications favour rating children as D/secure or D/insecure (Lyons-Ruth *et al.* 1999).

Main and Cassidy (1988) refer to 'controlling' behaviour patterns in kindergarten children previously rated as Disorganised; others (Crittenden 1995; Lyons-Ruth *et al.* 1999) describe bimodal controlling-caregiving and controlling-punitive behaviour patterns beyond infancy. We observe such controlling behaviours in many of the school age children with whom we work. They may be understood as adaptive attempts to exclude distressing representations of self as helpless and needy (Liotti 1999) or to redress the original relational imbalance (Lyons-Ruth *et al.* 1999). In our experience these apparently organised behaviours are transferred to subsequent parent-child dyadic relationships. They are frequently triggered by underlying distress, consistent with Porges' (1998) polyvagal theory of hierarchical stress responses (see also Chapter 4). Use of actively hostile 'fight' or 'flight' strategies, or the passive helplessness and hopelessness of the 'freeze' response, indicates dissolution to developmentally earlier survival strategies (Porges 1998). Entry into these altered, or dissociative, behaviour states reflects fundamental, representational disorganisation in the child.

Main and Cassidy (1988) used doll play and story stems of attachment-related scenarios to examine the mental representations of children with disorganised attachments. They found that this group differed from the other attachment groups: their attachments tended to be based around the theme of hopelessness. In Main and Cassidy's study, stories of children judged to be disorganised were of two distinct types: either containing pronounced elements of danger and chaos or inhibited and devoid of play and people. According to Teti (1999) these distinct groups are associated with the sub-groups 'controlling-punitive' and 'controlling-caregiving' respectively. There is evidence (George and Solomon 1998; Lyons-Ruth et al. 1999) to suggest that children in these sub-groups demonstrate qualitatively different, unresolved caregiving histories: the former experiencing hostile parenting or physical abuse, the latter parental withdrawal or sexual abuse.

According to Main and Cassidy (1988):

> The first (group) are characterised by the depiction of chaotic, frightening events leading to separation and often the disintegration of the family. At the level of content the themes are frightening, explosive and angry. This is consistent with Main and Hesse's hypothesis (1990) that fear lies at the heart of disorganization. When the children tell their stories they are often unable to control or organize their story. They appear 'driven' or 'flooded' by the content which depicts evil people and monsters which appear to arrive from nowhere or vanish and will rise again. These characters often transform themselves. There is a nightmare quality to the story. (p.417)

In contrast, in the second kind of story, the child's helplessness is not depicted directly; instead the child's story demonstrates an absence or marked inhibition of play. It is as if the child is struggling to flee the situation mentally as quickly as possible. Their play is often constricted; their stories barren and devoid of people.

Interestingly, dissociative qualities in adults have been associated both with heightened capacities for fantasy (Aldridge-Morris 1991; Hilgard 1977), linked to attempts to escape painful reality (Ross 1997), and constricted fantasy play (Mollon 1996), where fantasy and reality are all too distressingly similar. The two, very diverse, story stem outcomes reported by Main and Cassidy (1988) are consistent with both these interpretations and could be understood as children's attempts to dissociate themselves from the chaos and fear inherent in their family relationships. The research carried out by Main and associates, and Solomon and George, over the past 20 years is also consistent with Bowlby's original 'segregated systems' attachment model (1979) and Lyons-Ruth and colleagues' (1999) unintegrated 'hostile-helpless' relational model.

Braun (1984) defines dissociation as 'the ability to make unpleasant thoughts and feelings go away'. Under extreme duress, he continues, 'whole experiences can be put away'. Dissociation in childhood is considered to be a normal, developmental process (Putnam 1997). As the child matures, his disjointed, state-dependent perceptions of the world become integrated (Putnam 1997; Siegel 1999) and he acquires a more holistic, associated perspective. Thus Liotti (1999) suggests that dissociation can be described as a lack of associations, initially a natural, adaptive part of the integrative developmental process, associated with developmental, metacognitive deficits (Main 1991) and maintenance of multiple internal working models (Liotti 1999). Dissociation can also provide the primary auto-hypnotic defence response available to youngsters (Mollon 1996), enabling children mentally to step around scary information and to survive otherwise unsurvivable experiences (Herman 1992). Either way, information relating to these experiences will not be stored within narrative memory, involving the proposed integrative functions of the mid-brain hippocampus (Bremner et al. 1995b) and readily available to conscious, verbal recall and reflection. Instead traumatic information is processed discretely by the mid-brain amygdala (Balbernie 2001; Siegel 1999) and stored primarily as sensori-motor and sensori-affective data, or implicit, procedural memories (Balbernie 2001; Schore 1994; Siegel 1999) (see also Chapter 4), that are highly immune to modification (LeDoux, Romanski and Xagoraris 1991).

Dissociation becomes problematic when it becomes chronic and behavioural pathology such as forgetting, lying, stealing, acting out and destructive behaviour (Shirar 1996) becomes apparent. According to Shirar (1996) these are frequently not recognised or treated as dissociative defences: instead they are perceived as problem behaviours. For example, when a child cannot remember what he has just been doing, he will naturally tend to fabricate a narrative (Waites 1997), which will appear to the observer to be 'lying'. Since the traumatised child is likely to have a poorly developed orbitofrontal cortex (Schore 1994, 2001a, 2002; Siegel 1999), the mismatch between subjective and objective versions may be compounded by weak 'mindreading' capacities (Baron-Cohen 1999) and fragile autonoetic consciousness (self-awareness) (Siegel 1999), associated with dysfunction in this area. When challenged he may simply be unable to recognise that his story is contradicted by observable evidence. Furthermore he is unlikely to learn from experience that his confabulation is unconvincing, or revise his inner working models to become more coherent and integrated, since learning will remain state-dependent and fail to be generalised (Putnam 1997; Shirar 1996).

Infant Behaviour States

In babies there is no sense of 'self'. Instead the infant experiences various 'discrete behavioural states' (Putnam 1997) of consciousness (see also Chapter 4). Initially, regulation of these behavioural and affective states is the caregiver's job, since immature infants lack the capacity to self-regulate (Schore 1994, 2001a; Siegel 1999). Through co-regulation with the primary caregiver and repeated experiences of smooth transitions from state to state during the positive attachment cycle, the youngster gradually develops a sense of continuous being and unified identity. Maltreated children will, by definition, not experience the consistency and containment of attuned, attachment interactions necessary: their representations of self and others will therefore remain segregated in dissociated, altered states of consciousness (Liotti 1999). Moreover, children who are traumatised in their early years may actively maintain these highly-charged, distressing experiences outside their 'normal consciousness', by entering discrete, dissociative states (Putnam 1997; Shirar 1996). Access to these traumatic memories may unwittingly be triggered by re-experiencing, or even contemplating, any part of the original traumatic event (van der Kolk 1996b): since they are state-dependent experiences they are unlikely to be integrated. Dissociative disorders are therefore not so much about children 'coming apart' as about never having been 'joined up' (Archer 1999b; Liotti 1999; Putnam 1997).

Chronic dissociation can also be understood in terms of the dissociogenic environment of confusion and deception inherent in distorted family systems (Liotti 1999), or as 'learned helplessness' (e.g. Herman 1992) or hostile control: the contradictory behavioural options observable within approach-avoidance situations (Lyons-Ruth et al. 1999). Since approach-avoidance, in both parent and child (Lyons-Ruth et al. 1999), is central to the attachment paradox, it is not surprising that a high proportion of dysregulated, abused and neglected youngsters demonstrating disorganised relationship patterns, also display dissociative behaviours. For many, this equates with Terr's Type II trauma typology (Terr 1991), during which dissociative strategies are employed, since these chronically traumatic situations possess some measure of predictability. Dissociation involves alterations in consciousness that affect perception, thinking, emotional expression, somatic state and underlying neurobiological regulation (Liotti 1999; Lyons-Ruth *et al.* 1999; Perry 1999; Putnam 1997; Schore 1994, 2001a; Solomon and George 1999a) and is a significant feature of post traumatic stress disorders (van der Kolk 1996).

Post Traumatic Stress

Verbal, declarative or explicit recall does not develop until a child reaches 28 to 36 months, as the hippocampus matures (Siegel 1999; Ledoux 1999). Reflective functions develop as connections to the orbitofrontal cortex mature (Balbernie 2001; Baron-Cohen 1999; Carter 2000). Memories of pre-verbal and traumatic events are stored as body sensations, movements, feelings, sounds, smells and images (Levine 1997; Waites 1997). Traumatic events leave behavioural, implicit or procedural memories which may take the form of intrusive dreams or nightmares, repetitive post traumatic flashbacks, re-enactments, during which the youngster is effectively 'doing unto others what was done to him', hypervigilance and hyper-reactivity (Perry 1999; van der Kolk 1996b). Core symptoms of post traumatic stress syndromes also include avoidance, psychic numbing, depression, poor concentration and alterations in attention (van der Kolk 1996d), all of which are dissociative symptoms.

Van der Kolk (1996a) draws attention to this characteristic biphasic pattern of post traumatic response, consistent with Solomon and George's descriptions (1999a) of flooded or constricted segregated systems and Lyons-Ruth and colleagues' (1999) bimodal 'hostile-helpless' model. Whilst psychic and behavioural reactivity, representing the hypermnesia of the biphasic traumatic memory system (Mollon 1998), can be considered to be part of a psychic approach strategy, to facilitate mastery of distressing material, dissociative amnesia, especially for explicit material, can be considered as psychic avoidance. Thus events, even mundane ones and their associated feelings, can remain out of awareness until triggered by a seemingly benign situation. For example, a youngster whose sexual abuse included hair stroking as part of her 'grooming' could find herself re-experiencing state-dependent memories of that abuse when her adoptive mother attempts to brush her hair. However, since the original traumatic events do not form part of declarative or autobiographical memory, the child can neither begin to discriminate, or make essential connections, between past and present, nor effect symbolic transformations (Hughes 2002). Instead she may be retraumatised by the current, benign experience (Mollon 1998) and, simultaneously, reinforce her repertoire of dissociative strategies (Mollon 1996).

Unravelling Tangled Threads: Therapeutic Intervention

A major element of the therapy used at Family Futures is the use of experiential narrative and storytelling with traumatised children. We encourage youngsters to tell their own stories, or use disclosure of information available to the therapist or the children's parents, to help children gain conscious access to vital, personal information. This enables youngsters to update and integrate their autobiographical narratives (Hughes 2002; van der Kolk 1996b; Waites 1997), and feel understood by, and more connected to, their adopters (Hughes 2002). There are considerable implications here for the work that social workers do in preparing life storybooks for adopted children, work that is often, in our view, effected very superficially. Frequently there is insufficient detail; the truth about the child's traumatic past tends to be glossed over and adopters are not routinely involved. It is also not uncommon for life story work to be suspended once a child becomes distressed. We interpret this reaction as indicating that traumatic memories are being reawakened: the youngster may be re-experiencing the trauma in the here-and-now, or become distressed as the incongruity of his beliefs about his past are exposed.

These are very significant processes that need to be integrated within an informed, proactive, therapeutic approach, with the deliberate intention of enabling children to integrate their parallel, or segregated, internal working models. A secure 'holding' environment, involving current caregivers, is fundamental to this very powerful work (Hughes 2002). Complex issues of contact are also relevant here, since beyond the life storybook, real-life or imagined ongoing contact with birth relatives may be occurring. Arranging facilitated contact (see Chapter 11) can in real time and real life facilitate this process of integration and healing. However, this too needs to occur as part of a planned and integrated therapeutic process that includes the adoptive parents, not as something that exists in isolation or for its own sake.

In our experience, under stress, for example following a placement transition, children revert to their earliest internalised models, or 'road maps', and behaviour patterns. As a result, adoptive parents may initially be faced with a child whose attachment patterns and internal working models relate to his birth family, or earliest foster family. Over time new, more positive, attachment patterns may develop which will enable him to deal with, and process, previous traumatic events and deconstruct, then integrate, earlier internal working models. The major implication here is that to address the therapeutic needs of the child, primary attachment issues need to be seen as paramount and must be addressed before dealing with specific issues of trauma. The child needs to develop more positive attachments and internalise more secure parental models if he is to access sufficient, healthy ego strength to integrate his existing internal working models (Hughes 2002). This is an essential prerequisite for therapeutic healing. Following is a summary list of the preconditions for therapeutic change:

- permanent good enough parents
- one to two years within a stable family environment to facilitate some positive attachment to new parents
- therapeutic opportunities for the child to integrate his working models
- therapeutic help for the child to process traumatic experiences, with parental support
- therapeutic support for parents to process any traumatic life experiences that may resonate with the child's
- access for parents to information about, and interpretation of, child's history in the context of trauma, attachment and child development theories
- a parental support programme incorporating effective, developmental reparenting strategies.

The first and second points are reciprocal processes, since children need 'new parents' to do this work within therapy; as they do the work with their parents their attachment to them increases. The latter process equates to a positive paradox of parenting, an approach-approach model that is the converse of the approach-avoidance of the disorganised attachment model. The final points ensure that parents are able to provide the better-than-good-enough parenting that traumatised children require in order to effect lasting change and healing. In our experience, lack of understanding and support for adoptive parents can lead to secondary traumatisation (Cairns 1999) in caregivers and actively inhibits the child's healing process. This complex interweave of essential therapeutic elements will continue to be explored throughout this volume.

Summary

It is clear that recent changes in the nature of adoption have increased the complexities of placement and emphasised the need for increasingly sophisticated, integrated post adoption services. Fortunately our understanding of attachment theory, and especially disorganised attachments, has continued to develop and has become increasingly linked to developmental and trauma theories. Teasing out the implications of these interrelated fields is no easy task but can provide us with an effective working model for family and therapeutic interventions. Thus embracing the experience-dependent organisation of neural pathways (Perry 1999) allows us to connect failures of early caregiving with the initially adaptive evolution of distorted, segregated internal working models (Liotti 1999; Schore 2001a), distorted relationship interactions (Lyons-Ruth *et al.* 1999) and observable dissociative symptomatology. Since learning occurs optimally within healthy attachment relationships (Perry 1999), and needs to be integrated across states (Putnam 1997), we can understand why the intellectual and academic development of traumatised children is also likely to be compromised. Work at Family Futures has attempted to integrate all these areas of concern and to ensure that the essential therapeutic elements we have identified are met in coherent, collaborative, rationally organised and functional ways.

CHAPTER 4

Weft and Warp
Developmental Impact of Trauma and Implications for Healing
Caroline Archer

I love to give myself away
But I find it hard to trust
Got no map to find my way
Amongst these clouds of dust.

Setting the Scene

One of the most exciting experiences of the closing years of the 20th century has been, for me, the increase in robust research-based evidence, demonstrating the dramatic effects of traumatic experience on human neurobiology. Simultaneously there seems to have been a sea change in approach within the crucial areas of attachment, child development and clinical practice, as groundbreaking clinicians like Schore (1994, 1998), Hughes (1997, 1998) and Siegel (1997, 1999) breathed new life into old ways of thinking. With these inspirational developments, I too was able to gain the strength of conviction necessary to connect my own experiences of being parented, and of being an adoptive parent, with both logical and 'gut feelings' about these issues and to synthesise them into some literary coherence. One major outcome for me was the publication of two volumes of 'developmental reparenting strategies', written for the adoptive parents of 'children who hurt' (Archer 1999a, 1999b).

Concurrently, the founder members of Family Futures Consortium were creating their own unique blend of therapeutic interventions and family support measures for a similar population of children and families. Understanding the cycles of attachment, abuse and neglect in terms of fundamental organic change, and its inevitable impact on the developmental life cycle of the child, has enabled us to begin to 'close the circle'. Hence we can begin to integrate predominantly left-brained scientific knowledge with intuitive, holistic right-brained perspectives from adult adoptees, adoptive families and their sensitive therapists. This is a theme that is being explored not only in 'serious literature' but also in novels, such as Pat Barker's fascinating *Regeneration* trilogy (Barker 1993, 1995, 1996).

Telling the Story

Traditionally, attachment theorists, including Bowlby, proposed that attachments between parent and infant begin beyond the first six months of a child's life. However, whilst the classic, external signs of 'separation anxiety' (Bowlby 1988) may not become evident before an infant reaches six months, more subtle observations point to much earlier, global responses to distress (Murray Parkes 1997; Perry 1993a, 1999; Schore 1994, 2001b). Spangler and Grossman (1999) observed neurobiological dysregulation in neonates, which they suggest may be the result of uterine exposure to maternal distress. Drell, Siegel and Ganesbauer (1993) allude to symptoms of post traumatic distress disorders in early infancy, emphasising that infants may be particularly sensitised, and therefore highly vulnerable, to sensory and affective stimuli, whilst lacking mature cognitive capacities to comprehend or modulate their subjective distress. Schwarz and Perry (1994) refer to the developmentally maladaptive, generalised activation of the alarm response in babies and young children, leading to exaggerated hypervigilance, avoidance or re-enactment behaviours. Acknowledging both genetic and micro-environmental contributions to this neurobiologically based adaptation to survival, they identify the long-term effects of early traumatic experience, including depressive, dissociative, eating, identity and personality disorders, which become particularly apparent during adolescence, often potentiated by the developmental demands of that stressful, transitional period. This pattern of enduring psychopathology is confirmed by Fonagy (1999a); Putnam (1997); Schore

(1994, 2001a, 2001b, 2002); Siegel (1999); van der Kolk (1996) and Waites (1997).

Exploring the developmental implications of early trauma, both Schwarz and Perry (1994) and Drell *et al.* (1993) describe modified response patterns dependent on an infant's level of maturity at the onset of distress, in particular the disruption of the good enough parent-child relationship. This may be secondary to parentally experienced trauma or result directly from separation, loss, or maltreatment. Such experiences have been shown to be particularly overwhelming when associated with primary caregiving, since they create an inescapable paradox within which the youngster must seek vital comfort and security from the very source of his distress (Perry 1995a; Solomon and George 1999a; van der Kolk 1996d). They are also highly correlated with disorganised attachment patterns (Liotti 1999; Solomon and George 1999a) (see Chapter 3).

Whilst infants may respond with disturbances to global functioning, evidenced by excessive crying, disturbed eating and sleeping patterns, hypervigilance, neurophysiological lability or muted responses, lethargy and failure to thrive, toddlers may additionally demonstrate difficulties associated with the age-appropriate tasks of separation, individuation and autonomy. They may display increased anxiety, sleep disturbance, motor activity and aggression or, alternatively, appear unresponsive and apathetic. Additionally, older toddlers may show problems with somatisation, socialisation, repetitive play, dissociative state changes, clinging, regression, shame, cognitive and language development whilst, conversely, exhibiting precocious linguistic and pro-social coping skills at times (Drell *et al.* 1993; Schwarz and Perry 1994). Moreover, I would suggest that a child's organic developmental pathway commences in utero, mediated by the maternal micro-environment (Perry 1999; Schore 1994). We must therefore consider the potential for maladaptive neurobiological changes during gestation, when the infant may be deemed most developmentally sensitive to interruptions to the, literally and metaphorically, life giving foetal-maternal relationship. Mother and baby do not exist in isolation, rather they interact in many subtle and complex ways, at levels which may extend from the physical through the existential towards the spiritual.

Talking Neurohormones

More than 20 years ago Verny and Kelly (1981) began to explore the foetal-maternal relationship and to suggest that during pregnancy the mother's longer term emotional states could substantially affect the well being of her unborn child. More recently, Borysenko and Borysenko (1994) have demonstrated how this uterine 'dialogue' is mediated through the exchange of neurohormonal messages. Perry (1994, 1995a, 1999) has proposed that such traumatic exchanges can, in their turn, lead to genetic alterations. In maturing offspring this could certainly be considered adaptive, since babies exposed to distress in the womb would come into the world expecting to encounter stress and optimally prepared to survive such an environment. Evidence to support this claim is provided by Fisk (2000), who demonstrated that an 18-week foetus reacts to uterine distress with increased secretion of the stress hormone cortisol. Perhaps the ongoing debate as to whether or not a foetus experiences pain is spurious, since in all events the foetus clearly suffers considerable dis-stress.

In animals, elevated cortisol levels are associated with helplessness (Lyons-Ruth, Bronfman and Atwood 1999). The release of cortisol is known to affect human energy levels and immune system function (Schore 1994; McEwen 2000), as part of the 'fight, flight or freeze' response to stress (Perry 1995a).

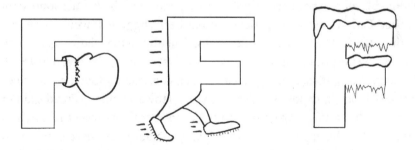

Figure 4.1 Fight, flight, freeze – responses to stress

Schore (2002) suggests that the direction of the the stress response may be gendered genetically. He also postulates that abuse and neglect may have differential effects on its neurobiological and behavioural expression.

Corticosteroids have also been shown to have adverse effects on cell growth (Sapolsky et al. 1990), maturing neural pathways (Begley 1997; McEwen 2000; Schore 1994; Siegel 1999) and long-term psychoneuroimmuno-logical responses (Schore 1994; McEwen 2000). Spangler and Grossman (1999) found associations between elevated cortisol levels and attachment disorganisation in infancy. Areas of the developing brain that may be affected by excess corticosteroids include fronto-temporal areas, leading to mentalising deficits (Fonagy 1999b), and the hippocampal system (McEwen 2000; Panksepp 1998; Schore 2001a). This last leads to difficulties with verbal memory processing, according to Glaser and Balbernie (2001), who also report ongoing difficulties with attention and concentration in nursery-age children demonstrating elevated cortisol levels. As a function of the relative dominance of the earlier maturing right limbic amygdala (Schore 1994, 2001a; Siegel 1999), somatic, sensory and affective memories become more intense (Drell et al. 1993), and the youngster's traumatic responses more generalised (Siegel 1999; Waites 1997) than in more mature individuals.

Creating Memories

It has been argued that since the hippocampus, a key structure within the limbic system responsible for explicit (verbally recalled) memory, does not become myelinated until the child's third or fourth year (van der Kolk 1996a,b), then experiences prior to that period will have little long-term impact. Early traumatic experience, it has been suggested, would have few lasting effects. The term 'infantile amnesia', denoting the relative inability to recount events prior to age three years, was first proposed by Freud in 1899. Nelson (1988), in examining research data, consistently found evidence of memory block in children under four years. However, just as Freud did not discount the lasting impact of events beyond recall, so recent researchers propose that the apparent absence of early memory may have more to do with integration (Mollon 1998) or retrieval difficulties (Waites 1997) than with failure of initial memory storage itself.

There is certainly growing evidence that memories are laid down from the pregnancy period onward. For example, De Casper and Fifer (1980) have shown that newborn babies are able to discriminate between their mother's voice and that of a stranger, suggesting that prenatal auditory exposure and retrieval play a major part here. Neonates will also show a preference for breast pads bearing the smell of maternal breast milk (MacFarlane 1975). Reciprocal social smiling is evident by two months (Waites 1997), whilst haptic (touch related) memory is also believed to play a large part in very early memory formation. Catherwood (1993) demonstrated the capacity of babies at eight months old to sustain tactile memories, even when other touch experiences intervened. Hopefully, as we become more adept at creating subtle measures of foetal and neonatal sensory and motor responses, we will become increasingly able to demonstrate the infant's capacities for very early memory function.

Discussion of the validity of early memory is by no means academic, since in very substantive ways memories themselves form the basis of self-awareness at every level. For Perry (1999) memories are carried in every human cell; van der Kolk (1996a) contends that 'The body keeps the score' and Pert (1999) proposes an intelligent body-mind information system, which integrates our awareness. According to Waites (1997), attachments form the social matrix of memory, providing both the context for the burgeoning awareness of self and repeated, shared conversations with primary attachment figures, from which the individual derives his personal narrative: his 'own coherent story'. Thus attachment relationships provide not only the powerful emotional milieu and valence for the child's first memories but also the sensory, motor and linguistic templates for encoding essential personal information, from which the child derives an increasingly integrated sense of self.

Dancing to the Tune

There is growing evidence, from developmental neurobiological studies, that an infant's very earliest interpersonal experiences inform the selective development of neural pathways within the brain and nervous system (Balbernie 2001). Thus consistent, healthy attachment experiences from good enough parent(s) lead to the formation of well organised, well regulated 'baby brains' (Schore 1998). The infant acquires his regulatory capacities, including basic functions such as respiration and heart rates, sensory, motor and emotional modulation and integration, and higher, cortical self-regulation, through the 'dance of attunement' with primary caregiver(s), beginning before birth. From infant observation studies, Trevarthen (1979) describes a sophisticated sensory and emotional dialogue between mother and baby, which he terms 'primary intersubjectivity'. The parent's capacity to 'tune in and turn on' their infant provides vital co-regulatory experiences (Schore 1994) of shared stimulation, comfort and transition (Archer 2001b). These form the templates ('road maps') for the youngster's ability to regulate his own states of body and mind, to develop mentalising capacities (Fonagy 1999b, 2002) and to manage essential transitions between states (Putnam 1997; Schore 1994; Siegel 1999). Hence connecting with the caregiver literally provides the youngster with the organic, structural connections that form the lifelong basis for his socio-emotional functioning. These include the development of healthy internal working models (Bowlby 1973, 1988) of his environment, both internally and externally, and his global sense of self, including self-esteem, self-control and self-efficacy.

The child's internal 'road maps', symbolic representations of organic brain structure, are functional and energy conserving (Siegel 1999), since they allow the individual to make rapid predictions about the future, based directly on past experience. This is, essentially, a highly adaptive process: the economy of response facilitating developmental survival, giving the individual a functional 'edge' in performance terms. Simultaneously it confers a greater sense of autonomy on the individual, enhancing his sense of self-efficacy and well being. Hence healthy attachments have profound, positive effects on a child's resilience, providing in-built protection against subsequent traumatic and distressful experiences (van der Kolk 1996d).

Establishing Pathways

We could visualise this in terms of laying down footpaths across a familiar stretch of land. Once we have walked these paths repeatedly and the undergrowth has been trodden down they will become well established, easy to follow and easy to maintain; there would be plenty of interconnecting pathways. The sketch maps of the area we could draw up would be simple and relatively easy to follow. If the paths have been well planned and remain in continuous use they would lead us to most places we need to go. They would also provide a flexible, basic framework from which we could explore new territory with relative confidence, since there would be considerable 'goodness of fit' between the familiar old and the unfamiliar new ground.

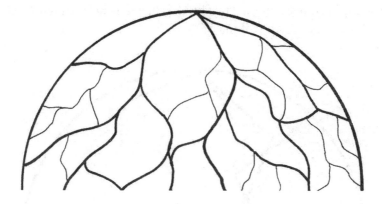

Figure 4.2 Healthy 'road map'

Conversely, poor, inconsistent or traumatic early attachment relationships have been shown to lead to the establishment of very different brain and nervous system structures. These are associated with poor capacity for self-regulation (Schore 1994), reflective function (Fonagy 1999b) and concomitant emotional and behavioural difficulties (Archer 1999c; Balbernie 1999, 2001; Hughes 1997, 2002). McEwen (2000) refers to the 'pruning' of nerve cells and neural connections that are not regularly used; Perry (1995a, 1999) speaks of the 'use dependent' nature of development, by which the infant selectively establishes neural pathways in line with previous experience. In the traumatised child the loss of potentially healthy neural networks and the creation of distinct, distorted neural pathways serves to provide him with the best possibility of survival. His body will be set on 'red alert', primed for high levels of stress, and his internal 'road maps' will be limited and rigid: hardwiring him to respond selectively to perceived threat rapidly, through 'fight, flight or freeze' stress responses.

Continuing our footpath metaphor, we might imagine a pattern of heavily worn pathways criss-crossing portions of our patch of land, with fewer interconnecting pathways, little global coherence and reduced flexibility. The sketch maps we would draw up would reflect this relative lack of connection and organisation but would readily facilitate 'navigation' through chaotic new territories. However, there would be little 'goodness of fit' when applied to more ordered, less familiar areas. The traveller would find himself in seriously uncharted waters. In adhering to his well-worn routes he would encounter much adversity, both real and perceived. This would further confirm his beliefs that the world is hostile, unpredictable and potentially life threatening and that he must therefore hold to these tried and tested 'road maps' against all the odds.

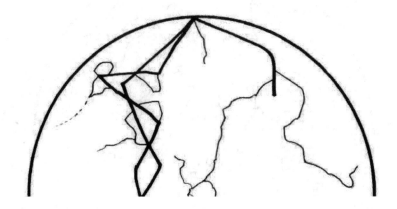

Figure 4.3 Unhealthy 'road map'

The Response Hierarchy

According to Porges' (1997, 1998) polyvagal theory, mature human beings have access to a hierarchy of responses to new or difficult situations. The 'highest', and developmentally most recent, level of response is unique to human beings, involving the 'smart' vagus, allowing mediation and resolution of such challenges through reason, language and the parasympathetic moderation of automatic body-based reactions via the ventral vagal complex (VVC). Thus predominantly left-brained higher thought processes can be used to modulate and integrate socio-emotional behaviours and successfully negotiate the unfamiliar. The second level of vagally mediated response is the mid-brain 'fight or flight' response, which is common to all mammals and, as a high arousal, neurobiological sequence, is adaptive to survival, whether as predator or prey (Levine 1997). These autonomic reactions are familiar to many of us and are popularly associated with increased adrenaline secretion. The most primitive level of response is related to brain stem survival functions, such as respiration, body temperature and heart rate. Evolving first in reptiles as 'feigning death' or 'freezing' behaviour, it involves a dramatic fall in energy available to the organism, through activation of the parasympathetic nervous system. These unusually low arousal body-mind states have been closely linked with dissociative states in humans (Perry 1999).

Whilst the evolution of this phylogenetic, hierarchical response pattern has clearly been adaptive, the impact of traumatic experience, particularly traumatic experience which impacts our species-specific development, can render it highly maladaptive. In such circumstances the child's capacity to integrate each level of vagal response and select the most appropriate strategy becomes severely compromised. Under stress he is likely to decompensate and utilise more primitive response patterns (Porges 1998). Since neurobiological adaptation 'programmes' us to see what we expect to see (another adaptive economy of function (Siegel 1999)), the abandoned, abused or neglected child is likely to continue to perceive threat within his environment where none may exist. The inevitable precipitation of the physiological 'fight, flight or freeze' reactions, in their turn, confirm the youngster's distorted 'road map' of beliefs that the world is inimical. These states form the basis for the child's distorted self-perceptions, ranging from feeling abandoned, helpless, overwhelmingly needy and shame-filled, through to self-contained, all-powerful, self-sufficient and blameless (Archer 1999b; Schore 1994), reflecting the 'helpless-versus-hostile' dynamic proposed by Lyons-Ruth *et al.* (1999).

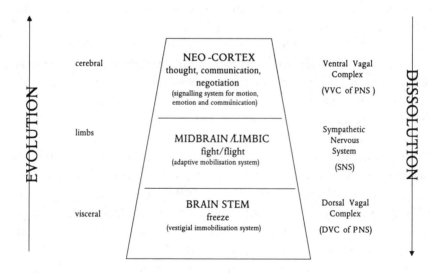

Figure 4.4 Response hierarchy (after Porges (1998))

These 'segregated' states (Bowlby 1979) are by no means mutually exclusive but, in practice, many traumatised children identify themselves, and hence become identified by others, with one dominant ego state (Archer 1999c; Putnam 1997). Recent sophisticated alterations to attachment classifications recognise this apparent organised *behavioural* overlay in children categorised as 'disorganised', as they mature, whilst acknowledging the persisting disorganisation of underlying mental representations (Lyons-Ruth *et al.* 1999). Hence, over time, what begins as a relatively transient physiological and behavioural state becomes a more or less permanent personality trait (Perry 1995a; Siegel 1999). This is supported by observations by Spangler and Grossman (1999) that neurobiological dysregulation in neonates is significantly associated with the disorganised classification in infancy and with 'controlling' behaviours, both 'caregiving' and 'aggressive' (Lyons-Ruth *et al.* 1999) in school age children. It can be understood in terms of repeated state-dependent triggering of traumatic memories eliciting chronic neurobiological dysregulation, leading to behavioural disorganisation.

Dissociative Connections

Due to the associated phenomena of neurophysiological 'triggering' and state-dependent memory it requires very low levels of stress, or the somato-sensory recognition of a small element of these survival-based response patterns, in order to set off an entire, neurobiological chain reaction, over which the child has gained little conscious control. He may then be catapulted into extreme states of mind and body, with predictable patterns of expectations, perceptions and reactions, quite inappropriate to the actual circumstances he is encountering. Although his internal 'road maps' are out of kilter with his surroundings, the child's well established but distorted internal working models will prevent him from recognising this lack of coherence, or learning from his mistakes so as to alter his cognitions or behaviours (Perry 1995b; Siegel 1999). His poor capacity for self-regulation, including the modulation of arousal and transition between states of body-mind, mean that he will find it difficult to return to more normal states readily (Perry 1999; Putnam 1997). Thus the 'fight, flight and freeze' responses are essentially dissociative responses, meeting Putnam's criteria for discrete behavioral states (Putnam 1997):

- marked 'distance' from normal states of consciousness along dimensions such as heart rate, respiration, affect (emotion), and level of arousal

- profound state dependency of the accessibility/retrieval of information, feelings and memories

- 'architectural' structure of the pathways connecting states. Direct pathways are postulated to be closer in state space than pathways that must traverse a series of intervening states

- pronounced lack of integration of knowledge and sense of self at the metacognitive level, which would facilitate integration and continuity of identity and behaviour across daily fluctuations in behavioural state.

Whilst there can be no question that these organic adaptations were originally adaptive, they become major barriers to change within the more caring environment of an adoptive family. The child may regularly misperceive his adoptive mother as a 'hostile monster' or, conversely, a 'helpless mouse': reflecting his earliest parenting experiences. He will then continue to use his primitive survival strategies, using his internalised 'road maps' to 'survive the familiar threat', since for the great majority of traumatised children this threat previously occurred within intimate family relationships. Thus, sadly, the 'transplanted' child will be unable to make consistently good use of the nurture and security offered to him by good enough substitute parents (Delaney and Kunstal 1993), whilst his survival-based behaviours are likely to distress his new family and challenge their perceptions of themselves as competent parents.

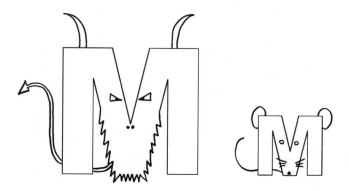

Figure 4.5 Distorted perceptions: Mother – monster or mouse?

Implications for Interventions

The idiosyncratic neurobiological organisation of the traumatised child has major implications for effective therapeutic interventions. His disorganised attachment patterns, the somato-sensory and affective dominance of his implicit memory, his distorted perceptual and cognitive systems, and his fundamental lack of self-integration frequently render direct, language-based approaches ineffective. The child's typical 'road maps' will not enable him to make sense of traditional 'client centred' approaches, since he lacks basic internal and external sensory, and socio-emotional, literacy and his expectations of interpersonal relationships are founded on insecurity, mistrust and unpredictability. We can understand these difficulties, and begin to explore more appropriate interventions, in the light of the complex, interconnected, neurobiologically-based traumatic phenomena addressed briefly below. Although here I identify several separate areas, they are discussed together, since it is vital to recognise their complex, dynamic interconnections:

- attachment-based difficulties
- developmentally-based distortions
- traumatic memory storage – pre-verbal/non-verbal
- experience-dependent maturation of neural networks.

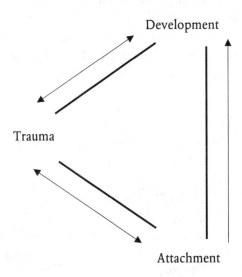

Figure 4.6 The trauma triangle

Early attachment experiences determine the child's internalised perceptions of himself and others. In particular they impact the child's expectations of self and others in terms of security, trust, predictability and efficacy. They are highly implicated in the development of internal working models (Bowlby 1988; Siegel 1999) and the organisation and integration of these multiple representations of self and others (Fonagy 2002; Liotti 1999).

Attempts to forge a therapeutic alliance with the traumatised child are likely to be built on rocky foundations, since the child may share few common perceptions of the world with the therapist: lacking fundamental self-awareness and possessing distorted 'road maps' by which to negotiate his healing journey. Many traumatised children have been shown to demonstrate disorganised patterns of attachment (Lyons-Ruth and Zeanah 1993) and will therefore lack an integrated, coherent sense of self and others across time and context.

Attachment forms the basis for the organic development of the brain (Schore 1994). Essentially, in the first three years of life, this involves 'right brain to right brain' (Schore 1998, 2001a) communications. These are rapid sensory and affect-based exchanges which, when shared with a sensitively attuned caregiver, provide developmentally appropriate co-regulatory experiences (Schore 1994, 2002). Over time, the youngster acquires the capacity for self-regulation of (reptilian) brain stem and (mammalian) mid-brain-limbic arousal (Schore 1994, Siegel 1999).

Connections to higher brain functions, such as symbolic semantic representation and verbal expression, are also facilitated in these interactions with the good enough parent (Siegel 1999). The asymmetric development of the right orbito-frontal cortex, the 'senior executive' connecting the mid-brain and limbic system with the neo-cortex, has been demonstrated to be pivotal here (Schore 2001a, 2002). This area has been shown to be developmentally compromised in autistic children (Baron-Cohen 1999), in severely maltreated Romanian orphans (Federici 1998; O'Connor et al. 2000) and in traumatised children generally (Schore 2001b; Siegel 1999). The attachment relationship forms the basis for the maturation and integration of the child's reflective and metacognitive functions (Fonagy 1999b, 2002).

It will be difficult for traumatised youngsters, lacking vital somato-sensory, emotional and linguistic connections (Parnell 1999; van der Kolk 1996d), to engage meaningfully in verbal therapeutic interactions.

Their poorly developed reflective capacities will also interfere with the acquisition of appropriate insights through dialogue.

Traumatic experience in young children leads to selective development of survival responses, based on 'fight, flight or freeze' (Perry 1999). These sensitise the youngster to generalised perceptions of threat (Schwarz and Perry 1994) and result in state-dependent responses becoming neurobiological, and hence characterological, traits (Perry *et al.* 1995). Such children are predisposed to hair trigger over-reactions and find it difficult to engage maturely in the 'normal world' (Parnell 1999).

The traumatised child's capacities for cognitive re-structuring primarily through cognitive and verbal approaches will be limited. Attention should first be given to addressing the child's somato-sensory and sensory-affective regulatory capacities and distorted 'road maps' through the recapitulation of early attachment sequences (Archer 1999c).

Under stress the youngster's access to areas of higher consciousness has been shown to be reduced (van der Kolk 1996d, 2000). Sophisticated scanning techniques indicate that blood flow to the frontal cortex, and the language area in the left hemisphere (Broca's area), is substantially reduced (van der Kolk 1996d). Hence access to sequential and logical reasoning (Parnell 1999; Schore 1994) and the inhibition of impulsive reactions (van der Kolk 1996d, 1999) will be compromised.

During therapy, efforts to enable the child cognitively to understand his traumatically distorted perceptions will not override the body's automatic stress response (van der Kolk 1999). The application of recent, verbally acquired, knowledge to essentially infantile ego states will be compromised (Putnam 1997; Watkins and Watkins 1997). The dissonance between recent, cognitively acquired information and the child's prevailing neurobiological reality may cause additional distress and self-blame (van der Kolk 1999), which further inhibit desired therapeutic change.

The youngster's experiences of early traumatic distress frequently occur pre-verbally, before his explicit, declarative memory systems, requiring hippocampal maturity, are fully operational (Le Doux 1998; Siegel 1999; van der Kolk 1996a, b; Waites 1997). Memories from the first three years are predominately implicit (emotional, behavioural, somato-sensory, perceptual, non-verbal) memories (Parnell 1999) mediated by the earlier maturing right-hemispheric amygdala (Schore 2001a; Siegel 1999), which attributes emotional valence to experience. Implicit memories lack the 'hooks' of time and place conferred by the hippocampal system (Waites

1997) and are frequently re-experienced as if they are happening 'in the here and now' (van der Kolk 1999, 2000). They are associated with significant shifts in heart and respiratory rates (Perry 1996, 1999; van der Kolk 1999), tend to carry overwhelming, negative affect (van der Kolk 1996d) and tend to lack congruence and integration across the hemispheres (Parnell 1999).

Retrieval, and hence effective processing of such traumatic memories through 'the talking cure' will be extremely problematic, in part because the cortical activity of thinking will preclude activation of the amygdala (Carter 2000). Since traumatised youngsters may spend their lives trying to 'forget', they may also actively resist 'remembering' (Shirar 1996). In addition, retraumatisation during therapeutic retrieval is highly likely (Briere 1996; Levine 1997; Parnell 1999).

Traumatic experiences at any age are essentially non-verbal, somato-sensory and affective experiences, since the hippocampus and Broca's area are 'short-circuited' as part of the adaptive stress response. Language-based interventions are fundamentally left-brained, neo-cortical communications (Schore 1994). Traumatised children tend to have fewer healthy connections between their left and right cerebral hemispheres (Schore 1994), so that appropriate insights are inhibited. Where such children appear to have developed precocious verbal skills these frequently remain disconnected from sensory and emotional knowledge areas, both physiologically and psychologically (Archer 1999b).

Lack of good enough parenting, and disrupted attachments leading to 'synaptic pruning' (McEwen 2000; Schore 2001a, 2002), particularly in the ealier maturing right in the orbito-frontal cortex, leaves the child with ineffective self-regulatory capacities, weakened empathic attunement and poor cognitive functioning (Schore 2001a; Siegel 1999; Lyons-Ruth and Zeanah 1993). He will lack a coherent sense of self across mental and behavioural states (Putnam 1997; Shirar 1996; van der Kolk 1996): retrieval of essential historical information through 'the tyranny of language' (van der Kolk 1999) will therefore be problematic.

In the therapeutic relationship, the traumatised child will be further disadvantaged in utilising opportunities for engaging in verbal exchanges and for 'feeling felt' (Siegel 1999). He is unlikely to be able to experience the security of the holding environment, 'connect' with the therapist or express his fear and vulnerability directly.

Cognitive-behavioural approaches address the child's higher brain functions and rely on a maturing capacity to modulate attention and impulsivity. The traumatised child's neo-cortical, self-regulatory and verbal reasoning capacities have been compromised (Glaser and Balbernie 2001; van der Kolk 1999; Schore 2002) whilst his limbic and mid-brain sensory and emotional literacy remain developmentally weak and labile. The youngster's sense of self remains fragmented and his self-perceptions distorted (Parnell 1999; Fonagy 1999a).

Social learning and brief cognitive therapeutic interventions are unlikely to succeed with traumatised children. Therapeutic repair must first occur at the level of the original damage (Hughes 1997, 2002; Schore 1994; van der Kolk 1996, 1999) and in ways that recapitulate the sensitively attuned primary attachment relationship (Hughes 1997, 2002; Archer 1999a, 1999b, 1999c, 2001b). This can be understood in terms of Braun's (1988) BASK model of dissociation, where dissociation is defined as lack of normal associations (Ross 1997). Hence affective and sensory modalities form the core of self-awareness from which behavioural and conscious, knowledge-based connections, and hence mature controls, are derived subsequently.

Developmental maturity of the brain and nervous system evolves 'from the bottom up' – recapitulating phylogenetic evolution, through vegetative to reptilian to mammalian, and hence essentially human, states of being. Neurological development also displays hemispheric asymmetries (Schore 2001a, 2002; Siegel 1999). Thus the final part of the cerebral jigsaw to be put in place will be the higher cognitive, language-based reasoning competencies we have come to associate with mature human beings. Optimal fuctioning here is very much dependant on good levels of function at earlier developmental stages.

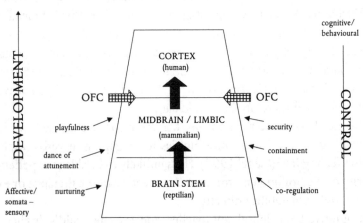

Figure 4.7 'Bottom up' developmental hierarchy of the brain

Since modulation of arousal and somato-sensory and affective literacy (all 'mammalian' brain functions) are seriously compromised through disruptions to attachment (Schore 1994; Siegel 1999), it is here that neural remodelling needs to begin. Furthermore, since it is via good enough, primary attachment interactions that such competence is achieved, it is through recapitulating the normal, developmental attachment processes that healing can optimally occur. If core psychobiological deficits have not been addressed the traumatised child cannot be expected to exert 'mind over matter' and will continue to respond with developmentally immature behaviour (see above).

Summary

It is clearly vital to engage the traumatised youngster initially through 'right brain to right brain' communications (Schore 1994, 1998, 2001a). In doing so parents and therapists aspire to replicate essential early developmental stages that have not been satisfactorily completed. Since failures of healthy attachment interfere so fundamentally with the infant's global development, attempting to intervene at hierarchically more mature levels is analogous to applying mortar to a crumbling building lacking adequate foundations. Brain development occurs from 'bottom up'. So, too, the healing process must begin with the earliest parent-child co-regulatory, somato-sensory and affective sequences (Schore 2001a, 2001b, 2002; Siegel 1999; van der Kolk 1999), facilitating brain stem and mid-brain maturity. This would include playful movement, touch and family cradling experiences (see *Introduction* and chapters 8, 9 and 13).

Thus the therapeutic parent, or supporting psychotherapist, provides the sensitively attuned responses, nurturing, playfulness, security and containment that the child did not experience in infancy, in order to replicate the exquisitely synchronised 'dance of attunement' and co-regulation of the mother-infant relationship.

For the therapist, an additional challenge is to provide these essential vitalising experiences (Schore 1994) without compromising the still tenuous attachment relationships between the youngster and his adoptive parents. In the child's mind, with its distorted inner 'road maps', these primary attachment relationships remain the greatest single threat to his well being, yet they are simultaneously what he most craves, and certainly requires, above all others. Southgate's (1996) schematic representation of the attachment hierarchy places the mother-infant attachment centrally and moves outward through increasingly peripheral, concentric attachment 'spaces': through extended family and community to global relationships. Without this original parent-child relationship in place, there may be little true, integrated connection with the inner world of the self or the outer, social world (see also Chapter 15).

Failure at this fundamental level predisposes the individual to serious 'early forming personality disorders', acknowledged to be highly refractive to therapeutic interventions (Schore 1994; Ross 1997; Fonagy 1999a; van der Kolk 1999); the perpetuation of disorganised, dissociative responses; and persistent failures in relationship formation. The cost to society is high; the costs to individuals and their families are inestimable. To avoid losing youngsters in a 'Bermuda Triangle' of psychopathology it is advisable to address the complex implications of the 'trauma triangle' (see p.90) with some diligence. Ideally, 'remodelling' of internal 'road maps', through developmentally-appropriate somato-sensory and emotional input (Archer 1999a, 1999b; Hughes 1997), should occur as early as possible, whilst the child's neural networks are most plastic and before states become fixed traits (Perry *et al.* 1995). Issues of therapeutic efficacy are explored in greater depth throughout this volume and discussed in Chapter 15.

CHAPTER 5

Clinical Concepts
and Caregiving Contexts
A Consultant's Perspective
Jeanne Magagna

Introduction

A major role of a consultant is to attempt to link existing theory and practice with practitioners' experiences and innovative practices, informed by new areas of research. In my role as supervising consultant to Family Futures I endeavour to make connections between conventional psychotherapeutic concepts and the eclectic, dramatic and integrative approach the team is evolving. In this chapter I describe three types of primitive identification, namely adhesive, projective and introjective identification, that can impede or facilitate children's psychological development and appear crucial to the understanding of adoptive families.

For many years I have worked in the National Health Service as a child, family and adult psychotherapist. Currently I work in the Department of Psychological Medicine at Great Ormond Street Hospital for Children. Over the past few years I have been meeting regularly with Family Futures, discussing with members of the multidisciplinary team their experiences of working with adoptive families. In working with Family Futures I have been struck by the therapeutic effectiveness of their treatment model. At the time of approaching Family Futures, adoptive family members are generally in crisis, or facing particular difficulties in relation to the child placed with them. The family is initially seen for a comprehensive assessment, often followed by further therapeutic work solely within Family Futures, or in collaboration with other agencies. The child's, and the couple's , life stories are carefully and sensitively explored, since dysfunctional histories may inhibit the development of good relationships within the family and compromise school achievement. Histories of emotional, physical or sexual abuse are common both for the children and their parents. Finding the best ways to understand and meet the child and family's needs and strengthen the links between family members is a central focus of the work.

Characteristically, families come to Family Futures seeking repair of fragile connections between caregivers and children. The beauty of the Family Futures' intensive encounter is that, often, sufficient understanding and emotional support is provided to enable the family to continue thinking about their difficulties, bear them and consider the best ways of handling them, thus pre-empting placement disruption. Unlike conventional treatment centres, Family Futures' approach avoids many of the problems of initiating in-depth work within the therapeutic hour and then facing interruption and rebuilding of defences between sessions. More importantly, the child is never taken on for individual therapy without simultaneously helping his adoptive parents to develop their skills as caregivers. Nor are parents seen independently, without the child receiving some therapeutic help, either within the family or on an individual basis. An on-call system means that families know there is someone available in off-duty hours should an emergency arise, enabling families to feel really connected to Family Futures and supported by them during the most critical periods with their troubled child. The crisis intervention service is much more comprehensive and containing than that provided in most social service departments and child guidance clinics, which may lack the necessary resources to provide such a service.

Family therapy services are often perceived as critical of parents. Adoptive parents report feeling that therapists seem to forget that they have adopted a child whose interactions, influenced by past trauma and defences, have been interfering with potentially healthy family relationships (Archer 2000a). Parents can feel misunderstood by those family therapists whose technique is to consider current interactions without respect for the child's history, implying that the adopters are primarily responsible for family dysfunction. Family Futures endeavours to provide a comprehensive, inclusive therapeutic service that both takes account of past history and enhances current relationships.

Key Identificatory Processes

Regular discussions with the Family Futures multidisciplinary team have drawn my attention to three key identificatory processes: adhesive identification, projective or intrusive identification and introjective identification. I shall describe these processes in detail, with particular reference to developmental attachment and trauma theories.

Adhesive Identification

Adhesive identification describes a process of searching to adhere to a light, a voice, a smell or some part of the self, such as muscular firmness, intellect or the thumb, to provide a 'psychic skin' to hold together unintegrated parts of the infantile self (Bick 1968). Here the catastrophic fear of falling-into-space and annihilation haunts every demand for change and creates an anxiety for sameness, stability and support from the outside world. Habitual use of adhesive identification makes it difficult for therapists to engage with children and families and involves many of the symptoms that Hughes (1997) suggests are common in attachment difficulties. Typical behaviours include: denial, muscular rigidity and immobility, non-stop movement, eroticisation, primitive omnipotence and primitive omniscience, congruent with the bimodal controlling behaviours of attachment-disorganised children (Lyons-Ruth, Bronfman and Atwood 1999).

DENIAL

'The abused child is likely to deny the existence of his abuser's mind, since not to do so would be to face the unacceptable fact that those one loves and on whom one depends have malevolent intentions towards one' (Holmes 2002). Denial allows survival, for it seals off the heart from the self, to protect the self from unbearable memories of trauma. Denial is used where there is a breakdown in the parents' protective shield, either internally or externally, and is essential when a child is being physically, emotionally and/or sexually abused. However, it also obliterates loving and aggressive feelings.

With massive denial there is apparent loss of capacity to use the mind to focus, to attend, to think. Some children who appear intellectually impaired regain some of their mental functioning capacity, once the intensity and nature of their distress is understood (Sinason 1988b, 1992). If sufficient emotional space is allowed to consider what the child has gone through, memory can return. A child with learning disabilities still has emotional intelligence: somewhere the child knows and understands what is happening within and around him. Once thoughts are made bearable to him, psychological and intellectual growth is possible. This concurs with research on the plasticity of brain circuitry (Glaser and Balbernie 2001) and the concepts of 'joined-up thinking' explored throughout this volume.

NON-STOP MOVEMENT

An infant faced with a life or death struggle, in the absence of a firm, containing mother who can hold him both physically and psychically, may adopt one of the earliest modes of protection, non-stop movement. It is as if the baby is trying to hold himself together, holding onto movement to prevent the terror of a dead end (Bick 1968). Hunter (2001) describes how, in the absence of a containing mother, non-stop movement continues to function as a kind of 'second skin' container, even after the child has been removed from an abusive home and placed in a secure environment. Non-stop movement forms part of the 'fight or flight' physiological state responses to stress that, according to Perry *et al.* (1995), eventually become relatively fixed traits.

MUSCULAR RIGIDITY AND IMMOBILITY

If a baby, traumatised in early infancy, is not supported by his primary caregivers, his method of survival is to retreat, both psychically and physically. The infant fears disintegration, falling to pieces, dissolving into a state of nothingness with no *thing* existing, no body, no self. Often trauma occurs from the mother's self preoccupation, or sometimes from the mother being over-identified with an older, dominant sibling. The traumatised child, lacking solid attachment to a protective mother, may fail to cry, resorting instead to his own primitive protections against terror, including muscular rigidity. It is as though the child fears annihilation and lacks sufficient experience of a mother upon whom he can depend. Pseudo-independence, remaining still, not crying and using a rigid muscular shell to hold himself together replace emotional dependence on the mother (Bick 1968). A slightly older child may use hard objects that are held tightly in place of the muscular 'shell', making him feel hard, impenetrable, in absolute control and thus safe. According to Tustin (1990) he seeks this hard object when he feels solely responsible for his own safety. These descriptions are characteristic of the 'freeze' or shame dissociative responses to distress.

EROTICISATION

Engaging in activities generating sexual excitement can represent holding onto pleasure, to prevent falling into a painful, traumatic sense of loss and depression. Sexual acting out and maintaining inappropriate boundaries may also be used as a defence against emerging dependence on caregivers or therapists. Thus it may represent part of the controlling behaviours evolved by traumatised children with disorganised attachment patterns.

PRIMITIVE OMNIPOTENCE

One powerful way of surviving intolerable distress is through primitive omnipotence, demonstrated in studies of feral children raised by wolves (Newton 2002) and research on children from severely abusive and neglecting families (Boston and Szur 2001). Primitive omnipotence involves the thought: 'I can only trust what comes from me, what I can do for myself. I must depend on myself. I can do everything for myself!' This is very characteristic of children described as attachment disordered (Cline 1992; Levy and Orlans 1998) and typified by Archer (1999b) as 'Superkid' behaviours. Primitive omnipotence allows the child to survive, rather than dying from overwhelming trauma to the self. Using omnipotence the self becomes idealised as a source of permanent comfort, and 'the other' within the self becomes a recipient of all the destructive impulses. Gradually an intense split emerges between the self as 'the idealised caregiver for the Self' and 'the other' experienced as dangerous or untrustworthy. The internalised other itself now holds the threat of destroying the omnipotence of the self. This is consistent with descriptions of extreme affect states in children with segregated, or dissociated, systems (Bowlby 1979; Liotti 1999) and disorganised attachment representations.

According to Hunter (2001), a child using primitive omnipotence also demonstrates 'avoidant' attachment patterns. If caregivers or therapists offer understanding, intimacy or love, this is experienced as a threat, just as aggression or abuse would be experienced as threatening. The child clings to primitive omnipotence like a shield for protection, fearing that under-standing and loving contact could melt his armour of omnipotence. He is terrified that his armour will be broken and that he will fall into confusion, disintegration, become overwhelmed with feelings that are too painful and intense and thus disintegrate. Often caregivers and therapists describe such a child as aggressive when, in fact, the child is defending himself, by pushing away the threat of love and understanding. The approach-avoidance dynamic is pivotal to attachment theory and, in 'disorganised' children, is described in terms of 'frightened/frightening' (Main and Hesse 1990), or 'hostile-versus-helpless' dynamics (Lyons-Ruth *et al.* 1999).

Children raised in maltreating families resort to primitive omnipotent control as a protection against relationships with people and as a substitute for caring and protective internal parents. However, omnipotent control functions as a kind of internal 'prison guard', a controlling force which restricts the experiencing of difficult feelings, as well as pleasurable moments and intimate relationships. It protects the child from becoming too overwhelmed by intense infantile feelings and anxieties aroused in intimate relationships with parents or peers. The control of the 'prison guard' involves identification with an inner 'super-parent figure', a model of tough self-sufficiency obliterating human frustration and even basic physical needs. Since control is omnipotent it also obliterates the experience of pleasure. Such an internal 'prison guard' features prominently in descriptions of adults (e.g. Fonagy 2002; Ross 1997) and children (Shirar 1996) with dissociative disorders.

In a therapeutic encounter with an individual using primitive omnipotence there are only two feelings: love and fear (Leunig 1990), encapsulated in the sub-title of this volume, *Fear Can Stop You Loving*. As the child utilising primitive omnipotence makes therapeutic progress he often draws or describes a sensation of the self with feelings being locked inside. Simultaneously he experiences a vicious debate between two conflicting emotions: the love of being understood and the fear of being touched emotionally, reflecting the underlying approach-avoidance conflict.

PRIMITIVE OMNISCIENCE

Research (Hunter 2001) shows that children who have witnessed domestic violence, or have been the recipient of direct physical threat or abuse, or other maltreatment, are hypervigilant to all cues which could be connected to something which could arouse fear. These cues could be a particular smell, sound or movement, or another's gaze. They are associated with a raised heart rate and feelings of anxiety in response to minute cues (Glaser 2000). The hypervigilant child attempts to navigate a sea of potentially terrifying objects in order to survive. He learns to watch very carefully from a distance, while avoiding direct eye contact at all times. He memorises every minute detail that could indicate impending disaster. The child holds onto knowledge of all facts, including auditory, olfactory and somato-sensory mood states from the past, to use as 'danger' signals. Vital details, including perceptions of caregivers' state of mind, are clung onto tenaciously. Every change in the current caregiver, in the environment, or in routine feels potentially dangerous. The omniscient, hypervigilant self feels 'I must know everything and rely on myself because there is no one, no mother to pick me up and save me' (Magagna 2002a).

Primitive omniscience is used to protect the self in lieu of an internal secure parent, enabling the self to bear anxieties about sudden change. Predictability and a sense of security are usually derived from the primary caregiver's ongoing, reliable emotional state and reliability in caregiving. When the caregiver is unreliable, the child develops dysregulated stress responses, involving excess cortisol secretions (see Chapter 4). These are known to interfere with the planning and organising of actions, using 'working memory', and the inhibition of attention to distractions and inappropriate responses (Schore 1994). The baby-self of a maltreated child requires that absolutely everything be understood in terms of whether it presents a danger to the Self, since the baby-self is terrified of the unknown, fears falling apart, fears dying (Bick 1968).

The primitive protection of omniscience consumes enormous psychic and physical energy, in order to scan minute, non-verbal details from faces and body language, read the emotional climate and try to anticipate situations. There is such a mass of information that the thinking mind almost becomes transformed into a static space, in which information is stored and sorted to aid the search for survival. As a result, very little mental space remains for thinking about emotional experiences taking place inside the self. This is supported by sophisticated brain scanning techniques that indicate marked reduction in blood flow to higher cortical areas linked with language and thought (van der Kolk 1996b). Change and flexibility bring the fear of affect, catastrophic anxieties and imagination from the infantile self that threatens destruction of the fragile, more adult parts of the personality (Magagna 2002a).

A child who has relied on primitive omnipotence and omniscience to survive feels that he needs to know, and be good at, everything he does. While in school, he can feel shattered or persecuted by the realm of learning experiences that confront him with what he does not know, or requires time to master. This can prove equally problematic at home, where every instruction or new challenge can overwhelm him, causing him to 'shut down', or freeze, or lead to escalation of defensive controlling behaviours, through 'fight' or 'flight' neurobiological mechanisms.

WORKING WITH PRIMITIVE OMNIPOTENCE AND OMNISCIENCE

It is essential that parents and teachers recognise that the child's infantile omnipotence and omniscience are being threatened by the global learning process and creating major anxieties for him. Finding ways of assisting the child to develop a sense of self-esteem, while letting go of these protective mechanisms in order to learn, is one of the primary tasks of caregivers at home and teachers in school. The child is always looking to see if adults value him and support him emotionally. It is important not to shatter the child's primitive omnipotence by putting him in situations in which it is clear he will be unable to meet expectations, since this can lead to psychiatric disorders (Maughan and Yule 1994). Parents need both to experience sufficient security and informed support and to be provided with a clear understanding of their child's difficulties with learning. Often children need to be considered in developmental terms, so that they are not asked to undertake apparently simple challenges, for which they are not developmentally ready (Archer 2001a; Hughes 1997, 2002).

When approaching Family Futures almost every distressed child uses omnipotent control, distrusting the goodness, strength and adequacy of the therapist, just as they distrust these qualities in their adopters. The child feels simultaneously relieved and threatened by the intimacy and understanding offered, reflecting the underlying approach-avoidance conflict. An understanding of the conflict between wanting to be dependent and maintaining omnipotent control must inform all therapeutic interactions both at home and in therapy. For a child with a history of maltreatment by loved parents, becoming dependent is terrifying. It is therefore important to distinguish between a child simply being aggressive and a child using hostility in defence of the 'omnipotent self which he has been using to protect himself' (Cornwell 1985).

The use of spontaneous play, art, puppets, sand-world and psychodramatic techniques are described throughout this volume. Often these techniques are invaluable because the child is freed from the 'spotlight' as he looks at an intermediary space with the therapist or parent alongside him. For example, looking at or using puppets, or drawing and describing a character, enables the child to feel that people are not penetrating him with their eyes and understanding. Schore (1994) explores the urge to 'avoid the gaze of the world' in shame-filled children, leading to typical downcast body posture, immobility and loss of thinking capacity, proposing that the caregiver, or therapist, must effect 'interactive repair' through gentle touch and modulated voice tone.

In the initial stage of work with a child using primitive omnipotence, it is often much less intimidating and more facilitating to consider the state of mind of the therapist, caregiver or internalised parent or a puppet representing someone significant to the child (Alvarez 1992). Sometimes playing at the side of a silent child and talking to oneself or a co-worker allows the child to observe and get to know the therapist's thinking process. The child is free to attend or not, but his omnipotent control will not inhibit thinking about emotional issues. This technique forms a major facet of Hughes' clinical work with children with disorganised attachments (1997, 2002).

Projective or Intrusive Identification

Projective identification is a phantasy that some part of the self has been separated off and relocated in another person; there is an alteration of the self, with a depletion of actual feelings or abilities. In projective or intrusive identification, unconscious, primitive emotions are often projected while the child or adult identifies with a good or bad internalised figure. This can be expressed in several ways, including: identification with an idealised object, projecting distress onto the body and identification with the aggressor.

IDENTIFICATION WITH AN IDEALISED OBJECT

The 'Jack-in-the-box' Relationship

In the 'jack-in-the-box' relationship one individual receives projections from another (the 'jack-*in*-the-box'), coming to feel imprisoned both by his own feelings and the projected feelings of the other. All sorts of unwanted aspects of the personality, such as loneliness, depression, incompetence, neediness, helplessness and hostility, can be projected onto the 'imprisoned' person, by the other (the 'jack-*out*-of-the-box'), who is identified as 'super-competent'. This 'super-competent' self lacks knowledge of many parts of her true self, and suffers feelings of emptiness, since so many aspects of the self have been projected outwards. The super-competent 'jack-out-of-the-box', be she spouse, parent or therapist, may be drawn into compulsive caregiving, advice-giving and protecting the 'jack-in-the-box' (Magagna and Black 1985) because the vulnerable, needy or unwanted parts of her 'super-competent' self have been projected into the 'jack-in-the-box'. When a 'jack-in-the-box' relationship occurs, it is harmful to the integrity of both individuals. This is true whether it be from the moment of the idea of conception, during pregnancy or birth, within an adoption or fostering situation, or within the therapeutic relationship.

'Super-parent' Phantasies Surrounding Conception

A woman may conceive in identification with an idealised mother, while projecting into the foetus needy parts of the self. The biological parent who gives birth to a child has phantasies around the conception and birth that script the child into a role for the parent's internal drama. This is supported by research, including Verny and Kelly's (1981) exploration of the effects of ambivalence and rejection on the unborn child. It may also be obvious when one hears prospective parents talking about the 'child-in-the-womb'. Some phantasies are clear from the outset, as in studies of pregnant women and their male partners, where a sizeable minority expressed wishes to hurt their unborn child (Condon 1987). Kent *et al.* (1997) studied depressed women who repeatedly punched their own pregnant abdomen and acknowledged powerful negative feelings towards their unborn children. Here it is obvious that the unborn baby had been scripted into a conflictual relationship with the mother. Archer (2001b) explores the neurophysiological implications of such traumatic experiences for the unborn child, including raised cortisol levels, affecting developing neural pathways (Glaser and Balbernie 2001).

'Super-parent' Phantasies Surrounding Adoption

The urgent need to repair hidden damage to the self can be the unconscious agenda for anyone in a caregiving role; this can include identification with a super-parent who will be marvellous in every aspect of caregiving. Sometimes, for fear that disclosure would lead to rejection by a partner or placing agency, prospective adopters conceal their own histories of emotional, physical or sexual abuse or other traumatic experience. Concealment of previous damaging relationships could be said to represent a conscious wish to be accepted to look after, and perhaps love, a child. Unconsciously, the damaged child within the adult self may be projected into the adopted child, despite the conscious wish to repair the damaged child.

Such parents may be thwarted in their reparative wishes and feel emotionally injured once again when they encounter a child who is intrusively identified with the aggressor (see below) or his past, and is unable consciously to acknowledge his own wish for love. The child may also have a compulsion to re-experience hurt that fits with his internal drama. In such cases it is not only that the child projects rage but also that the parent becomes angry because she feels impotent to repair damage, both within the child and herself. Moreover, the parent is scripted into responses to the child which re-awaken and amplify the rage and hurt from her internalised conflictual links in her own family. As we are all, to a greater or lesser extent, damaged this may apply to most adopters, child care practitioners and therapists with rescue phantasies.

WORKING WITH 'SUPER-PARENT' PHENOMENA

Words are like a cracked bell, never giving full richness of meaning. The speaker brings alongside him a feeling state that needs to be understood in the body and psyche of the therapist or parent. Descriptions of the child may include references to what has been split off and denied in the couple's own personalities. This could be described as 'the-child-in-the-parent', that is unresolved pain from their own past parenting experiences, that remains alive in current relationships with the child or therapist. It is through the experience of narrating one's personal story and having the therapist understand and experience its full impact that parents' good and bad memories become transformed into a conscious narrative (see also Chapter 2). After a parent has recounted her story, it can be helpful to integrate unconscious sentiments by having her speak directly, as the child of her parents, to an empty chair, representing the grandparents: expressing what she would like to have said, as a child, to them and what she would say to her parents now. Relationships with previous therapeutic teams may also need to be explored. It is essential to encourage parents to withdraw inevitable projections of their own infantile self from the adopted child; this will enable parents to see the child as smaller than they are, rather than as a huge, potent emotional threat to their parenting capacities. The family's eventual capacity to face and bear their own emotions, respond to each other's needs and help their children depends on the internalisation of the experience of being helped to bear their emotions and think about them with the therapeutic team.

PROJECTING DISTRESS ONTO THE BODY AS RECEPTACLE

There is a psychological self, an entity distinct in some ways from the body self. It is important to recognise this in trying to understand the various ways in which each affects the other. A baby without a good attachment to a caregiver will often respond somatically, rather than by crying out. A young child might head-bang when angry, feeling that there is no containing parent who is strong enough, or understanding enough, to accept rage. Neglected, abused children and children in very disturbed emotional states may attack their bodies, rather than cry out to someone for help or endure the psychological confusion or pain threatening to overwhelm them. In these situations the psychological self projects the inner wound onto the body, thus damaging the body, yet claiming psychological relief, as with children who self-harm. It thus makes inner pain tangible and it can be shared with others, albeit in dysfunctional ways. Children may use self-punishment and suffering to avoid what for them is feared as even greater suffering and danger, namely their perception of the damaged state of their inner world (Riesenberg-Malcolm 1999). Self-punishment can also be directed towards the internalised parents with whom the child feels unconnected, for they have not protected the psychological self from this psychic pain.

Identification with the Aggressor or Victim

A child depends on caregivers to protect him, through the attachment relationship: gradually he internalises, or introjects their protective qualities. A child will introject his parents either as protective or as harmful if his parents have maltreated him. Hence there are contradictory possibilities for introjective identifications. One introjective identification results in the child feeling like a passive, frightened victim, leading to depression, guilt, despair and rage at unmet needs, along with a deep suspicion of any offers of help.

Alternatively the child may identify with the life threatening, introjected parent, who is experienced as powerful, aggressive and frightening, in an attempt to rid himself of unbearable psychic pain, or out of rage at what has been done to him. He is then likely to perpetrate abuses on others (Williams 1998). When identifying with the aggressor, a child is seeking to obtain mastery and to defy others, and cannot tolerate depression, guilt or shame (Krystal 1988). These two patterns are consistent with the bimodal, 'frightened/frightening' (Main and Hesse 1990), or 'hostile/helpless' (Lyons-Ruth et al. 1999) patterns of controlling behaviours observed in 'disorganised' children, reflecting patterns of early, dysfunctional caregiving experiences (see also Chapter 3).

Evocative projective identification

Here, the child disposes of a part of the self by splitting it off and exporting it into a person important to him. Projective identification is part of normal infant development: the mother gives meaning to the baby's emotions communicated to her and attempts to understand and respond to them. In this way the baby's distress becomes more bearable to him. A child exposed to unresolved trauma, maltreatment, maternal depression or pre-natal drug or alcohol abuse will often use projective identification to control, or possess, an important person or communicate unbearable states of mind (Fonagy 2001). He is repeatedly confronted with intolerable levels of confusing and hostile caregiving and is forced to internalise aspects of his caregiver that he is incapable of integrating. In an attempt to experience himself as coherent, the child forces the alien, unassimilated parts of himself into others, so that he can maintain the illusion that these parts are now outside, through subtle manipulative control of the other's behaviour (Fonagy and Target 1997). These descriptions, too, are congruent with current material on attachment disorganisation (Lyons-Ruth *et al.* 1999) and the control issues discussed by Cline (1992), Hughes (1997) and Levy and Orlans (1998) in relation to attachment disordered children.

Of course the process of projective identification can backfire in the case of a caregiver being a 'super-parent' (see above). Initially there may be enormous relief of distress on the part of the super-parent, who identifies with an idealised parent and projects distressed parts of her self into the baby. She is able to take care of these in the baby and experiences relief because her own distressed baby parts, when projected into the baby, tend not to overwhelm her. However, when the baby cries, as he inevitably will, the caregiver experiences not only the baby's cries but also the distressed parts of herself that she has split off and projected into him.

Similarly, faced with the projective evocations of a traumatised child, the adoptive parent is likely to feel overwhelmed and may be unable to understand or meet his needs appropriately. Often, with evocative projective identification, parents and therapists end up receiving unbearable states of mind from their children. They need to understand that these evoked feelings represent part of the child that cannot be acknowledged or verbalised by him. They must hold these feelings within themselves until the child is ready to make sense of them, with the caregivers' help. Parents and therapists also need to make sense of their own relationships, past and present, which may influence their emotional responses to the child's projections.

WORKING WITH PROJECTIVE IDENTIFICATION

Therapeutically, the individual's self needs to become differentiated from these internalisations of abusive or neglectful parents. Therapy is a place where the child, like a baby, externalises an internal situation linked with past or present situations in his life; the distressed part of the child is received by the caregiver or therapist. Their task, as recipients of the projection, is to receive the emotions, try to make sense of them and give them back to the child, divested of the psychic pain suffered when his experiences were neither shared nor understood by anyone.

According to Meltzer (1967), the hypervigilant child is deeply attuned to the states of mind of his parents or the therapist; their capacity to bear his psychic pain must be genuine and cannot be counterfeited. Eventually the child will then be able to reflect on his emotional state, rather than project it outward; initially, however, he simply projects unbearable mental states into the caregiver. These are traumatic states of mind for which there are often no words: simply unbearable psychic pain and anger over being maltreated. There is a risk, of course, that the caregiver or therapist will become hurt and angry about being 'mistreated', rather than emotionally accepting and understanding the child's unbearable rage and pain and helping him find more suitable ways of expressing his feelings. However, once adopters are helped to understand and recognise this pattern they are able to provide the sensitive feedback their child requires, in the 'dance of attunement' (see chapters 9 and 10).

Introjective Identification

Introjective identification describes a process of taking in aspects, qualities or skills of another person in such a way that they are gradually identified with, and inform, the character of an individual. This forms a part of the normal, developmental attachment process. Eventually the individual carries his parents and siblings in his heart and can continue an internal dialogue with them in their absence. In order to internalise the parents it is important to acknowledge their separateness and their freedom to come and go as necessary.

THE INTERNAL WORLD AND THE EXTERNAL, PAST AND PRESENT WORLDS

Much of the behaviour of parents and children becomes more understandable if one gains a detailed picture both of their internal world and past and present external worlds. The key components of the inner psychic structure are composed of an internal mother, internal father and internal siblings. Much of the current literature on therapeutic work with adopted children identifies the child's history as creating current problems in families, including aggression, fears of closeness, perceived rejections and self-doubts that impede the formation of deep attachments to subsequent caregivers. Sometimes there is a reluctance to consider in detail all factors within the current family system that might ameliorate their relationship difficulties. This may be for fear that the professionals or the child will begin blaming the caregivers, or parents will blame themselves, rather than acknowledging the complex interactions between them. It is crucial to assess the states of mind and needs of every family member. In this way the family's strengths and difficulties can be identified and understood, as part of the therapeutic process of facilitating attachments between child and family and repairing fractured connections between family members. A non-blaming, receptive environment is crucial. Here parents can use the therapist to strengthen their adult self, away from their child, so that they do not need to 'protect' him from their own vulnerabilities.

Looking at past and present external worlds, as well as these three key types of identifications, is important for each family member. Schore (1994) describes how the mother begins to help her infant to regulate somato-sensory and affect states, poorly developed at birth, by alleviating distress and reinforcing positive affect. This is a recursive, reciprocal process that depends on the mother's sensitivity and attunement to the infant's cues (Stern 1995).

> This includes an accurate appraisal of the infant's feeling state, synchronicity with the infant and the appropriate intensity of the mother's response. Regulated affect allows the infant to engage in exploration of his environment and in learning. (Glaser and Balbernie 2001, p.81)

Clearly, it is therefore essential to explore these issues for adoptive parents, as well as for their children. In doing so one of the most important questions to explore would be: 'What kind of mature, loving and thoughtful parent is residing internally in these parental figures?' Adoptive parents need to be enabled to provide many additional experiences of love, understanding, security and containment that dysregulated, 'disorganised' children will need, to achieve reasonable levels of self-regulation.

INTERNALIZED SIBLING RELATIONSHIPS

The child also introjects relationships with siblings and peers. It is important to note the way in which conflicts between love, jealousy and anger are expressed in these relationships. It is also vital to explore their capacity to acknowledge the existence, supportive functions and needs of these siblings. The value of facilitating, or detrimental, aspects of sibling relationships throughout the life cycle has been seriously neglected in studies of child development (Mitchell 2000).

Summary

This chapter has examined the three, key identificatory processes of adhesive, projective and introjective identification. Perhaps most important in therapeutic work with the child, or 'the-child-in-the-parent', is to enable him to release his adhesive identification, involving the stranglehold of primitive omnipotence and omniscience. These 'Superkid' behaviours are amongst the most challenging to adoptive parents (Archer 1999b). When the child feels secure enough to let go of his protections against anxiety he can gradually begin to depend on his parents and the therapist. Eventually he can introject their capacities (co-regulation), contain his own anxieties (self-regulation) and achieve freedom to develop (self-agency). The Family Futures approach is to acknowledge these patterns of identification as they occur within relationship interactions, whether between individual family members or family member and therapist. In time, from their developmental trauma and attachment perspective, the team endeavours to explore these issues sensitively, respecting the defences of child or adult. Gradually they 'lead' them towards greater self-awareness and enable them to process their hurts without becoming overwhelmed.

After being involved in therapeutic work with the Family Futures team the adoptive family is never left as it was. Family members are provided with sufficient insights and ways forward, understanding that fear has 'loosened its grip and opened its hands' (Leunig 1990), opening up possibilities for love of which they may have only dreamt.

CHAPTER 6

'A Hard Day's Night'
A Parent's Perspective
Lucy Greenmile

In order to get across to readers the intense physical and emotional challenges of living with a traumatised adopted child, we asked an adoptive mother to write an account of everyday life in her adoptive family up to the point of their referral to us. The 'drama of adoption' is only too evident as she tells her story. These are her words and her thoughts on what lay behind the difficulties her son experienced within his new family.

This is the all too real story of our family's struggle with our adopted son, Jason. The past four years with this traumatised child have been an escalating, passion-filled war of attrition, for which absolutely nothing had prepared us. Many of the passions on our part, as parents, have not been soul enhancing, and certainly not the kind talked about in polite company. The sweet moments were very few and far between, and even these were so easily tainted by the guilt-ridden, isolating, and hateful slog of surviving our son's challenging behaviour.

My husband, Simon and I came to the adoption process believing that we were a reasonably 'child friendly' couple. We were honoured to be godparents to ten children (one jointly) by then, and took an active role in many of their lives. We had been trusted to care for many of these children, even as small babies, for whole weekends sometimes, offering their parents much needed time off. We were not only delighted to do so, but also felt hugely privileged. We hoped that we would bring to our new family a small but realistic understanding of the hard work involved in caring for children.

We also hoped that we might know the same intense pleasure our friends and family so obviously derived from their children. At the beginning, sharing the same dreams as every hope-filled adoptive parent, we really believed that commitment, love and stamina would work magic and make a little boy truly part of our family. During the next four years of adoptive family life, despair, exhaustion and alienation almost drove us to the wall on at least four or five occasions.

Beginning our Story

Jason's current difficulties are for the most part the result of extremely neglectful and abusive parenting over the first four years of his life. This seems to have followed the familiar pattern of disrupted and chaotic living, with grave concerns voiced by professionals and neighbours. Allegations were made, some substantiated, most not, of unintended neglect at best and intentional abuse at worst. However, we were not remotely aware of the extent of this when Jason arrived to live with us.

Jason is the middle child in what was initially a sibling group of four. He was four years old when he was eventually taken into care, with his three older siblings. These siblings were eventually placed for adoption separately; we understand from Jason's shared social worker that they all still struggle to cope, just as Jason does. Jason was eventually placed with us, with a fifth sibling Jessie, born after her siblings' removal and removed at birth.

From the start of their placement with us we had a nagging unease that something was just not quite right when Jason and Jessie were together. It had the feel of something much more sinister than sibling rivalry or jealousy, and was borne out by numerous tiny events, each perhaps insignificant in itself. Before she could talk, Jessie would turn and show us stinging nettle marks around her mouth, or all over her hands, if we left them alone for a second. In the sand-pit she always ended up with sand in her eyes or mouth as Jason's spade would 'accidentally' slip. Football sessions in the garden inevitably resulted in Jessie being hit by the full force of the ball, again 'by accident'. These things continued to happen even though we began to shadow them constantly.

We witnessed Jason taking a dinner knife and quietly telling Jessie to put it in her mouth, or run her finger down it. We caught Jessie being 'helped' up to the very top step of the slide, and over a fence with a steep drop on the other side. Riding in a little pedal car she was carefully lined up and told to pedal directly under swings that were in use. Mishaps would repeatedly happen in which she was always the one falling, tripping, or being landed upon. Whenever she cried Jason would (and still can) laugh maniacally. On one occasion, from our first floor bedroom, Jason spotted a fire engine passing by. I was behind the children, dressing. Jessie could not see over the window ledge, so Jason offered to push her *out* of the window so she could see the engine. He then dramatically announced 'Oh no, I'm not allowed to do that, am I?' He would repeatedly tell Jessie that she was stupid and useless when she could not do something, even when we reasoned that she was far too little. Pursuing this further would result in a tirade of invective against Jessie. We very soon realised that she could not be safe around Jason unless we stood bodily between them.

The emotions engendered in us by this behaviour ranged from bewilderment and sadness to anger. We understood that Jason's aggressive attitude resulted from feelings of deep insecurity and we would make a point of reassuring and supporting him, whilst giving him the clear message that aggression towards others, Jessie in particular, was not acceptable and solved nothing. We were careful to be scrupulously fair to them both, setting aside special time for each of them, yet nothing we did seemed to make a difference to Jason's hostility. We were shocked by the scope of the unrelenting unpleasantness he acted out on Jessie.

Jason's tragedy was further compounded by the fact that Jessie, following a first year of quiescence, subsequently appeared to be forming healthy attachments to us. Her lack of engagement in that year went without remark at the time, so entrenched were we in dealing with her hell-raising brother. Perhaps because she was so much younger when she came to us, and had not experienced the same degree of trauma as Jason, she was more able to allow us to parent her. She seeks cuddles and she comfortably regresses into babyhood. Jason desperately needs and indeed, at a subconscious level, craves to be able to do the same. Her ability to do so rubs salt into his every wound.

Living with a Twister

Jason's wounds became our wounds as his dysfunction and anger were dumped into our family's life like a time bomb. He had lived through, and survived, severe trauma and as a result had become a whirling twister, terrifyingly out of control inside, but sucking in the time, emotions and energy of everyone around him in his desperate effort to control everything outside. He is unable to allow himself to need or trust anyone. Living with Jason is living with perpetual 'NO': whether expressed through verbal or behavioural challenges. Constant dissent is an exhausting weapon. Defiance and apparently senseless actions have frequently led him into life-threatening situations and me into near terminal shock.

Our son would often, in temper, throw himself into busy morning traffic on the walk to school (me, being firmly attached to him, and the pushchair, being firmly attached to me, nearly following suit each time). At six years of age he sought out Dad's razor (taking a chair into the bathroom to reach the shelf) and sliced his thumb open with it. Another day we were chatting in the garden with our neighbours, one of whom was leaning on an axe, when Jason sidled up behind us and ran his thumb the full length of the blade. (We had just been discussing with Jason how to use tools safely.) At seven years of age he created a very precarious pyramid, during a few unsupervised minutes in the garage, and balancing on this while groping blindly two feet above him, stole the bonfire lighter stored on a high beam. Having concealed it successfully during the day, he experimented with setting fire to his teddies after lights out that night. Soon afterwards he climbed onto the glass roof of an elderly neighbour's conservatory, terrifying her and us. At nearly nine years he stole and ate pills that had been tucked well out of sight on a saucer at his grandparents' house.

The parents of any child with serious attachment difficulties might be familiar with this tiny sample of chaotic behaviour patterns. For us, so far, these have been the extremes, and in some ways we have been lucky. Jason was not mown down by a car; he used his thumb for surgical practice, not his wrist; his burning teddies did not set fire to him or his bed; he did not fall through the conservatory roof, which would have sent him crashing through the hothouse plants to the hard tiled floor below; the pills he picked out and ate just happened to be grandpa's diuretics and not his more dangerous beta blockers.

However, these behaviours produced a constant chill atmosphere of uncertainty around Jason, paralleled by an anxious sickness in the pit of my stomach about what he would get up to next. Jason *cannot* trust us as adults or parents, or take our word for things. He must have taken in our warnings at some level that the razor and the axe were sharp, but could not resist running his thumb down them just the same. He did not just touch them and remove his thumb, either: he really *ran* his thumb down both – full length! Plaster applications are an additional battlefield: a child so traumatised does not allow comfort. My hugs or shows of concern are treated as additional damage; Jason will wince, shout and push me away if I go to him. Simply showing that I care about his health, welfare, or safety, is so utterly threatening to him that he will use any means at his disposal to keep me at bay. Events are often played out very publicly, so not only do I *feel* like a rotten inadequate mother, I must also look like a rotten, inadequate *and* brutalising mother for Jason to be so vociferous about refusing my ministrations!

Jason's instinctive reaction to perceived stressful situations is aggressive. A stressful situation can be defined as anything requiring some form of compliance from him. This could be as simple as being asked quite calmly to finish his breakfast, put his shoes on, or brush his teeth. Most mums will say that these are familiar grounds for a tantrum from any irritated or tired child. The difference with Jason is that he consistently fights on every single one of these and similar issues, every time, sequentially and inexhaustibly, seven days out of seven. We now understand that emotional stress can throw him straight back into the traumatic experiences that originally damaged his attachments and normal development. He is then lost in the fight or flight mode that allowed him to survive in his birth family. He is supremely tuned into the moods and atmosphere surrounding him, and often chooses to control the situation by creating chaos. Then, he *had* to be a master in assessing what mattered to the people around him, and an even greater expert in manipulating these issues to survive. If only he could use his unique skills in more healthy ways today!

Twisting the Knife

Jason's frequent aggression towards others ranged from deliberate punching, kicking, or stabbing with pencils, to a more generalised rage, where anyone within reach was targeted. On one occasion when he was upset he announced to the class that he *did* know how to carry scissors correctly, but that today he was choosing to carry them 'unsafely, like this'. A little classmate was caught by the sharp-ended sweep just under her eye; thank God it was not a centimetre higher. His outbursts were so common, at his mainstream primary school, that as soon as Jason seemed 'about to blow', his shoes would be promptly removed, for his own, and his schoolfriends', safety. On many days he would return from school looking as though he had gone several rounds with a particularly hungry tiger. His sweatshirt would be in tatters where he had chewed the cuffs and collar. He would gnaw at his nails and cuticles and, when beside himself, gouge his arms and face. If he ever laid hands on a pin badge he would draw blood, working away on his cuticles. On one occasion he worked our very tolerant dog into such a complete frenzy that I found Jason's face and arms a mass of bleeding welts where the dog's claws had been scrabbling at him.

I lost count of the sleepless nights we spent as parents wondering how we ever came to this, what we were doing wrong and how on earth we were going to get through the next day. A cold knot of dread and depression accompanied the alarm clock bell every morning and a common refrain from other parents on the school run was: 'Cheer up – things can't be as bad as all that'. In fact, they were, and worse! However hard I tried to be upbeat, and to seek out and praise something really good about Jason's day, my reality was dreading what Jason was going to get up to (very publicly) in the playground and guessing which aggrieved parent I would have to appease. Our long walk home was repeatedly overshadowed by wondering what on earth we could *do* with this child. By the children's bedtime I was usually drained. This, however, mostly went hand in hand with a 'high' of adrenaline-fuelled anxiety. Discussion with Simon of Jason's day often ended in pointless rows, recrimination and tears, as I sought to relieve my frustration. Simon felt isolated from our daily hell, and powerless to help me. It is a testament to the resilience of our relationship that coping with Jason did not tear us apart.

Ordinary days with 'ordinary hell' at either end of the school day were bad enough but the toxic icing on the cake was the regular telephone call from school telling me that Jason was so out of control, or had done something so heinous, that I was to come and collect him immediately. (I was required by his primary school to be available at the drop of a hat; that became an additional personal load.) It had become unthinkable that we could risk inflicting Jason, at his worst, on unsuspecting neighbours or friends. (The support network of adults we had carefully mapped out on paper before the placement began had been rendered redundant by Jason's behaviour from day one!) On his way out of school, screaming and swearing, Jason would try to wreck the school secretary's office, attempt to break the windows, throw over plant pots, and strip himself while being manhandled into the car. This would be in addition to a determined battery of physical and verbal abuse against me.

Once secure in the car he would lie on the rear seat trying to kick the side window out with both feet, or hammer the driver's seat with both legs at full strength. (Audi build-quality has proved highly impressive!) All this had to be managed whilst keeping Jessie out of Jason's reach and trying to drive home. Once I got him out of the car he would rage around, kicking and wrecking anything that lay in his path, stripping off his remaining clothes while continuing to spit and swear at me. It could take hours to calm him. I mostly achieved this by holding onto him securely and rocking him; we were usually both in tears. At these times Jason would swing violently between loathing me or loathing himself and goading me to hurt him or kill him. 'I wish I was dead' was, and continues to be, a common and heartbreaking refrain. Jessie and the dog were particularly at risk when Jason was in his enraged state. Jessie, understandably, was often extremely distressed by these episodes and would try to stroke *me* while I held *him*.

The aggression aimed at others was difficult enough to live with but Jason's attempts to hurt us personally, particularly me, were devastating. 'I hate you and X (family members). You're all useless/mean/horrible' were permanent features. My 'love you' as I left his bedroom one night was met with a singsong 'fuck you'. Stroking his head gently one morning to wake him up was met by a half-opened eye and a vicious dig in the ribs when identity was established. The Valentine card made traditionally at cub scouts for Mum was deliberately, and very publicly, given to the cub scout leader. A Mother's Day card made under duress at school had 'love from' crossed out and 'I hate you' scored over the top. At primary school Jason would sail through the gates chatting animatedly with absolutely anyone but me and then, without so much as a backward glance, fling himself straight into a loving embrace with the playground assistant. My friends informed me that on Jason's authority all I do at home is sit and drink tea all day, that I never remember or celebrate his birthday, and that I am a useless mother. On a sleep-over with us my nephew appeared in tears at the awful things Jason was saying about me.

I regularly find Jason's teddies eviscerated, usually through the genital region, and soaked in urine. Action Men and Barbies violently lose their full complement of limbs. Before we learned to buy Velcro fastened shoes, shoe laces would be removed at night and used to bind and hang naked Action Men in ferociously tied knots. Jessie's Barbie dolls are found unclothed in all sorts of bizarre sexual poses. A Mickey Mouse picture on the front of a jumbo writing pad was gouged viciously through its full thickness in the genital area, and a plastic 101 Dalmatians pencil case had each animal's eyes carefully stabbed out. The really spooky thing about these acts is that they are always performed unseen, often in brief moments whilst I am out of the room. Even presented with the evidence littering the house, Jason vehemently disclaims all knowledge and responsibility for them. At six years old he spent nearly an hour trying to get the mother of a school friend to agree that 'pussy' was not necessarily feline. The sight of a small animal suckling would lead to a stream of unpleasantly suggestive comments. We always tried to discuss these issues openly and appropriately with Jason, but this would lead to him pursuing his argument in mock innocence until we would end the conversation in exasperation. He seemed to have no 'off' button, even when the subject had been long closed.

The level of aggression at which Jason functioned was utterly foreign and totally unexpected to us and was, indeed, one of the most difficult things we had to adjust to in living with him. Teething troubles and settling in we had expected, given what little we knew of his 'neglect'. Jason gave classes in the finer nuances of the British expletive (to the enthralled infants playground whenever he could get away with it!) and estranged our family and friends as they watched him target us. We ourselves could not help but empathise with the enraged mother or father of that day's victim.

Jason shows no hesitation in lying, blaming others, or arguing that black is white. Possessions disappear, or are found in bits. He thrives on the adrenaline-rush of anger, even more satisfying when induced in Mum and Dad. We later made the connection that this recreated the familiar feelings of the atmosphere within his birth family; with the help of the Family Futures team Jason too has since been able to recognise that he uses this tactic. However, the slog of coping with his distorted behaviour came close to driving a wedge through our family.

It appeared to us that Jason lurched from truly dissociative behaviour, where he was relatively disconnected from reality, to extreme manipulation, where he knew exactly what he was doing. We subsequently came to understand that, never having been 'joined-up' and having adopted dissociative responses as a crucial early survival strategy within his family of origin, he had now learned to utilise similar strategies consciously. Thus a stolen packet of sweets found in his pocket at the supermarket will be disowned in absolute amazement (mumbled through the sweet actually being consumed at the same time). Provocative behaviour witnessed in triplicate is vehemently denied. Having belted his 'best' friend in school,

Jason could not see a single reason why neither this child nor his mother would be instantly delighted by an invitation to tea the same afternoon. (Not surprisingly, we were never a part of the after-school 'tea and play' circuit: another lonely stretch along the road of difference.)

On our own and unsupported we eventually ran out of ideas and the energy to help Jason control his behaviour. We tried ignoring negative behaviours and cuddling him anyway; we talked to him and we re-enacted the problem scenario, practising a 'better' ending. 'Every day is a new day' became stuck in the groove and every new day produced new horrors. We tried removing treats, which did not work, then rewarding good behaviour with star charts and presents earned with the stars. Some things worked sometimes, albeit with a genuine air of 'I have no idea what you are talking about but I'll go along with it' from Jason, yet there was no consistency. We eventually fell into a numb belief that nothing we could do was going to change Jason or his behaviour. Our lives were twisting into a downward spiral of hatred and delinquency. We listened miserably as he would cry himself to sleep or wake in terror, yet brooking no comfort.

A Twist in the Tale

We realised that we really must act immediately when one night, patient, loving and supportive Simon came in from work with exhaustion already etched on his face and I seriously, if briefly, considered lying to him that actually we had had a good day and that everything was fine. I was just not able to say this. (If I had even tried this strategy it would have had little effect, since every day, hour, minute and second with our son was clearly written on my face.) Jason would have succeeded in his strategy of 'divide and rule' had I been capable of lying.

We were fortunate indeed, during the crisis meeting following this realisation, to have been referred to Family Futures Consortium, one of very few therapy teams offering support to the whole adoptive family and addressing its specific problems in an integrated way. The referral came about through the gentle but utterly unwavering persistence of our family support worker, who had been party to the escalation of events and our feelings of hopelessness. She insisted that Family Futures was one of only two teams who could offer the kind of specialised help that we so desperately needed. We realise now that we could so easily have been sent down the road of traditional child-based therapy, once a week, with the child attending in isolation from the family and with very little feedback or support offered to us as parents. Had this happened we would definitely not still be a family unit now. Family Futures re-armed us with some effective guerrilla tactics, which have helped in some measure to counter the eerie survival strategies to which Jason clings. Under the team's gentle guidance we also came to understand that our child was not in fact 'mad and bad', as it seemed, but traumatised and in great emotional pain.

Our one abiding sadness is that the referral took place so late: 18 months post placement. By this time Jason had so consummately sabotaged relationships with us that we now had our own 'Everest' of family baggage to scale, as well as tackling the monsters of his past. This might have been avoided had sufficient, specialised, preparatory work been offered both for us and for Jason, in conjunction with a comprehensive therapeutic post placement support package. Now all we can do is hope that this help did not come too late: only time will tell.

Part II

State of the Art

Theory into Practice

Jenny and Marty's Story

Jay Vaughan

Jenny and Marty's story has been created to represent the typical history of many of the children and their adoptive families who consult Family Futures. This is a composite, fictionalised family, not to be confused with Lucy Greenmile's real life family story. The Saunders family's experience provides realistic examples of the background and current difficulties which face many permanent families and will be used by many of our contributors in Part II as the basis for their working examples and discussion. We recommend that chapters in Part II are read in order, to gain a comprehensive, coherent family narrative. Any resemblances between the Saunders family and adoptive or foster families known to social work agencies is purely coincidental.

The Saunders family's story begins with an advertisement in 'Be My Parent' (a publicity service, provided by British Agencies for Adoption and Fostering, on behalf of placing agencies seeking families for children for whom they are responsible):

> Jenny and Marty are brother and sister. Jenny is nine years old. She is a quiet child who loves to spend time in her room, reading and drawing. She sometimes has trouble sleeping and likes to have the light on as well as the radio. Jenny is very attached to her brother and they have a close and caring relationship. Marty is eight years old and a lively little boy. He loves active games and can at times be very physical. He has a lovely smile and is great fun. He would be a challenging but rewarding child to parent. Jenny and Marty are currently placed separately but the plan is to

reunite them in an adoptive family. If you feel you would like to be Jenny and Marty's parents please contact Borsettshire Social Services.

What Mr and Mrs Saunders were subsequently told about the children by Borsettshire Social Services:

Jenny (date of birth: 26 February 1992) is nine years old and her brother Martin (date of birth: 12 June 1993), known as Marty, is eight years old.

Jenny and Marty came into care because their birth mother could not care for them; their biological fathers' identities are unknown. Jenny and Marty were placed on the Child Protection Register on 3 August 1995, when their birth mother was picked up by the police for begging.

Attempts were made to keep the children with their birth mother and over the next two years they attended a family centre. In December 1997 Marty was taken to the casualty department of the local hospital by his birth mother, following a head injury. Subsequently both Jenny and Marty were taken into care under an Emergency Protection Order.

They were placed with emergency foster carers, Mr and Mrs B, for two nights, whilst a short-term placement was found for them. Jenny and Marty then moved into Mrs G's home, where they remained for six months until some family difficulties arose. They then went to live with Mr and Mrs W and remained there for a further six months, until December 1998, when the two children were placed in separate foster homes.

Jenny was placed with Mr and Mrs Q. They found her easy to parent and she fitted well into their family, which consisted of three younger children, aged seven, four and two years old. During this time Jenny was showing some concentration problems in school but everyone was optimistic that these would resolve themselves within the security of a permanent family.

Simultaneously Marty was placed with Ms P, with whom he remains, whilst he waits for an adoptive placement. Ms P has found that despite Marty's difficult early history he has settled well and is managing in school.

Throughout this time Jenny and Marty have maintained regular contact with their birth mother, and with each other through fortnightly contact meetings.

What Mr and Mrs Saunders were *not* told about the children by Borsettshire Social Services:

Jenny and Marty's birth mother was known to be a drug addict. (It was later revealed, through detailed exploration of family case notes, that she had also been working as a prostitute.)

The children were living in a squat with their birth mother and a number of other people. Their mother often begged for money for food, which was frequently in short supply. However, she sometimes elected to buy drugs for herself, rather than food for the family.

When Marty went to casualty it was felt that the bruising to his eye was probably a non-accidental injury. The doctors also expressed concern about Marty's low body weight, other injuries to his body (cuts and bruises) and his infestation with head lice. On examining his sister, Jenny, evidence of a sore vagina and bruising to her buttocks raised concerns about sexual abuse.

School was problematic for Jenny because she lacked concentration, often appearing to be in a world of her own. Marty also proved difficult in school: he was regularly reported to hit, kick and bite other children, and sometimes teachers and playground supervisors.

The relationship between Jenny and Marty was not an easy one. They constantly fought with each other. Jenny tended to try to parent Marty and make all his decisions for him.

The placement with Mr and Mrs W broke down because Jenny alleged that the carers' teenage son had sexually abused her. It was at this point that social services personnel had taken the decision to place the two children separately.

For both children, contact with their birth mother had been spasmodic, as she frequently failed to keep appointments. When she did visit she was often tearful and the children appeared to take responsibility for looking after her. Following contact Jenny and Marty's behaviour became substantially more difficult. In particular, Marty would cry and would become inconsolable.

Jenny experienced night terrors, walked in her sleep and regularly wet the bed. She also had a tendency to avoid eating. Marty's food difficulties frequently resulted in him overeating, to the point of making himself sick.

The initial referral to Family Futures in December 2000:

At this point Jenny and Marty had been living with Jean and Jack Saunders for two years. The couple had decided to adopt after undergoing several years of unsuccessful treatment for infertility. They were struggling to parent Jenny and Marty effectively and had not yet finalised the adoption. In particular, they were facing many difficult challenges with Marty and were unsure if they would be able to continue the placement.

Jean and Jack felt that although Jenny had begun to form an attachment to them, Marty had not. They found his violent behaviour increasingly threatening. At times it had put their marriage under extreme stress and they had sometimes questioned their original decision to adopt. They felt that the Intensive Attachment and two-year Follow Up programmes provided by Family Futures were their last hope of holding their family together.

CHAPTER 7

Assessment
A Multidisciplinary Approach
Alan Burnell

The Saunders Family Assessment

We utilise a combination of individual, couple and family work during our assessment process. In addition to the assessment consultation itself, a prior, paper assessment is carried out and often a network meeting follows, where the outcomes of the assessment are discussed with relevant parties. What follows are two accounts of the Saunders family's assessment day. One focuses on the beginning of the day, 'Beginnings', the other focuses on 'The Family Painting' exercise. Examples of individual sessions, including sand-tray work, and the 'Trust Walk' can be found in Chapter 9.

Beginnings

The assessment was scheduled to begin at 10.30am; prior to this the team spent an hour in preparation. Now they checked the file: the date and time on the letter to the family confirmed that this was definitely the right day. At 10.45am they rang Mr and Mrs Saunders at home and found their answering machine switched on. They then agreed to wait until 11.15am before ringing the children's social worker to see if she had any idea why the family had not arrived. At 10.55am the family came in, clearly very stressed, and immediately launched into a complicated explanation of what had happened to make them late. The team endeavoured to reassure them that this was not a problem: everyone was just glad that they had arrived.

Jenny and Marty were quiet and watchful. Jenny smiled a great deal at everyone and looked calm, although she continually fiddled with her fingers, lacing and unlacing them; Marty looked very scared and refused to remove his coat. One of the therapists approached Marty and asked his name and age. Marty replied quietly and then asked her if this was her home. When she replied in the negative, Marty commented, 'I would like to live here.' The family was then given a guided tour of the building and drinks were made for them. Subsequently they were invited to join the assessment team in the large family room, containing two large sofas and some chairs. Jack Saunders sat with Marty and Jean with Jenny; everyone looked very uncomfortable and anxious. The team co-ordinator explained that the day would consist of an introductory meeting, followed by some separate sessions for the parents and children. The children were also informed that their individual sessions would not be completely confidential, since they would be shared with their adoptive parents. Lunch was planned for around 12.30pm, to fit in with the children's usual school lunch time; this would be followed by a family session.

The children were invited to say why they thought they had come to Family Futures. Jenny and Marty were both very quiet and said that they did not know. Jenny then responded, 'It's because Marty is difficult and hits Mum.' Jean looked horrified and interjected with an account of what she and her husband had explained to the children the previous evening. The children had been told that, as a family, they all needed some help because they were not always happy together. Family Futures was a place where adoptive families could come to get help. Marty asked, 'Could I live here?' Mum smiled and said, 'It is a nice building.' One of therapists took this opportunity to explain to the children that Family Futures is not like social services and does not remove children from their parents; Marty looked visibly relieved. Jean asked Marty if he had thought he would be moving to a new family and whether that was what he thought the day was about. Marty was unable to answer but it was clear that he had been concerned about this. Jenny smiled throughout this conversation and continued to lace and unlace her fingers. The co-ordinator suggested that this could be a good point at which to separate out. Jean and Jack were to remain in the family room whilst the children were to go to separate playrooms, with a therapist each. Further reassurance was provided by showing the parents where their children were going to be and showing the children where Mum and Dad would be concurrently.

Jean and Jack still appeared very tense. They apologised once again for being late and said that they hoped it did not matter too much. Jean looked tearful; when the therapist acknowledged this she began to cry. Jack sat still beside her while she cried. Jean talked and talked through her tears about how awful things were at home and how hopeless she felt. She explained how desperately they had wanted the children and how hard they had fought to be accepted as adopters. To her mind this fight now seemed pointless, since she did not think she could be a mum to these children: they did not want her. She added that she was now beginning to feel that she did not want them. Jean looked embarrassed and ashamed; she hung her head, shaking it and repeating over and over again, 'I can't do it. I can't do it!' Jack reached out, held her hand and stroked it, saying, 'No, I don't think I can either.'

Some moments of silence elapsed before Jean could look up. Jack said, 'Look, we've been to child and family therapy for six sessions. They seem to think that it's because our relationship is in tatters that we aren't really able to connect with these children. I don't know much about therapy but I don't think anyone could connect with them. I'm not saying we're perfect and we've had a tough few years, what with all the miscarriages and IVF, but we were getting along OK. We were coping. Now look at us! She's not sleeping. I dread coming home. I know the moment I do all I'll hear is what they've been doing that day. We argue all the time about them and the right way to treat them. Surely this has something to do with the kids? Child and family hadn't even read the papers we sent them before our session. They didn't even know the children were adopted. I mean, it's hopeless! Is it us? Perhaps they'd be better in another family?'

The remainder of the session was spent reassuring Jean and Jack that many parents feel this way. The therapist explored the complex reasons for this in more detail: the children would certainly have triggered all sorts of feelings for them as parents and, inevitably, they would often not feel good enough, since the children had brought their traumatic, birth family history into their adoptive family. At that moment Marty burst into the room shouting, 'I want to live here! They've got lots of toys and I can do whatever I like.' The therapist tactfully brought the session to a close.

The Family Painting

After lunch the family were invited to attempt a family painting together. The children were hugely excited by this idea; Marty danced excitedly over the paper, tripping at one point and ripping it. Jenny sighed and found the sellotape. No one knew quite how to begin, so Jean drew round Jack, to help get them started. The children watched this process, although Marty found this hard and fiddled with the paints, desperate to get the lids off and begin. Jean then worked very hard to engage both children. Firstly, she drew all round Marty; he loved this and giggled throughout, saying it tickled. She then drew around Jenny, who lay extremely still with her legs tightly closed. Mum then asked Jenny to draw round her but Jenny refused; Dad appeared not to hear this and was occupied helping Marty colour in his outline. Jean began to colour in Jack's outline.

With half an hour left, it was a full-time job for Dad to keep Marty occupied painting his outline and simultaneously protect the rest of the room, and himself, from the flying paint. Throughout this Jenny sat painting in her outline carefully, in the palest shade of pink, so that it was hardly noticeable. When the family were informed that they had ten minutes to finish off, Jean again asked if someone would draw round her. Marty came in her direction, with a large paintbrush dripping with green paint; Jack swiftly intervened, removing the brush from his hand. He picked up felt pens and suggested that they both draw around Mum. In order to complete this in time it was rather rushed, so that when Jean stood up parts of her appeared to have been missed and other parts looked deformed. Jean's only comment was, 'Oh well, never mind. Let's quickly finish off.' Jean had been drawn lying at Jack's feet and Marty's form was indistinct and unrecognisable. The parents started to clear up, while Jenny continued to paint. Marty took off his shoes and socks, dipping his feet in the black paint. In one dramatic move he slid across Jean's image, leaving her as one large, black smudge at the bottom of the painting. Jean turned, looked at herself in the picture, smiled sadly, and said quietly, 'Yes, that's me!'

These two vignettes are intended to give a flavour of the holistic assessment process we have developed at Family Futures.

(Jenny and Marty's story by Jay Vaughan)

'If You Want to Go There, I Wouldn't Start from Here!'

It is an historical accident that social workers are the main providers of services to adoptive parents and their children in the new millennium. Over the centuries, babies abandoned on the doorsteps of churches and foundling hospitals had led to the tradition of infants being cared for by the Church and its hospital offshoots. Clerics, nuns, doctors and nurses were the forbears of an adoption service, which became a legal entity in the United Kingdom in 1926. At that time the placement of babies in 'good families' was the province of an embryonic social work profession growing out of earlier philanthropic provision. Hence there was a certain logic to social workers being invested with the responsibility of caring for these babies and finding them new homes. However, present day adoption is very different, where children are older and often placed in sibling groups (see Chapter 1). Frequently they have experienced trauma, which we understand affects their psychological and physiological development and may further challenge their often-compromised genetic inheritance. Their needs are far more complex than simply the perceived need for love and good homes. The task of defining and meeting the needs of today's adopted children has become so complex that this task can no longer be fulfilled adequately by any one profession.

As we know, genetic and environmental influences on children are interactive and highly complex. Severely traumatic environmental influences may include uterine distress, early separation and loss, neglect, physical, sexual or emotional abuse, dietary deficiencies, dysfunctional patterns of family interaction, poor educational achievement and social disadvantage (Archer 2001b, 2002). Thus the need for a multidisciplinary assessment process begins to emerge clearly. The real future for adoption and family placement services demands a radical break with historical links to Church and social work. A new multidisciplinary team approach is also essential, if the needs of adopted children and their families are to be met in comprehensive and integrated ways.

Significant Factors in Assessment

At Family Futures we have identified what we believe are significant factors, when assessing children and their families, under three broad headings: factors in the child, factors in parents and factors in the family.

Factors in the Child

TRAUMA HISTORY

We embrace an increasingly forensic approach in our search for information about the early experiences of children with whom we work. From what we have learnt about the first three years of life, and its significance both for the organisation of attachment patterns and the organisation of the brain, we recognise the vital importance of obtaining a detailed picture of the child's history during this crucial period in his life. Increasingly, as part of our assessment process, and routinely as part of our treatment programme, we devote a great deal of time and energy to researching original file material. First-hand accounts, not only of events but also of the quality of life experienced by the child during those early years, are vital to gaining an understanding of the degree, duration and type of early traumatic experience. When information is gathered from summarised material the information inevitably becomes stylised, stereotyped and jargon-filled. As we know, 'the devil is in the detail'. It is only when original source documents are read that the detail, and hence the individuality of the child and his experiences, emerges.

In order to understand fully why a child has developed in a particular way, specific information from a variety of sources, including police, medical (including obstetric) services, education and social services, is essential. Having collated a detailed profile as part of our pre-assessment, it is important that this material is not only used factually and chronologically but also imaginatively. It is the essence of this information that feeds our creative understanding of children's early experience, the beliefs that they have about themselves and the world, and their expectations. Hence, as part of our therapy programme, a rather dry chronology becomes the script for a drama that enlightens both the child and his adoptive parents as to the true nature of his early experiences.

PATTERNS OF ATTACHMENT

We use a number of indicators to examine this central issue. Firstly, we ask adoptive parents to complete our attachment questionnaire, which itemises specific behaviours associated with reactive attachment disorder, according to DSM IV. The version that Family Futures uses is a composite of two American ones drawn, with permission, from Beechbrook and the Attachment and Bonding Center in Ohio. In conjunction with the questionnaire we use direct observation of the child during the assessment day, the parents' verbal account of them and their subjective responses to them. In our individual sessions with children we also use sand-tray and miniature world work (Landy 1986) as media through which children can express their inner worlds. These techniques are similar to 'story stems' (Main and Cassidy 1988), which are increasingly being used in the assessment of children's attachment patterns. We have also adapted the 'strange situation' test (Ainsworth *et al.* 1978) to provide another, more age-appropriate, indicator of attachments during the assessment day.

Our aim is not to diagnose *per se*, but to gain as clear a picture as possible of the way each child has formed attachments to his adoptive parents (see also Chapter 3). In addition, we consider patterns of attachment between siblings, using the sibling attachment framework devised by Bridge Child Care Consultancy (1991). We avoid using diagnostic terminology, in favour of looking for common patterns of attachment to significant figures, which not only provide a precise and detailed picture of the child and his relationships but also one that is meaningful and useful to his parents.

PROBLEMATIC BEHAVIOUR

For this information we are heavily reliant upon first-hand accounts provided by parents, teachers, social workers and the children themselves. We have devised a useful framework, in a form entitled 'A Day in the Life', which we ask parents to complete. This breaks down the child's day into significant events, from getting up to going to bed (see also Chapter 12). Our assessments involve five hours of face-to-face interaction with the family, during which the child's behaviour can be compared with parental accounts and parents' perceptions of the child discussed with them.

CONTACT ARRANGEMENTS

Although contact is discussed in some depth in Chapter 11, it is also a very significant issue in compiling a comprehensive assessment. Areas explored here include:

- frequency and form of contact arrangements

- changes in arrangements over time

- evidence of 'farewell' contact with birth family members, at what age and with what outcome for the child

- the nature of the transition from previous foster carer(s) and any ongoing contact arrangements with them.

One of the important issues to address in an assessment is whether there is too little, or too much, contact and its meaning for the child. Our experience has led us to identify a 'golden rule of contact' for children who are not forming attachments in their new families: put simply, if the child *is* having contact he is having too much; if he is *not* having contact he is having too little. Although this may appear simplistic, even flippant, I believe that on closer examination it highlights the essence of what we hope to establish during an assessment: namely whether contact arrangements are enhancing or inhibiting the child's current, significant attachment relationships.

The issue of 'openness' in contact should also be considered during an assessment. Although practice in adoption over the past 15 years has moved away from the 'closed' nature of baby placements, it is important that we are not seduced by the myth, or magic, of openness. Whilst many contemporary adoptive parents are able to talk openly with their child about his birth parents, are comfortable with 'letterbox' contact, and even some level of direct contact, in our view, contact and openness *per se* resolve nothing.

Contact arrangements alone cannot resolve the child's unrequited longing, his unresolved ambivalence or his denial and idealisation.

During individual assessment sessions it is very common for children to express these feelings about their birth parents and to display a degree of confusion about their pasts. When fed back to their adoptive parents, this is often a cause for surprise. Many adopters believe that their children can recall experiences in their birth families, or have taken on board what they have been told; often this is far from so. Clarifying the discrepancies between adoptive parents' beliefs and those of their child can itself be a positive, therapeutic outcome of an assessment. It goes without saying that, for some children, the above issues apply equally to the attachments, beliefs and contact needs relating to other previous, significant caregivers. In our experience, an infant removed from his birth family in his first year often imbues his first 'short-term' foster carers, who may have cared for him for the next 12 to 18 months, with all the attributes of 'real' parents. He may feel he was 'stolen' from these caregivers by his adoptive parents. The sense of unresolved loss can be as strong in respect of previous foster carers as for birth parents.

EDUCATIONAL ISSUES

Educational issues for children who have been traumatised and are experiencing attachment difficulties are reviewed more fully in Chapter 14. We believe that, as part of our assessment, a full educational assessment of the child should be carried out. If an educational assessment has already taken place it may need to be reviewed by an experienced educational psychologist, within the broader perspective of attachment and development. In gathering information we routinely ask parents and teachers to complete a short version of the Connor's Questionnaire and to provide examples of the child's schoolwork, school reports and SATs results. During their individual session with the child the therapist will be mindful of the child's:

- concentration
- comprehension
- language development
- developmental play
- ability to draw and write in age-appropriate ways.

In the past some professionals have been reluctant to assess children formally, perhaps for fear of labelling, or because of potential resource implications. In our opinion it is helpful for children as young as five years to be tested by an educational psychologist: in many cases long before the class teacher expresses any concerns about the child's abilities. We identify a high incidence of specific learning difficulties in the adopted children we see and believe that it is vital that parents and teachers, as well as therapists, identify potential educational difficulties as early as possible. In the short term this may have no bearing on resources *per se*, although primary age children with whom we have worked have often been allocated classroom assistance already. Classroom assistants are often unaware of children's specific learning needs and are therefore not able to adopt appropriate strategies for dealing with them. While in general we welcome this additional input, it is regrettable that the full benefits of additional help are being neither appraised nor achieved. Most parents welcome the additional information we obtain: naturally they have a right to know as much about their child as is feasible. They should also be given as much advice and assistance as possible in order to enable their child to reach his full potential. Failure to do so frequently leaves parents feeling frustrated by their child's apparent laziness, unwillingness or oppositional behaviour: behavioural strategies which often mask underlying educational problems.

Furthermore, practitioners working therapeutically with children, or engaging them in life story work, need to have an accurate picture of their ability to conceptualise, comprehend and work at symbolic levels, in order to tailor their work to a particular child. We find that an educational assessment of a child informs, and often changes quite dramatically, our therapeutic approach with him. It ensures that we convey concepts and meanings in ways attuned to his ability to make sense of them. Moreover, we are becoming increasingly aware that a child's educational needs cannot be considered separately from his psychiatric and paediatric appraisals. In our complex assessment process, disentangling coexisting psychiatric, paediatric and educational issues is central to accurate and comprehensive assessment. For example, it is often difficult, without this interdisciplinary dialogue, to ascertain whether a child's hyperactivity in the classroom is due to hyper-arousal in response to classroom invoked stress (Perry *et al.* 1995) or is symptomatic of attention deficit hyperactivity disorder (ADHD). Similarly, a child's daydreaming, passivity and under-performance in the classroom could be dissociative behaviour, or the result of limited intelligence and failure to comprehend, due to traumatic, neural pathway disorganisation (Perry *et al.* 1995).

MENTAL HEALTH CONCERNS

From the inception of our service we have been indebted to Dr Paul Holmes, our consultant child and adolescent psychiatrist, who has helped us recognise the role and relevance of psychiatry in the assessment and treatment of children with attachment difficulties. Ten years ago, when we first began our work with older-placed adoptees, the psychiatric diagnosis we met most frequently was 'conduct disorder'. As a result of our growing familiarisation with American perceptions and practice with this group of children, we began to employ the term 'reactive attachment disorder'. In the early 1990s this was a useful step forward, since it validated many adopters' experiences: that attachment difficulties were central to the problems they were experiencing with their adoptive children. However, as discussed in chapters 4 and 15, recent, rapid developments in the field of psychoneurobiology have led to a broader understanding of the impact of trauma on youngsters' neurological development.

In our view, the greatest challenge for any psychiatrist currently working in this field is grappling with the issues of complex symptomatology and co-morbidity of disorders. The population of looked after children being adopted bring with it genetic and environmental legacies: their histories of pre- and post-birth traumas, which are expressed at physical, physiological and psychological levels. As a result, the children with whom we work cannot simply be regarded as attachment disordered. Many of them, because of their birth parents' lifestyles, are at high risk of foetal alcohol, or other drug, effects. Moreover, during an assessment we often become aware of previous concerns about autistic spectrum disorders; the hyperactivity that some children exhibit may have been fashionably diagnosed as ADHD. For any one child it is conceivable that all, or several, of these diagnoses may apply. Of course, in addition, the children we see invariably demonstrate attachment difficulties of varying degrees of severity. Often during our treatment programme children also exhibit depressed behaviours, as they begin truly to feel their feelings. Others have previously exhibited suicidal behaviour, which has prompted the assessment request. Very careful risk assessment from a psychiatrist is then needed, regarding the safety of the child, and the potential benefits of anti-depressant medication.

What has emerged over recent years is how complex the interweaving of all these variables is and just how important and helpful a considered and collaborative psychiatric perspective can be to our work. However, we believe that the psychiatric assessment should form part of an integrated and multidisciplinary team, in the context of an understanding of this particular group of adopted children and their parents. In our view, this population is significantly different from the mainstream of families seen by local child and adolescent services and therefore needs input from a psychiatrist with expertise in the field of trauma, attachment and family permanence.

PHYSICAL HEALTH CONCERNS

All children placed for adoption will have had a medical assessment. However, in the context of post adoption service provision these examinations may well have occurred several years earlier and can demonstrate varying degrees of thoroughness. If there are any health concerns, or any information arising out of our research of file material, suggesting genetically transmitted disorders we immediately refer to our consultant paediatrician.

Through our practice of paediatric consultation, we are also becoming increasingly aware that many looked after, as well as adopted, children have not had thorough paediatric assessments and have underlying, undiagnosed conditions. Paediatric assessments are at their most rigorous when questions of injury or neglect are being debated in the legal domain. Beyond the court order, or where none exists, a global comprehensive assessment is rarely carried out with full background information available to the paediatrician, regarding the child's genetic background and his pre- and post-natal environment. Children are then placed in permanent families without clear information available to their new caregivers of the child's current medical status and potential. In our experience it is vital to establish whether a child's behaviour, for example bed-wetting, soiling, clumsiness or 'laziness' has a physiological, as well as a psychological, origin so that appropriate remedial help can be accessed.

On a more mundane level, we believe it is important to consider traumatised children's current diet and sleep patterns. Adopters frequently lack experience or basic information about the relationship between types of food, food sensitivities and chronic low-grade nutritional deficiencies and their children's behaviour and general health. They may also struggle with establishing sound sleep patterns, since they often lack experience and awareness of the physiological basis for the development of sleep patterns in infancy. Education in effective strategies for altering these patterns in age-appropriate ways is essential.

PREVIOUS THERAPY HISTORY

It is important to establish immediately whether the child or adoptive family has received therapeutic help in the past. With the consent of the adopters, we then contact previous therapists or counsellors, requesting summaries of their work. This can be particularly important where previous therapeutic experiences have been unhelpful or distressing.

CURRENT THERAPY NEEDS

Taking into account all the information acquired throughout the assessment, the therapist working alongside the child during the assessment day should consider the child's:

- willingness and ability to co-operate
- ability to engage with the therapist during the assessment day
- ability to use symbolic play
- access to a coherent and authentic narrative regarding themselves and their history
- developmental stage in their play and ways of relating
- preferred expressive arts activity (e.g. drawing, storytelling, puppets, drama)
- ability to tolerate messy play
- response to boundary setting by the therapist
- ability to engage with their parents in discussions
- preference for working at verbal or non-verbal levels
- physical contact sought by the child from the therapist, its extent and appropriateness
- response to difficult issues raised during the assessment and typical defences employed under stress
- nature and quality of current parent-child interactions.

This assessment is made both during the child's individual session and throughout the assessment day. It is a team process, since the observations of other team members, in a variety of contexts, are taken into account. What is often most telling is what transpires during parent-child negotiations over lunch, or whilst putting on shoes at the end of the day, rather than what happens within the therapy sessions.

CULTURAL AND RACIAL ISSUES

For children of a different ethnic background from their adoptive parents, beliefs about cultural heritage and racial identity need to be explored as part of the assessment process and be incorporated into our treatment approach. We also believe it is important that our team should reflect the racial and cultural diversity of our families, to enable parents and children to identify with and have confidence in us as service providers. Our assessment considers:

- the child's knowledge and beliefs about his cultural, religious and racial heritage
- the child's attitudes towards his birth parents' cultural and racial provenance and the impact this has upon his own sense of self and identity
- the child's ability to distinguish between his feelings towards his birth family and current family and his feelings relating to racial origins, colour and culture
- the impact of the child's early experiences that may compromise his internal working models, self-organisation, sense of self and personal identity
- adoptive parents' belief systems around these issues.

Factors in the Parents

During the assessment it is essential to acknowledge to parents the powerful impact that parenting a traumatised child (who brings with them a history of pathological attachments) can have on parental self-esteem and relationships. Many parents with whom we have worked approach 'helping' agencies with caution. Many embarked upon parenting with enthusiasm and optimism, yet when faced with the realities of parenting a challenging child, found their confidence severely knocked, even when preparation for adoptive parenthood was adequate. This can lead to self-doubt and a growing sense of personal failure; like many of us they find this hard to face or acknowledge publicly (Archer and Swanton 2000). It is therefore essential, as part of our collaborative approach, that parents are helped to feel they are part of the solution and not part of the problem, despite any difficulties they may be experiencing currently.

Parents who have sought help from non-specialist sources lacking understanding of contemporary adoption have often experienced their 'help' as blaming, if not persecutory. One of the unintended consequences of conventional family therapy services is the assumption that problems presented by the child are symptomatic of current parental failure. This can leave adopters feeling very rejected or angry, often with their relationships compromised and understandably reluctant to engage in a therapeutic alliance with the team. Parents benefit greatly if, as part of our therapeutic contract, we clearly acknowledge that their child brings with him a legacy of pathological behaviour patterns, which previously helped him survive.

We stress to parents that ours is a team approach: they are invaluable members of the team and part of our role is to help address and repair any damage incurred during their transition to adoptive parenthood. This is informed by research into the transition to parenthood (Cowan and Cowan 1991) and the psychological impact this has, both upon the individual parent and their relationship as a couple. We recognise that, in addition to the normal transition, adoptive parents have to cope with the projections and post traumatic stress behaviours that the child brings to their new family. It is frequently the mother who feels the greatest challenge, since the mother-child relationship is central to attachment behaviour (Bowlby 1969, 1979; Winnicott 1971). It is therefore important during the assessment to ensure that:

- A collaborative relationship is developed within which parents are given explanations at every step.

- A positive therapeutic alliance is formed with parents.

- There is appropriate acknowledgement of parents' histories, their transition to parenthood, their experience of other agencies and the impact all this may have on them, both as individuals and as a couple.

- The assessment and treatment programme is as much an educative experience as it is therapy (Lowe *et al.* 1999). To this end, from its inception, our service has always incorporated adoptive parents into the team. Their task is to support and educate parents: providing a mentoring role. (See chapters 12 and 13 for further discussion of this vital element.)

ACQUIRED ATTACHMENT PATTERNS

Parents are asked to complete an autobiographical account of their own childhood and parenting experiences. Certain key issues are highlighted, such as adopters' perceptions of their attachment to their parents, parents' method of discipline, their experience of parental alcoholism or abuse and other significant losses. The value of such accounts as part of the assessment process is as much qualitative as quantitative. Two key qualities are considered in the first instance:

- Coherent and authentic narratives. Our knowledge base here has been influenced by work done on adult attachment interviews (see Chapter 2).

- Similarities or resonances between parents' histories and that of their adopted child.

We remain aware that, at this stage, it is unlikely that parents will be completely open. Difficult issues concerning the parents' pasts may only emerge once the treatment process has begun, when they have developed sufficient trust in us as a team and have become aware of the significance of their own pasts in relation to the current situation.

PARENTING SKILLS

During the course of the assessment day we identify, from parents' first-hand accounts, their 'Day in the Life' diary (see also Chapter 12) and family interactions taking place during sessions, the specific areas of their child's challenging behaviour with which they would initially like assistance. Sometimes during the assessment parents observe one of the team using particular strategies with a child and may feel inspired to experiment with different approaches. We encourage this where possible during the assessment, as it adds a dynamic quality to the day and enables parents to assess whether our suggestions are relevant and effective. The rationale for our parenting approach is discussed more fully in chapters 12 and 13.

Factors in the Family

We employ our Parent Child Interaction Checklist, which we devised in order to rate the quality of the parents' interactions with their child. Parental interactions are rated independently by members of the team and their perceptions compared. Although this is not a definitive or standardised protocol it does ensure that all members of the team are considering the same behaviours and achieving some degree of consistency.

TRUST BETWEEN FAMILY MEMBERS

The 'family painting' exercise, described at the beginning of this chapter, can provide a medium for assessing levels of trust between family members. We may also use the 'family trust walk', described in Chapter 9. The damage to trust caused by early trauma is so central to resolving both trauma and attachment issues that these family exercises are vital elements in assessing a child's repairing sense of trust in their adoptive parents. It is also an opportunity for adoptive parents to model the level of trust they have in each other to their child.

PARENTAL CONTROL

For children to develop a sense of trust in their parents they need to feel reassured that their parents are in control, both of themselves and of the family. The 'family painting' exercise provides a real world situation in which issues around control can be clarified. During the course of the day there are also many mundane, but more typical, parent–child interactions, where issues of control are tested: mealtimes, arriving and leaving often provide flash-points during which the child drops his guard and shows us how difficult he can be.

OPENNESS OF COMMUNICATION

The child's individual session invariably revolves around his understanding of his past and the difficult things that have happened to him. These individual sessions do not remain confidential. Information is fed back to parents by the child, with the encouragement of the therapist, throughout the assessment and the treatment programme. Children and parents are informed of this in their introductory sessions (see Chapter 8 for further discussion of our rationale). This provides an opportunity to test out how open the family is in their discussion of difficult issues. If neither the parents nor the child raise such issues during the assessment, the therapy team will deliberately interject issues that are known to be problematic, to assess how well family members can resolve these matters. In our dealings with children during the assessment it is very important that we convey to them that we are not afraid to explore difficult issues and will not collude with their attempts to deny difficult behaviours, distressing past events or anxieties about the future. Openness has to be seen not only as an attribute of healthy family functioning but also as characteristic of the therapy process.

INFORMAL SUPPORT NETWORKS

Parents who adopt children with attachment difficulties frequently find themselves becoming increasingly isolated as a family, due to their child's challenging behaviours. Support that may have been there from friends and relatives initially tends to fade, either because they find the behaviour itself too problematic or because they do not wish to expose their own children to these behaviours. The use of childminders can become increasingly inappropriate, either because of the age of the children or, again, because of the challenging nature of their behaviour. As a consequence not only do families become isolated but also parents lose access to the everyday forms of respite that most families enjoy. It is therefore important to explore what arrangements families can and do make to gain much needed support and to consider more formalised forms of respite, where informal networks have collapsed or are inaccessible.

The corrosive and draining effects of lack of support and isolation are profound. Strategies for addressing and reversing this process must be a central part of any post-assessment plan. This forms part of our rationale for network meetings (see also Chapter 13). Co-ordinating network meetings ensures a coherent, systematic response from the formal professional network and informs our work with informal family networks.

FORMAL SUPPORT NETWORKS

A similar process of attrition and alienation often occurs between the family and professionals with whom they have been engaged. It is not uncommon for families either to have opted out of social services networks or to have found them unhelpful in addressing their needs. They may also be fearful of returning to social services for fear of being judged as failures and risking their children being removed (Archer and Swanton 2000). Moreover, many parents find their relationship with the child's school deteriorates over time, as growing, mutual frustration sets in. Teachers may appear critical of parents for the behavioural difficulties they experience in the classroom; parents may feel criticised, unsupported and their requests for educational assessments and special needs provision unheard. We find that parents are reluctant to inform the school of the child's history or, if the child's history has been shared, that its true significance for the child is not understood, since staff may be unaware of the long-term impact of trauma.

With the consent of parents we involve the local authority link worker, the child's social worker and any existing therapists in part of the assessment day. By so doing we seek to work systemically and to model, from the outset, a collaborative approach. Early involvement of social services personnel often enhances their relationship with the family and strengthens their commitment to resource provision. It also maximises our access to information about the child's past: details that might otherwise remain inaccessible.

Summary

Our assessments of children and their families endeavour to consider:

- the inner world of the child, within historical context

- parents, as individuals and as a couple

- the family and their interactions as a whole

- informal and formal networks of support, from a systemic perspective.

The assessment provides a comprehensive and integrated understanding of child and family and a clear action plan addressing all the above elements (see Family Futures Planning Matrix in *Appendix*). In our experience, failure to address all these elements concurrently leads to valuable points being missed, or to one element being emphasised to the exclusion of other, equally valid, issues.

Typical outcomes from an assessment at Family Futures would be:

- a network meeting of the informal and formal networks of relatives, friends and professionals, designed to focus and integrate existing support and interventions with a clear plan for the future

- an invitation for the family to participate in Family Futures' Intensive Attachment Programme over an extended period.

CHAPTER 8

Rationale for the Intensive Programme

Jay Vaughan

In our experience, conventional therapeutic help for families, either in the form of family therapy or individual child psychotherapy, does not address the needs of contemporary adoptive families. The primary task of parents who foster or adopt children is to help them form new and positive attachments. This often presents a considerable challenge for children and parents alike. The child's early experience of relationships may have involved neglect, abuse, multiple caregivers and repeated separations. This makes it hard for children to trust or to relinquish control. They bring with them patterns of behaviour which may have been adaptive, enabling them to survive in the past, but which are inappropriate in the context of caring families. These may challenge even the most stable existing family relationships. Contact arrangements, if not properly planned and supported, can also add to the complexity of forming new attachment relationships, for everyone concerned.

Our Approach

Over the past four years the Family Futures' team has developed a new approach to helping children and their new parents cope with these complexities. Our approach is based upon the following beliefs:

- A family is the most important resource a child has. All therapeutic work should seek to build and strengthen current family relationships, using an attachment and developmental reparenting approach.

- The traumatic effects of children's early experiences frequently remain unexplored and inaccessible to them. As a consequence they defend against painful feelings and act out experiences they are unable to understand or verbalise.

- Change is possible, if parents and children are helped to work together to understand their pasts and to form positive attachments in the present.

- The role of the therapeutic team is to facilitate this process and provide ongoing support.

- Therapeutic help for adoptive families needs to be intensive and long-term.

Aims of the Attachment Programme

We aim to:

- address directly, and change, the child's attachment patterns

- increase parents' confidence and skills as caregivers

- incorporate the extended family and professional support systems in change maintenance

- provide ongoing therapeutic support to families, as appropriate.

Key Areas Covered by the Attachment Programme

Overall, the Attachment Programme is designed to address the complexities of contemporary placements. To achieve this our Programme has seven essential elements, which are explored and managed simultaneously:

- the child's early history and patterns of attachment

- the parents' relationship as a couple and their expectations of themselves, and of each other, as parents

- contact with birth relatives and siblings

- the child's current behavioural difficulties

- strategies used by parents to deal with these difficulties

- patterns of interaction and communication as a family
- management of the wider family support network, including extended family members, schools, social services and significant others.

In our experience these complexities must be acknowledged and changes effected in all seven elements, if significant changes are to be achieved in children and adoptive families coping with these complex issues. This requires a concerted and intensive approach to intervention, often involving all family members, over an initial period of five days. Ideally, families should participate in the Programme soon after permanent placement. With this approach it becomes possible to achieve sufficient momentum to reverse the negative spiral in which many families in crisis find themselves. Our Follow Up Programme is designed to maintain and build upon the positives gained during this intensive week.

Throughout the Programme we endeavour to tackle the complexities of each family situation through a process of parallel interventions involving individual child work, individual adult work, couples work, family work, parenting strategies, developmental reparenting, parent mentoring, advice on complementary approaches and network management. Prior to the inception of our Attachment Programme it was common for one of these approaches to be attempted but not all of them simultaneously. Furthermore, we have pioneered the innovative use of dramatherapy and creative arts therapies, introducing an essential new dimension to working with adoptive families that allows us to integrate the remaining elements in exciting and effective ways. Dramatherapy brings with it three essential ingredients: structure, focus and the use of non-verbal techniques of communicating. The current chapter will focus closely on these issues.

The drama that traumatised children bring with them from their birth families is the stuff of Shakespeare: it makes perfect sense of the Lady Macbeth dilemma, 'Here's the smell of the blood still. All the perfumes of Arabia will not sweeten this little hand' (*Macbeth*, Act V, Scene I). Children struggle with whether they will ever wipe away the smell of their abusers. It is the drama to which Cox and Theilgaard (1987) refer in their work with abused abusers at Broadmoor prison. They propose that Shakespeare's primitive and archetypal themes are played out in the lives of these prisoners: here are men who have murdered, mutilated and raped, who know feelings of rage, despair, jealousy and elation, as portrayed by Shakespeare, since they have truly lived these experiences. Similarly, the children we work with have experienced extreme forms of abuse and neglect and have witnessed the drama of life at its most intense, at an age too young for them to either comprehend or cope. They know more about sheer terror, murderous rage and the extremes of passion than most adults. As a team we have had actively to acknowledge the levels of maltreatment and degradation that children experience, and witness its profound impact on them and their beliefs about the world. In the face of such trauma we began to wonder what was possible. Could these children be helped to connect to new families; could they be helped to trust people other than themselves? What could dramatherapy offer these children and their parents?

Our Attachment Programme integrates our personal experiences, the experiences of those who have worked as part of the team, and those who do so now. Creating a performance for the theatre is a group experience involving many individuals other than the actors: some are on stage and some remain off stage. Similarly, dramatherapy is largely 'group therapy' training (Jennings 1987). At one time or another each member of the group introduces significant people in their lives: sometimes directly, at other times indirectly by projecting them onto group members. Children who have been traumatised and separated from their birth families bring with them the ghosts of significant people from their pasts, which continue to haunt their new families. Adoptive families form groups that involve not only themselves, but also other families off stage. Family Futures therefore works with the adoptive family and the 'off stage family' as a unit, symbolically and sometimes, where relevant, in reality. The Family Futures team joins with each family to create a unique process of its own.

We cannot state too clearly that the therapy at Family Futures, which is described in this book, belongs not just to us but to all those who have laughed and cried and been brave enough to join with this process: families and therapists alike. Inevitably, in trying to describe this process, some parts will be excluded and not all will be fully explained. However, it seems important to try and cover a number of basic working assumptions.

First Principles

The Team Approach

We believe it is imperative that parents who come with their children to work with us join us as part of the team. They need to know what is being asked of them; they need to understand why we are asking them to do what, at times, can seem some pretty strange things. Parents are also the people who will be doing most of the hard work, both in therapy and at home. They are the most important members of the team of adults trying to help their children: they are the significant figures to whom we are all trying to encourage their children to attach. For each family, the Family Futures team uses a unique combination of team members, all of whom contribute different skills. They bring together personal experience of the world of adoption, social work, teaching, parenting traumatised children and psychotherapy training. Moreover, team members contribute individual specialist skills, such as massage, hypnotherapy and other complementary techniques. Each team can also draw upon the resources of a wider team, including a psychiatrist, a paediatrician, an adult, child and family psychotherapist and an educational psychologist (see *Introduction*).

Confidentiality

Whilst children are offered individual sessions as part of the therapy programme, these sessions do not remain confidential in the traditional sense. At the beginning of the Programme, we explain to every child that the content of their sessions will be shared with their adoptive parents. Our rationale for this is two-fold. First, as the emphasis of this work is family work, it is important that what children say is shared with their family. Second, we believe that, for children who have often been asked to keep terrible secrets, it is essential that there are no secrets within the therapeutic process. In our experience, children do not struggle with this conditional confidentiality; rather they seem to find it a relief. Similarly parents are delighted with this concept and eager to know what is happening in their child's individual sessions. The world of therapy and the world beyond need to be integrated: it is the parent who mediates this process, with and for the child.

Frequently it is professionals who find this concept difficult, having held for years that children should have a private space in which to talk with their therapist. I suggest that this could be appropriate when working with children who are securely attached. However, when working with children who are struggling with attachments it is important that the primary attachment figure is clearly the parent, not the therapist. By having the therapist share confidences with their parents it gives vital messages to the child: that there are no secrets and that the most important persons for the child are his parents, who can be trusted to understand how he thinks and feels. It is through this process of open and authentic communication of thoughts, beliefs and feelings that healthy attachments are formed and maintained. The converse may well communicate to the child that his parents are unable to handle painful information, or would reject him if they really knew him.

Our model of confidentiality could be open to criticism, since it could be said to deny the child safe space within which to disclose abuse or concerns about his adoptive family. Conversely, we believe that, because of the intensive nature of our work, it is more likely that team members would be alerted to any underlying issues relating to abusive behaviour by parents or siblings. We are clear in our contracting with families that if disclosures are made, or if we have serious concerns about the safety or well being of any family member, we would discuss these with social services staff. The open nature of our work encourages children to feel confident enough, and to trust us sufficiently, to raise issues of concern in their current family, as well as disclosures of past experiences. We would also be very aware of any unresolved issues in the adopters' history, due to the emphasis we place on coherence of autobiographical narrative (see chapters 2 and 7).

A Developmental Perspective on Attachment

Attachment begins at the point of conception and extends beyond the grave. Hence it is impossible to ignore the importance of a developmental perspective in understanding the impact of attachment trauma and the healing potential of adoptive families. Our work therefore focuses on, and follows, a clear developmental sequence. Our thinking and practice have been greatly influenced by Daniel Hughes, both from his writing (Hughes 1997, 2002) and, perhaps more importantly, his teaching and training input to the Family Futures' team. Dan has helped us to integrate into this developmental perspective the work of writers such as Schore (1994, 2001a, 2001b) and Siegel (1999). There will be many references to these influences throughout this volume, since they have become defining principles of our work.

A developmental perspective is of great significance to our treatment programme, enabling us to determine the developmental stage an individual child has reached and the developmental deficits he has sustained. In turn, this helps to define the form that our therapeutic interventions with the child should take. We now place greater emphasis on the need for developmental reparenting (Archer 1999c) that systematically allows the child to regress, enabling parent and child to experience and repair mother–infant interactions and relationships, from birth onwards. The value of this approach is endorsed by research highlighting the continuing plasticity of the human brain, particularly during childhood, and its ability to 'refire and rewire' neural pathways (Perry 1999; Schore 1994; Siegel 1999). Reparenting is not simply a symbolic ritual, although this can be important; it can also heal hearts, change minds and rewire brain circuitry. Marshall Klaus (1998) demonstrates in his training video that the optimal period for babies to interact and learn is during the state of 'quiet alert'. This has encouraged us to try and replicate this state during therapy sessions with parents and their children. An awareness of the functional, as well as the dysfunctional, use of dissociation by babies and young children has also helped us greatly to facilitate meaningful communications between parents and their children.

Our growing knowledge in the field of child development is also leading us to adopt a less purely psychological view and increasingly to explore physiological and physical dimensions. We are excited by the pioneering work of HANDLE (UK) and the Institute for Neurophysiological Psychology (INPP) at Chester (see also chapters 14 and 15). These organisations are doing much to shed the body-mind dualism that has been the hallmark of traditional child psychology and child development theory.

A Post Traumatic Stress Perspective

Primarily we see our work as redressing the impact of early trauma on children, whatever form that trauma has taken. Part of the therapist's task is to appreciate fully the onset, frequency and degree of trauma that children have experienced. The one or two recorded incidents on social work files are invariably the tip of a traumatic iceberg with which the child has had to live. Consequently, we place great emphasis on detailed forensic research of file material and first-hand accounts of children's early experiences. Disordered attachments are essentially indicators of trauma, whether psychological or physical. Encouraging the child to share traumatic memories, body states and feeling states with their adoptive parents establishes the conduit for the development of new and healthier attachments (Archer 1999a, 1999b, 1999c; Hughes 2002). We have seen many adopted children who can tell 'their story' with a theatrical grace that would be the envy of any actor. However, the potency and power of retelling and re-enactment requires the re-experiencing of emotions associated with these events. It is when the intense feelings of fear, loathing, rage, shame and abandonment are shared that children and their adoptive parents can begin to form truly meaningful attachments (Pennebaker 1997; Schoutrap *et al.* 1997).

For past traumas to be reworked and resolved the child needs to be helped to revisit and re-enact them safely, whether verbally or non-verbally, consciously or unconsciously, in the presence of caring adults who are able to help him repair fundamental damage to his sense of self. Many children fear that if they recount their past experiences they will be rejected or vilified: hence they maintain their secrecy. The gradual unlocking of these secrets and the nurturing experience of receiving empathy and acceptance from caregivers becomes the primary healing component. In our view, there is a complex interrelationship between trauma resolution and recovery, and attachment formation: the two represent the yin and the yang of the therapeutic process. Dan Hughes (2002) speaks of reworking both in parallel: forming the dramatic 'dance of attachment'.

Trust and Control

Amongst other things, the trauma of neglect, abuse and abandonment destroys the youngster's sense of trust in parents, and other significant adults, as safe, nurturing caregivers. This profound break in the trusting relationship between child and parent leaves him ever fearful of being dependent upon, or controlled by, parental figures. Commonly, self-reliance, self-soothing, self-harm and dissociation become strategies for survival. A level of trust therefore needs to be re-established before adoptive parents can, in any meaningful way, parent their child, or therapeutic work can begin. The child's early adaptive response to the overwhelming anxiety of an unpredictable world is often to seek to control every, and any, element of his immediate environment as a means of securing his own safety. The initial challenge facing many adoptive parents is therefore of containing their child. Without experiencing loving, empathetic and appropriate parental control it is difficult, if not impossible, for the child to acquire a sense of trust in caregivers: rather than risk dependent relationships many children elect to remain isolated and self-reliant.

Getting in Touch

Sadly, for the majority of children who require permanent substitute families, their experience of mother-child relationships has been sub-optimal: often beginning from birth or even in the womb (see Chapter 4). Mothers who have experienced domestic violence, abuse or high levels of personal stress may unwittingly transmit these experiences to their unborn children. During the first critical months of life current interpersonal and mental health problems, or her own poor early mothering experiences, can seriously distort the quality of a mother's interactions with her baby. Unfortunately, these relationship deficits are the legacy that many children who are ultimately adopted bring to their relationships with their adoptive mothers. Children experiencing their birth mothers as 'frightened or frightening' (Main and Hesse 1990) or 'hostile or helpless' (Lyons-Ruth, Bronfman and Atwood 1999), where their source of comfort and containment is simultaneously the source of anxiety or threat, mistrust intimacy and may appear 'people-phobic'. It is an essential part of our therapy to supplant these 'bad baby experiences' with repeated 'good baby experiences', through the somato-sensory language of infancy (see chapters 4, 13 and 15). This is mediated predominantly through eye contact, touch, movement, voice modulation and nourishment.

We encourage parents, both in therapy and at home, to do with their adopted child what they would do with any new baby, regardless of chronological age. Ensuring good eye contact, counting fingers and toes, massaging, caressing, cuddling, rocking, singing, 'motherese' and playfulness are all essential elements of the 'good baby experiences' of developmental reparenting (Archer 1999c). It should be noted that where sexual abuse forms part of the child's history, this must be done with particular sensitivity – but it must be done, if the child's distorted inner models of self and others are to be altered (see also Chapter 4). Dan Hughes stresses that the optimal parenting style is one that is warm, empathetic, playful, and curious (Hughes 1997, 2002). We encourage parents to recreate Winnicott's stage of primary preoccupation and 'mother-baby' symbiosis (Winnicott 1971), even if this is only feasible for limited periods at the beginning and end of the day. Progressively, developmentally more advanced mother-child interactions, such as 'peek-a-boo', clapping and rhyming games and turn-taking, can be introduced, allowing caregivers to extend the natural dyadic sensori-affective repertoire (Buckwalter and Schneider 2002).

Body Language

Our practice is also informed by body-centred therapies. Pesso and Boyden-Pesso (1969) describe the process of micro-tracking: the conscious and intentional observation of body movements and language that can be employed by body-work therapists to ascertain the location of trauma held in the body. This resembles the natural and spontaneous observation of a young baby by his mother that we seek to encourage. Interestingly, Marshall (2001) suggests that the world of the theatre also acknowledges this need to consider the minutiae of non-verbal communications. Body movement therapist, Pat Ogden (1998, 2000), demonstrates the dynamic way in which trauma held in the body can be sensitively and helpfully explored at the client's own pace, whilst Levine (1997) speaks of the need to introduce these experiences very gradually to prevent retraumatisation. Developments throughout this area of therapy reflect the underlying principle that the therapeutic arts mirror nature.

Monty Roberts (2000) clearly makes this ethological connection, echoing Bowlby (1988). Drawing on his vast experience with unbroken and traumatised horses, he speaks of 'whispering' to children, engaging them in predominantly non-verbal dialogue, rather than 'breaking' them. We, too, have moved away from the notion of 'rage reduction' interventions for children with disturbed attachments (Cline 1992; Randolph 1994), towards the idea of inviting children to 'join the dance' and learn the new steps of healthy attachment. By moving with the child, initially mirroring his lonely dance, and then gradually introducing new steps at the child's pace, parents and therapists can lead him towards the choreography of secure attachment.

Veronica Sherborne's parent and child games (2001), revolving around themes of trust and physical contact, can also be used in age-appropriate ways to address early relational deficits. As part of our therapy we often encourage parents and children to play traditional, drama trust games (Boal 2001; Carnicke 2000; Scher and Verrall 1988; Brook 1975), either in pairs or as a family: games around mirroring, drawn from the world of theatre and dance. These are extremely useful, both in assessing the child and parents' relationships and in encouraging them to practise the intimacy that traumatised children find so difficult. The work of HANDLE (UK) and INPP (see also chapters 14 and 15) suggest that physical contact and movement stimulates neurophysiological connections, facilitating sensory integration. Since neurobiological disorganisation has been significantly linked to attachment disorganisation (Spangler and Grossman 1999) we can understand the profound, reorganising effects of developmentally appropriate somato-sensory parent-child communications in both individual and relationship terms.

Holding Feelings

A major challenge facing adoptive parents is the aggression, both physical and verbal, of traumatised children. The infantile rage of a hurt or neglected baby re-enacted by an eight-year-old is unexpected and frequently perplexing to parents. In our experience, parents initially respond using a permissive approach that is gradually replaced by pessimism and passivity. Such distressing scenarios of abusive re-enactment can leave adopters feeling all the pain, outrage and helplessness that their youngsters felt within their birth families. Eventually the adoptive parent can come to feel like the 'victim', with the child as 'persecutor'. Perhaps more unexpectedly, dealing with a 'helpless' or avoidant youngster can pose even greater challenges. The process of trying to engage with an ultimately rejecting, pseudo self-sufficient child requires parents to override their child's desire to reject or withdraw and, instead, to offer experiences of loving, engaging interactions. In our experience, this can take much longer to achieve, demanding that parents learn to empathise and work with the child's resistance before they can draw him into the 'dance' of attachment.

In either scenario, conventional strategies, such as sending the child to his room, are ineffective and inappropriate. For the overtly hostile child, not only may his room be damaged, since his feelings of abandonment and rage are triggered and uncontained, but also he is left to console himself: again replicating earlier maltreatment. Simultaneously, adoptive parents are left feeling helpless and perplexed. For the 'helpless' child, the temporary severance of fragile attachment connections during 'time out' can be equally intolerable. The triggering of overwhelming shame may confirm the child's internal models that adults are hostile or rejecting; dissociative behaviours, including self-harm, are likely. Here parents may find themselves in the role of 'persecutor' with their child replaying the 'victim' role. It is easy to identify the bimodality of the 'helpless-hostile' dynamic proposed by Lyons-Ruth *et al.* (1999) here, both in individual actors and within their dramatic relationships (see also chapters 3 and 4).

In more extreme situations parents may find themselves resorting to restraint and physical containment, which can be both alarming and potentially dangerous if not approached with a balanced and empathetic mindset. Cline (1992), Keck and Kupecky (1995, 2002), Levy and Orlans (1998, 2000), Welch (1988) and other American attachment therapists have for some years advocated the use of parent holding as a valuable strategy for dealing with out-of-control children. If done with confidence, under-standing and empathy, this can provide adoptive parents with an extremely effective physical means of providing essential psychological holding for their child (see also *Introduction* and Chapter 13), but we do not advocate that therapists hold children to elicit cathartic responses from them. This can not only be retraumatising but may also compromise the child's burgeoning attachments to his adoptive parents.

Furthermore, in our experience, parents frequently find themselves addressing numerous outbursts of uncontrolled rage within the context of everyday life. They need help to understand the significance of such outbursts and encouragement to respond in safe, containing and empathetic ways. Aggressive outbursts need to be understood as having been triggered by traumatic, state-dependent memories. Indeed, it is part of the inherent paradox of attachment that, when children are at their most rejecting, parents need to hold their children closer: confronting the rejection and avoiding inadvertent collusion with the child's distorted perceptions (Archer 1999b; Hughes 1997, 2002; Keck and Kupecky 1995, 2002). This is as relevant for children who utilise predominantly 'helpless' behaviours, such as role-reversed caregiving, compliance, withdrawal and dissociation (Lyons-Ruth *et al.* 1999), as it is for those whose overt presentation is 'hostile' and controlling.

Supporting parents to hold their child through the 'rage' (or shame) cycle, using family cradling, ensures everyone's safety and also provides the child with experiences of containment that have not yet been internalised. Simultaneously, through the quiet 'whispering' of sensitive parent to distressed child, he is helped to 'feel felt' (Siegel 1999), to recognise and begin to make sense of his feelings. Throughout this process of psychological and physical holding, either in therapy sessions or at home, it is the therapist's role to 'hold' the parents emotionally. It is essential that parents feel accepted and understood, so that they can accept and understand that the feelings projected onto, and into, them by their angry or shame-filled child are the product of the child's pathological history rather than a personal attack. If the 'battle' for control and containment is not 'won' by the adoptive parents then, rather than the child living in the adoptive family, parents eventually feel as if they are living in the child's birth family. Holding is a huge, complex and sometimes controversial area, which deserves a more detailed appraisal than can be given here. However, it is important to underline its significance in reparenting children who have experienced serious attachment trauma.

A Coherent Narrative

Life storybooks have become the stock-in-trade of social workers involved in placing children for adoption. In our experience many such books tend to over-simplify and sanitise the child's past, leaving him with an incoherent and inauthentic story line (see chapters 2 and 7). An extreme example of this was provided in the life storybook of a child who had been sexually abused by her biological father. It contained a photograph of him, bearing the text, 'This is the Dad that loved you'. The child slept with this under her bed. The message this gave the child perpetuated and compounded her confusion between a loving parental relationship and an inappropriate sexual one.

We believe that we must think in terms of life story *work*, not storybooks. Life storybooks used to be seen as the way in which social workers could help children understand their past. Our current thinking is that they frequently omit too much of the child's life that is hugely significant. In our experience children, just as much as adults, need to develop coherent narratives and that while this can be a difficult and complex process it is an essential one. A coherent and authentic narrative, however stark, painful and unpleasant, is essential for resolution and mature reflection (Main and Hesse 1990). For us it is also the essential starting point for any therapeutic work with a child and provides the framework for the adoptive parents' understanding of him.

According to Carter (2000) the brain tends to follow a standard narrative formula, with a beginning, middle and plausible conclusion, in the recalling and re-telling of past events. It seems that throughout life, as children and adults, it is necessary for this beginning-middle-end sequence to be put in place. It affects how we manage schoolwork and relationships, organise our day and parent our children: it is how we organise our thinking about ourselves and others. This coherence is the glue inherent in everything we do. Life books, when accurate, can provide a useful chronology on which to base therapy, with the aim of re-engaging the child with his past and putting it into words. In this process of revisiting, repairing and resolving the emotional subtext it is essential that adoptive parents are involved since, like any biological parent, they must own and share their child's history, warts and all.

Alida Gersie (1990, 1991) uses archetypal stories as a powerful medium for helping children to understand more about themselves and their past. Incidentally this process also helps the child to learn how stories flow: with a beginning, middle and end. The life stories of the children with whom we work are so archetypal that they do not require recourse to fiction. Many social workers have told us that they have begun life story work, only to be forced to stop due to the child's obvious distress. In our view this distress does not mean that therapeutic work should not take place but that it needs to be approached gradually and requires the presence of containing parents to hold the child emotionally or physically. It also demands careful thought on the part of therapists and parents about how to manage life story work so that it respects the child's natural defences and his fragility and does not cause retraumatisation. At Family Futures, life story work, as with the majority of our interventions, contains essentially right-brained communications (see chapters 4 and 15), which in the telling are symbolically transformed and re-stored as coherent, left-brain memories (Siegel 1999).

The Value of Play

Our play sessions with children, and sometimes their parents, always focus on attachment themes, such as trust, babyhood, fear, defence, and displacement. It is the structure and focus of this work that bring poignancy and relevance to the sessions; through contained and supported play, children can communicate and say the unsayable. Helping parents and children to read and share this language of play is a primary goal of our work, since it increases the potential for communication ten-fold. Play has two further primary roles. First, it provides opportunities for the child, or child and parent, to revisit and resolve interrupted developmental stages (Archer 1999a, 1999b, 1999c; Hughes 1997, 2002) and thence return to the normality of childhood. We encourage parents to play with their child at much younger age levels than their chronological age using books such as Silberg's Games to Play with Toddlers (2002a) and Brain Games (2002b). 'Thinking toddler' (Archer 2001a) recognises that traumatised children will have had insufficient early, positive opportunities for parent-child interaction. Second, learning about 'the language of play' helps parents understand 'traumatic play': the repeated sequences of ritualised play through which the child attempts to resolve trauma through re-enactment. Through redirecting this play, the parent or therapist can help the child recognise a range of different outcomes, enabling him not only to communicate but also to feel empowered to take control of his past and his feelings: to act rather than to re-act. Thus we use miniature worlds and small objects, which children can readily manipulate, contain and control, to begin to develop coherent narratives (Byng-Hall 2002; Hodges *et al.* 2000; Magagna 2002b; Miller 1988).

Acting Out Rather than Acting Up

Involving children and their adoptive parents in dramatisations of specific events from their past, for example, a remembered trauma or farewell meeting with a birth parent, can be a very powerful extension of the use of play for processing the past. In this case the child is not 'playing' but 'playing out' a real life event. Here the full force of dramatherapy can be seen. From the measured moving of small objects in a sand-tray, the progression to dramatic re-enactment of trauma and the reworking of outcomes and endings can be cathartic for many children. These are complex dramatic processes that use techniques from psychodrama (Moreno 1980) as well as traditional dramatherapy theories, such as those of Stanislawski (1981, 1985) and Brecht (Bentley 1999, 2000). Stanislawski's theatre style of method acting can imbue the dramatic process with depth and penetrating reality. At times our drama also uses Stanislawski's idea of the 'as if' of drama as a way of helping children and parents feel more in control of the process. Dan Hughes (1997) alludes to this, in placing great emphasis not just on using what did happen but also what the child would like to have happened. Brecht's theatre style, whereby the audience has control of the process, is another way in which children and parents are allowed to comment upon and interact with the drama. This particular way of working has many resonances with the concept of 'the dance of attachment'. The power of the drama penetrates and confronts dissociative defences that children may have learnt to use in the past and that are distancing them from their adoptive family in the present. Conversely, at poignant moments in the drama, the child can be helped to reach moments of 'quiet alert' where, with the help of his adoptive parents and the therapist, he can begin to process the real meaning of his past and the power he has over this in the present.

In using drama techniques the role of the therapist is to select an appropriate theatrical style for an individual family. The other important consideration is the degree of 'aesthetic distance' (Landy 1986) required by the child in order to engage with the process, without being so engaged that he becomes overwhelmed. The concept of aesthetic distance was developed in order to help the therapist define, and maintain, the fine line between fantasy and reality that the child has to walk during therapy. At one end of the spectrum lies miniature world work, where work is extremely distanced, with distance defined by the size and manageability of the medium. At the other end of the spectrum lies mask work where, by adopting a mask, the work becomes dramatically much closer and more powerful.

Although the child maintains centre stage throughout, it is essential that parents are equal participants in this process, with their roles and feelings woven into the script. Thus the therapy team resembles Brecht's audience, as an active chorus from the Greek theatre (Bentley 1999, 2000) responding to the ebb and flow of each unfolding scene. During this process the primary therapist takes the role of director, ensuring that here too there is a distinct beginning, middle and end. The concept of director draws on both the theatre model of working and the idea of the 'director' in psychodrama (Moreno 1980).

Summary

In broad terms our approach has sought to integrate current knowledge from the field of developmental child psychology and neurobiology, including an understanding of the impact of trauma on self-development, with attachment theory and research, to provide the content and focus for therapy. The form that our interventions take draws upon conventional, individual and family therapy, enhanced and augmented by the use of dramatherapy and other creative arts therapies. As in life, so in therapy we continue to explore, learn from, and make sense of, the world-stage around us in our search for coherent means of working with traumatised children and their adoptive families: drawing in as wide an 'audience' as necessary to contribute to this vital, integrative process.

CHAPTER 9

The Drama of Adoption

Jay Vaughan

Introduction

This chapter gives a detailed account of a fictional family, the Saunders, and their journey through an Intensive Week at Family Futures. A discussion of the theoretical basis for our work can be found in Chapter 8.

The Saunders Family – The Intensive Attachment Programme

The Intensive Week

Two months had elapsed since the assessment day. Mr and Mrs Saunders seemed to have coped much better during this time because they felt hopeful about beginning the Intensive Attachment Programme. However, the children's social worker was concerned that the parents were fixated on the idea that this week would solve everything and was understandably worried about how realistic this was.

MONDAY

The team for the Intensive Week consisted of four therapists and a supervisor who would be available for consultation throughout the week. On the first morning, the team met for a preparatory meeting to discuss plans prior to the family's arrival. A team member had also visited the children's placing agency with Jean Saunders, to collect more detailed information on the children's histories. Jean had been very distressed by the parts she had read and had not wanted to take this information home with her. It was agreed that it would be more appropriate for the parents to consider all the information during the Intensive Week.

The family arrived at the Family Futures offices early because they were so keen not to be late for their first day; they were agitated after the drive and an argument between the children in the back of the car. The family was immediately shown to a welcoming room and provided with drinks of their choice. The children seemed over-excited. Jenny and Marty immediately began to pull lots of toys out of the toy cupboard. Jean tried to stop them, first by asking them to stop and then by shutting the cupboard herself. The children ignored her and continued with what they were doing. Marty took some toy fighting figures out and acted out a fight between them, occasionally hurting his sister as he flung them around.

The family was asked to come and sit together while the plan for the week was discussed. This took approximately 30 minutes. Jenny and Marty complied and came into the designated room to sit with everyone. Once in the room Jenny chose to sit on a chair rather than a sofa: this chair being slightly removed from everyone else. Initially, Marty chose to sit on the sofa, beside Jack Saunders. He then moved to sit beside the male therapist whom he had only just met. Immediately Marty seemed to want to be in control of who was where and what was happening. A therapist intervened and acknowledged how difficult this was for both the children. She acknowledged that they had all come to a strange place and did not know exactly what was going to happen. The therapist recognised how scary this must be for them when they had already had so many changes in their lives. The children stopped what they were doing and became more still and focused.

Immediate practical details were then explained to the family, such as the timing of each day and places nearby for the family to go for lunch. The parents returned their consent forms to the team, giving permission for some sessions to be video-recorded and authorising the therapy team to provide physical support, should family cradling be recommended during the Intensive Week (see also *Introduction* and chapters 8 and 13). Some general discussion of the week followed: it was explained that most children enjoy the week, although they can find it hard at times. Asked how they felt about coming for the week, both children replied, 'fine'. They were then asked if they had any questions but declined. Their parents said that they had talked to the children about returning to Family Futures as a family, to see if they could be helped with their difficulties at home. Jenny and Marty remained very quiet during this. Jenny looked particularly worried and seemed unable to speak. One of the team asked her if she would be more comfortable sitting beside her Mum but she shook her head and looked at the floor. Marty was very fidgety and clearly desperate to get off his chair. In response, the team co-ordinator, following a swift exchange with her team, suggested that perhaps the children were finding the introductions difficult. She suggested that it would be a good idea for the family to do something together, to break the ice.

The family were invited into a large room and asked to use the furniture to create an obstacle course with a beginning and an end. The video camera was already running. The family was given 20 minutes to design the course: they were all invited to be as creative as they wished. Marty immediately said, 'I know what to do, come on', grabbed a chair and turned it upside down. He then took two additional chairs and continued to make a tunnel. Jack pointed out that there was no way either he or Jean could fit through this tunnel. Jenny began to giggle. Marty said that they could fit and Dad was just being a spoilsport. Jack suggested they should first make a plan together and agree how the course should be laid out. Jean proposed using the large flip chart to work out the course layout. Meanwhile Jenny wandered off to the other side of the room and began to play with some small shells in the sand-tray. Jack looked increasingly frustrated, whilst Jean wrote a title on the flip chart: 'The Saunders Family Obstacle Course'. Marty said this was silly and he was not going to join in. After much persuasion both children began to help their parents set out the course as Jean had planned it on the flip chart. Throughout Jenny seemed to forget what she had been asked to find and needed to be reminded repeatedly. Marty spent most of his time rushing around the course trying it out as it was being built.

After 20 minutes the family were asked to finish their course; they requested additional time to complete the finishing touches. During this time Marty dismantled the tenting Jack had carefully arranged but eventually they managed to finish. It was then explained to them that they were each going to be led around the course blindfold and were told that it would be best if they did not speak whilst leading or being led. First Jack was to lead Jean; Jean would then lead Jack. Jenny would follow, led by Jean then Jack, before Marty was led in turn by each of his parents. Marty immediately insisted, 'I don't need to be led. I can do it myself.'

The children were asked to sit on the sofa with the therapy team and watch their parents. Jean and Jack led each other round very carefully, being extremely gentle with each other. At one point Jack led Jean under a table and kept her crawling for sometime after she was clear; the children thought this was hilarious. The team felt that Jean and Jack were sensitive and caring to each other during this session and wondered how much time they had together, without the children, to be playful or sensuous with each other.

When Jenny's turn came she looked very worried, although she vehemently denied this. Jean reassured Jenny that she would be very gentle; the team co-ordinator added that if at any point she wanted to stop she just had to say so. Jenny allowed her mother to put on her blindfold. She stood very still. Jean then led her slowly around the course, holding onto her arm. At one point she moved to touch Jenny's head, to help her under a table; Jenny flinched and banged her head. When Jean tried to rub her head Jenny pushed her hand away and indicated she wanted to keep going. Everyone cheered when they completed the course and even Jenny smiled a little. Rather than finding it easier second time around, Jenny appeared to struggle more under Jack's guidance. In particular, she did not like him touching her. Jack had to use verbal rather than physical prompts to help Jenny around the course.

It was then Marty's turn: he was very keen, asking if he could do it alone and if he could lead everyone else around. By the time Marty was halfway round the course with his mother it became very obvious that he could see where he was going. The team suggested he start again, once his blindfold had been adjusted. Marty appeared much more worried after this and clung to Jean, although on several occasions he tried to climb or jump over obstacles unguided and had to be restrained, so that he did not hurt himself. Jack held on to Marty very firmly as he steered him through the course, changing the route so Marty could not manipulate where he was going.

It took about 45 minutes for all the family to complete the course. It was therefore agreed that there would be a short discussion together, after the course was cleared and before lunch. Marty was extremely disruptive during clearing up and Jack became quite angry with him; Marty responded by kicking the cushions around and refusing to co-operate. Eventually the clearing up was completed and the family sat down to talk with the team. They agreed they had all enjoyed the obstacle course; even Jenny seemed more relaxed. Marty insisted he wanted to do it again, alone this time. Just as the session was finishing Jenny said very quietly, 'I could have led you round better, Marty.' Her parents frowned but said nothing. There was a long silence before one of the therapy team asked the children how much they thought they trusted their adoptive parents. Jenny glancing quickly at them, began to reply, then stopped. When asked what she was about to say, Marty interjected, 'I trust Jenny.' Jenny followed this by saying, 'and I trust myself to look after myself. I don't trust anyone else'. Their parents looked sad; Jean told both children how sad this made her and how she hoped that one day the children would feel able to trust them, as other children trust their parents. This discussion continued for some time, as the children struggled to understand the concept of basic trust. The session ended for lunch, with agreement that parents and children would work separately during the afternoon.

In the hour immediately after lunch Jean and Jack talked about the morning session and plans for the week with two members of the team. Both parents felt that the obstacle course had been interesting and very much represented how things were at home. However, they had been surprised by the degree to which Jenny had struggled and by how difficult it was for her to trust them to keep her safe. This led naturally into a discussion about the plan to talk to both children about their birth family. Jean and Jack were given file information researched in preparation for the week, to read that evening. They said they knew very little about what had happened to the children and felt very angry at social services for not giving them all the information on file.

Concurrently, Jenny and Marty had individual sessions with team therapists, with the aims of reconnecting with the therapists with whom they had originally worked at the assessment, and contracting about the week's work. The therapists explained to the children that their individual sessions would not remain completely confidential, since what happened within them would be shared with their parents. This provides an essential message to traumatised children that *these* parents can be trusted with even their darkest secrets (see Chapter 8). It was also explained that if at any point the children became distressed, the therapists would consider bringing their parents in to comfort them. The therapists stated that they would ensure no one got hurt in these sessions: that if a child became angry and out of control the therapist would hold him to keep him safe until his parents could take over. The children's sessions focused primarily on how difficult things had been at home and whether they were willing to work together throughout the week to improve the family situation.

In her individual session Jenny played with the sand-tray while she talked, making patterns with her fingers in the sand. She said that she did not think things were that bad at home and that she was happy. Jenny then created a large face in the sand, using stones and shells; she did not put a mouth on the face. The therapist asked, 'If there were a mouth what would it say?' Jenny looked blank and stared at the face. She remained still for some time and then said quietly, 'I want my Mum.' When the therapist very gently enquired, 'Which Mum?' she replied, 'Paula', her birth mother's name. Following a long silence, Jenny said, 'I think about her all the time. Do you know if she is alright? I want to see her. I know she still loves me. She's waiting for me.' The therapist explained that she did not know Paula but agreed that these were very important questions that needed to be considered during the next few days. Bringing the session to a close the therapist reminded Jenny that her session would be fed back to her parents: Jenny replied, 'That's fine.'

In his session Marty immediately took out fighting figures and played with them throughout. He did not appear to be listening but focused his whole attention on trying to engage the therapist in play fighting and killing off the figures he was holding. During this play Marty did agree that things were very difficult at home and that he sometimes became very angry. He also acknowledged that he enjoyed getting angry: 'It's funny to see Mum getting all red in the face. If I go on shouting sometimes she looks as if she's going to burst.' Subsequently Marty admitted he was scared that if she burst there would be blood all over the floor and he might have to clear it up. When the therapist enquired what Marty would have to do to make Mum burst, he replied, 'Just be naughty like I always am!' He then changed the subject, enquiring how much longer the session had to run. Marty was becoming more and more agitated. Rather than let the situation escalate, and to maintain control, the therapist decided to end the session early, suggesting they put the kettle on and prepare tea for everyone, before their final session.

Finally, the whole family and the team came together for feedback from their separate sessions. Jean appeared surprised by both children's comments and seemed very hurt that Jenny had indicated that she wanted to be with Paula. A team member suggested that this had been a very full first day; some important things had come up which could be explored in more detail later. To conclude, everyone including therapists was asked to say one thing that they would remember about the first day. Jack began, saying he would remember building the obstacle course together; Jean said she would remember Jenny asking for Paula; Marty remembered the biscuits; Jenny recalled Mum and Dad going round the obstacle course and Dad making Mum continue crawling when she did not need to. Jean looked shocked, asking, 'Did you?' Everyone laughed. It was agreed that day one should end here.

TUESDAY

The family arrived looking much more relaxed. They said they had had a good evening together, choosing to have a take-away meal as they were late getting home. This had been difficult, as everyone had wanted different food; Jack had compromised by going to both the chip shop and the Chinese take-away. Jean reported that Jenny had had a nightmare the previous night, which was unusual. The children asked to do the obstacle course again but the team explained that the plan was to work separately, before coming together to work as a family after lunch.

Jean and Jack spent their morning session with two members of the team, going over the children's histories that they had been given to read the previous evening. The parents explained that it was very late when the children finally went to bed and they had not had as long as they would have liked to read the information. However, they had read some of it. Jean became very red in the face and said she felt sick; she wondered if it had been the take-away meal. On enquiry it appeared that she had begun to feel sick after reading the information and was feeling very nervous about the day. She had had no idea of the number of injuries the children had sustained. She asked, 'What if I cry? I can't bear to think of them being hurt.' The therapist acknowledged how painful this all was for everyone and reassured both parents that the disclosure of information would be done slowly and sensitively. Jack felt it was very important that both children knew exactly what had happened to them, as far as possible. The therapist concurred, adding that it was vital that both children understood that their adoptive parents knew what had happened to them. The next hour was spent going through file information, discussing exactly what each piece of information meant in terms of its effects on Jenny and Marty. The parents looked exhausted and a break was suggested. Interestingly, Jean said, 'It's funny but I don't feel sick anymore.'

After the break, the time leading up to lunch was spent discussing plans for the afternoon and just how the children were to be told of their birth family history. At the beginning of the session it had been explained that both children would be working individually with their therapist and thinking about babies.

In her individual session Jenny had been asked to make a clay baby. She had loved working with the clay and spent a long time working on the baby's details. Lovingly she moulded each of the baby's limbs, spending ages carefully adding its nose, ears and even a few locks of hair. She treated the baby with great care and, at times, seemed to be murmuring to it tenderly. After a short break the therapist considered with Jenny what babies needed to be happy and healthy. Jenny was absolutely clear what babies needed: listing love first, followed by food and clean nappies. She then asked to make a bottle of milk and a crib for her baby and requested a piece of cloth for a blanket. Jenny was given some material to make a blanket and more clay for the crib and bottle. Again she worked intently on these, looking sad and wistful.

The therapist asked Jenny what she thought she was like as a baby. She replied, 'I probably cried all the time.' The therapist commented that all babies cry and wondered why Jenny thought she would have cried a lot. Jenny explained that her birth mother had told her she cried all the time, this was how she knew. Jenny was clearly finding the conversation very difficult and asked how much longer the session would last. When the therapist explained that it was time to pack up, Jenny was happy to comply, working hard to clear all the clay from the plastic sheet covering the floor and then cleaning her hands. Rushing to carry some of the tools from the room, Jenny accidentally stepped on the baby. She froze and considered what she had done. There was a very long silence, then Jenny's lip trembled and she said, 'Who cares? It's only a bloody baby!' The sentence hung in the air as if spoken by someone else, not the girl who had shown such concern only minutes earlier. Jenny gave the clay a kick and left the room; the therapist sat for a few minutes by the broken baby and felt like crying. All that care and love Jenny had taken with the baby, and then all that anger and hatred directed towards it: she was shocked. The therapist left the broken baby and went out to find Jenny, who was washing her hands again. The therapist said how sad it was that the baby got broken and suggested that perhaps it was too painful for Jenny to really think about.

In his session Marty made a huge mess with the clay, splattering it over everyone, despite the therapist's attempts to contain the mess. Marty made a large, shapeless baby with a huge head. He stabbed two holes in it for eyes and a gash across its chin for a mouth. When Marty went to pick up the baby its arms and legs fell off; he stuck them back on saying, 'There, finished. Now what?' When the therapist asked him about what babies needed he replied, 'Cheese and egg sandwiches.' She then enquired whether he knew any babies and Marty said that his next-door neighbour had one named George. He thought for a while and said, 'George drinks milk out of a bottle, a milk bottle.' On being asked if babies needed anything else Marty replied, 'No. Now what are we going to do?' He then began to pull all the toys out of the cupboard. It was suggested that they should make drinks, after which they could negotiate what happened next.

After the break the therapist suggested making a deal that if Marty did what the therapist suggested for 30 minutes, he could then spend 30 minutes playing with the toys. Marty agreed but continued playing. When the therapist reminded him of the deal, Marty replied that he wanted his half hour first. She repeated that they were going to do her half hour first, then his. Marty sulked and kicked at the toy cars. The therapist did not respond but instead took out some puppets. Picking up a dog puppet she looked at the baby saying, 'Hey baby, what are you doing lying there alone?' Marty immediately became engaged and said, in a little voice, 'Go away, nasty doggie. You smell! I'm waiting for my Mummy.' The dog asked, 'Where has your Mummy gone, baby?' Marty replied, 'She's gone to the shops for beer and ciggies.' The dog commented, 'Poor baby. All alone.' To which the baby replied, 'You're a nasty, smelly old dog. I don't like you. Poo dog!' The conversation between the dog and the baby continued for some time but became fixed on the baby insulting and wanting to hurt the dog. Suddenly Marty turned around and began playing with the fighting figures on the floor; for the remaining 30 minutes of the session he played intently with them, ignoring the therapist. He seemed to be in a world of his own, although at the end of the session he did half-heartedly help to clear up. Interestingly, he took great care to put his baby on a shelf where it would be safe.

Before lunch the family came together, so that the therapists working with the children could share what had been happening in their individual sessions. Everyone was particularly shocked to hear about Jenny breaking her baby. Jenny smiled slightly at this point. Following this everyone agreed they had worked hard and deserved a lunch break: the family elected to go out for lunch but Jenny and Marty argued over pizzas or burgers. Eventually Jack suggested taking Marty for a burger whilst Jean took Jenny for a pizza.

After lunch everyone met in the large family room, whilst a therapy team member explained that they were going to spend some time thinking about what life had been like for Jenny and Marty when they were with their birth mother. Jenny immediately began to stare out of the window. The main emphasis of this discussion, which had been agreed in advance with their parents, was to go through the injuries listed by the hospital, when Marty was taken to casualty by his birth mother following a head injury. The paediatrician who examined them had recorded a huge number of bruises on both children. Although Marty was the identified patient, the doctor had also examined Jenny, since she had obvious bruises on her face. There were a total of 36 bruises on Marty, mainly on the top half of his body. A number of these were old bruises and some looked like finger- tip bruising. In addition there were some small, round scars, which looked like cigarette burns. The paediatrician felt that the injuries were non-accidental. On examination Jenny was found to have a large number of bruises covering her whole body. Sixty-five bruises were identified, consisting of both fresh and old bruising. There were bruises and cut marks to Jenny's face, as well as five round finger-sized bruises to each of her buttocks. Her vagina was sore and some discharge was evident.

It had been agreed that the bruises should be marked on each of the children as the records were being read out. It was made clear to the children that they would not need to take their clothes off but could remain in their shorts and T-shirts. Bruises to their genital areas would not be marked on them but would be mentioned. Both children seemed intrigued by the idea of using face paints to mark their bruises and Jenny became much more interested and alert. Their parents helped them mark on the bruises; it was not long before it was hard to find a clean place on the children's bodies. Jenny and Marty were both fascinated and worked hard at co-operating when the bruises were being marked on them. Not once did they seem to take in the marks on each other, being completely enthralled by their own. The atmosphere in the room was absolutely still and quiet.

Jean and Jack were clearly horrified by what they saw emerging on the children's bodies. When the therapist began to mention the marks on Jenny's bottom and her vaginal soreness and discharge, Jack began to cry; Jean also began to cry and held Jenny tightly. Jenny stood motionless, allowing her mother to hold her but did not respond. Marty squirmed onto his mother's lap and buried his face. They remained huddled together for some time. When one of the therapy team commented how terrible it was that someone could have done this to their children, Jenny blinked but said nothing. Her parents wiped away their tears and explained to the children that they were crying because they felt so sad about what had happened to both of them. Jean said she wished that she had been there when they were little so that none of this would have happened; Marty turned and looked straight at her, saying, 'Mummy!' There was silence as she leant forward and stroked his face, whispering, 'My Marty, my sweet little Marty. I'm so sorry I wasn't there to stop her hurting you, my Marty, my love, oh baby, little one.' Two big tears rolled down Marty's cheeks as he let his head drop onto her lap. She scooped him up and held him close. Jenny looked on horrified, then burst out, 'Shut up, shut up! You don't know anything. She didn't do it! She didn't do it!' One of the therapists said, 'This is so hard for you, Jenny. You so much want it not to have been your birth mother who hurt you. You miss her so much.' Jenny turned her head to look towards the therapist, maintained eye contact and nodded.

As everyone now looked exhausted it was suggested that drinks and biscuits should be brought in to them. The remaining 15 minutes of the day were spent discussing how difficult the last session had been. Jean and Jack sat with Marty on their laps; Jenny sat slightly apart, looking out of the window. One therapist commented that Jenny was finding this extremely difficult. Marty was the stillest anyone had ever seen him; both parents said how lovely it was having Marty quietly with them. It felt like the first time they had ever had this sort of contact with him. The parents were offered some warm water and soap to wash the bruises and cuts off the children. This was done very slowly, as a healing ritual. Marty stood still and allowed his parents to clean him. Before she was washed Jenny went to a large mirror and stared hard at herself, saying nothing.

Subsequently, when prompted, Marty said that he felt sad. He put his hands inside Mum's jumper and began to try and climb inside. Jean giggled and tried to stop him. One of the therapy team said, 'I wonder if Marty is thinking about what it would have been like to have been inside your tummy: to have been born to you. If he had been, then none of this would have happened.' Marty smiled and said he should have been born to them; Jenny turned round and glared at him. Jean said to Jenny, 'We wish you could have grown inside me too.' Jenny replied 'You're a fat old cow who can't have children. You stole us, I don't want to be with you!', which stunned her parents into silence. The team suggested that, although this was a very difficult point on which to end, it could be very important to stay with the reality that Jenny still wanted, and is perhaps waiting to return to, her birth mother. On the other hand, Marty was clearly saying he wanted to be part of the Saunders family and wished that he had been born to them. It was agreed that the family would have a quiet evening and would avoid talking about the day once they left. A team member suggested that perhaps Marty would need to stay very close to his parents that evening, whilst Jenny might well need to have some time alone. A very sad and tired family then left for home.

WEDNESDAY

On their return the family reported that they had had a very difficult evening. During the car journey home Jenny had poked and pinched Marty, who wanted to sleep. When they reached home Jenny spent the evening trying to engage Marty in games that took him out of the room, away from his parents. Jenny also refused to go to sleep that night and sat up singing loudly to herself, so that everyone else struggled to sleep. She was sulky and difficult on the way to the session, saying she did not want to go. Marty, however, was happy to come and seemed calmer than usual. If anything, his parents felt he seemed sad and subdued. It was suggested that Marty and his parents should work together in the morning, whilst Jenny had some individual time with a team member. Jenny smiled and readily agreed to this arrangement.

Jean and Jack spent 30 minutes discussing the plan for their session with Marty. They were to embark upon a game of 'mummy, daddy and baby': it would involve Marty getting some 'good baby experiences'. The idea was to provide an opportunity for Marty to pretend he had been born to his adoptive parents and to experience what this might have been like. It was anticipated that at times Marty would find this distressing, as control was such an issue for him. At this point his parents would be encouraged to continue to cradle Marty in their arms and talk about how difficult this was for him, because of his poor early experiences. Based on his response to distress on the previous day, it was anticipated that after a while Marty would be able to respond to them and become really close.

Marty spent some time with a team member preparing the room, gathering cushions together to make a den. Marty did not have the 'game' explained to him immediately but was asked to help collect the cushions so that the game could be explained when his parents joined them. By the time they did so, Marty had managed to gather together all the cushions; a large box of 'baby' things had also been placed in the room. It was then explained to everyone that they were to play a game about 'mummy, daddy and baby', which would involve them pretending Marty had been born to them. Marty immediately responded, 'What I asked for yesterday! Can I get up your jumper Mummy?' It was made clear to Marty that the game might make him feel upset, as it would remind him of how it had really been for him as a baby. Asked what feelings he thought he might have had as a baby, Marty replied that he would have been very sad and all alone. The therapist explained that if he felt like this when playing the game, this Mummy and Daddy would look after him, comfort him and keep him safe. He was also told that he would not be hurt during the game or hurt anyone else. Looking bored, Marty asked to get on with the game.

Marty climbed into the pile of cushions that, his parents explained, represented the womb. They began to talk about the baby they hoped for, a little boy, as they already had a daughter who would be his big sister. They planned to call the baby Marty if he was a boy. They felt the womb for baby movements and even heard a little cry of 'mummy' from inside. The womb of cushions began to move and shake as the baby inside kicked. Jean and Jack wondered whether the baby was ready to be born and became very excited. Suddenly the baby popped his head out and smiled at them. With the help of the therapist 'midwife', Jean and Jack scooped up their baby and sat on the sofa admiring him. Marty lay with his eyes shut, smiling and allowing them to count his fingers and toes, kiss him and talk about how perfect and beautiful he was. Mum began gently to rock her baby, as he lay in her arms, and softly sang a lullaby. This lasted around 20 minutes and was very beautiful. Jean and Jack looked absolutely intent on nurturing their baby; Marty seemed rather tense but was still smiling. He still had his eyes tightly shut but it did not feel appropriate to break the spell all three seemed to be under to encourage him to open his eyes. Jean thought her baby seemed a little tense and suggested washing him and massaging his skin with oil, to help him relax. The therapists felt that before this happened Marty needed to be encouraged to open his eyes, so that he could see his parents. Marty really struggled with this and looked through, or over, Mum's shoulder. Some 'peek-a-boo' games were proposed, to encourage eye contact; Marty giggled but found eye contact a little easier this way.

Warm water, soap, cotton wool, massage oil and a towel were brought in for the family. Marty loved being washed and made small gurgling sounds in the back of his throat. His parents were delighted with him. It seemed to everyone watching that Marty was revelling in the closeness and it seemed hard to imagine Marty becoming distressed or angry. Once he was dried, Mum began to massage him, beginning with his face. While she massaged his face, his arms, his legs and his feet, Dad passed the oil to Jean and kept the rest of Marty warm with a large towel. Once the massage was complete, it was suggested that the parents should just sit quietly with their baby, observing him, as up until this point there had been lots of activity. Immediately Marty became more restless and began demanding a bottle by opening and shutting his mouth noisily. When his parents did not respond instantly he began to speak in baby talk, saying, 'Bot bot'. Jean said she did not think her baby was hungry yet, adding that he had had a huge breakfast that morning. Marty became more and more insistent. He began saying, 'I don't want to play this game anymore. I'm not a baby.' His parents were encouraged to reassure him that he was safe and that they would not let anything happen to him. Marty shouted all the more and began to try to kick and punch his mother. This mood change seemed very sudden; his parents commented that this was just like the tantrums he had at home when he could not have what he wanted.

Marty was struggling with all his might to get down, while screaming for a bottle. He was desperately trying to hurt Jean, upon whom all his attention was focused. Marty began to cry huge choking sobs, like a very distressed, young baby. His parents were encouraged to continue holding him gently, as he was no longer struggling, and to repeat that they would keep him safe. One of the therapists began to speak very quietly, saying how sad it was that Marty had been so sad and scared as a baby. She explained that his health visitor had been worried when she visited baby Marty because he had not gained weight. She was also concerned because the flat they lived in was very dirty and his feeding bottles were grubby. The therapist continued, recounting how later on the workers at the Family Centre noted how fearful Marty was as a toddler and how he took any food he could get when at the Centre, describing one occasion when Marty ate so much food that he was sick. They had also recorded that Marty always looked dirty and had bruises that his birth mother blamed on his clumsiness. The therapist kept repeating, 'Poor baby Marty. Poor baby Marty. So sad and so alone!' She then spoke of the bruises the doctors found on him in hospital and the head injury that had taken him there. Records showed that Jenny had told the doctors that Marty had fallen over and hit his head on the table, splitting it open so that blood went all over the floor. She said she had blood all over her dress and was in trouble for getting into a mess. At that time Marty told the doctors that Mummy had pushed him because he was naughty.

At this point Marty stopped crying and began listening to what was being said. He looked at Mum and said, 'There was blood all over the floor. My head had burst.' He then began to cry softly, clinging to his parents. Jean also began to cry saying, 'Oh, my poor baby, my poor little darling!' After a while Marty looked up and began to touch Mum's tears saying, 'Why is Mummy crying?' She smiled at him, explaining that she wished Marty had grown in her tummy and then she could have him safe. Looking directly at her, Marty replied, 'I wish I'd grown in your tummy, then you would be my tummy-mummy.' Then his face changed and he looked cross, saying, 'Why weren't you there? I was so scared in the hospital. Mummy shouted and shouted at the doctors. They looked scared. They left me on my own in a room and I cried. I thought Mummy would be so angry with me because I said she pushed me.' Jean remained quiet for a while, then said, 'You were *so* brave to tell them. You're safe now.' They remained cuddled together for the next half hour, after which a team member brought them a bottle of warm milk for baby Marty. Marty lay back and relaxed while Mum fed him. He looked up into her eyes and the two of them were lost in each other. Dad sat still with his arm around his wife's shoulder watching. At times he wiped away a tear.

It was difficult for the family to move on from this session. It was therefore suggested that Jenny should have her lunch with the therapy team, whilst Jean, Jack and Marty had lunch quietly together. Jean commented that this was the first time she had felt really close to Marty and emphasised how special it was for all of them. Marty was becoming restless but was encouraged to sit with his parents over lunch.

Meanwhile, Jenny had been creating an elaborate make-believe story about a little girl called 'Bruise'. She worked very hard to develop this tale of a girl with a dark, purple bruise inside her that nobody could see. Once she had written it down she began to act out the drama, which was to be video-recorded. In the drama Bruise ran away from a wicked witch who had cast a spell over her. The witch's spell was very strong. Bruise could feel the spell in her tummy: the only way she could stop her tummy pains was to make holes in herself with a stick and fill the bloody holes with mud. The spell meant that Bruise could not make any friends, because if she touched them they would melt into the earth. She therefore made friends with, and talked to, all the animals that lived in the forest. Bruise said she was lonely because, although the animals were kind to her, she really wanted to be free of the witch, whom she described as 'cunning and cruel with incredible powers', so that wherever Bruise was she knew what she was doing and saying. Bruise felt she was becoming like the witch: if she did not kill the witch she was afraid the witch would kill her. Bruise began to see the witch everywhere, in the trees, in the wind and even in the little squirrels in the forest. She began to hurt the little squirrels because she was frightened that they were the witch; she began to feel that maybe even these little friends were messengers from the witch, sent there to watch her. Bruise began to run madly round the forest screaming at the witch to go away; she began to laugh and smile at everything and to become the witch. Finally Bruise collapsed on the forest floor and lay still with the wind washing over her and the rain falling on her. She lay as if dead; birds came by and began to peck her, trying to wake her. Bruise began to cry and wonder whether she would ever be at peace: maybe if she died she would finally be free of the witch.

Jenny indicated that she would like to share this story with everyone; it was agreed that this should happen after lunch. Although Jenny seemed happy to have lunch with the therapy team it was noticeable that she ate in a very ritualised way. First she pulled out the filling from her sandwich and nibbled the edges of the bread. It seemed as if she had hardly eaten anything. Then she said she wasn't hungry but wanted sweets and a can of drink. As it did not seem appropriate for her to have both, it was agreed that she could choose one or the other. The issue of her eating would be raised with her parents at a later date.

Jean and Jack were informed that they would have an opportunity to talk about their experience with Marty on the following day. Meanwhile they were asked to sit with both children and watch the video drama Jenny had created that morning. Jenny was very excited and pleased with her creation. Her parents sat and watched the story unfold, immediately becoming aware of the metaphor, in the story, for Jenny's life. Afterwards they said they felt very worried about Bruise and wondered how she could be helped. Immediately Jenny responded, 'Nobody can help Bruise.' The therapist intervened here to say that Bruise did have choices but perhaps it did not feel like that right now. She continued, saying that Bruise made her think about little Jenny and how scary her birth mother must have seemed at times. Marty burst in, 'You told the doctors I fell over. You lied, Jenny.' When Jenny looked shocked and her lower lip began to tremble, Jack explained that no one was cross with her; she would have been too scared to tell the truth.

Jenny replied, 'There was blood all over me. Mummy said I was not to tell or she would deal with me later!' Jack reassured her that everyone understood; she had been a good girl to look after Marty when he had hurt his head. Jenny went quiet, so Jack went over and put his arm around her.

The day ended with everyone considering what they would remember about the day. Marty demanded to go first, saying 'I'll remember being born to Mummy and Daddy.' Mum said she would remember 'Marty looking into my eyes and the sad story of Bruise'; Dad said he would remember 'Jenny sitting all alone and Marty crying like a little baby.' Jenny said she could not think of anything. Eventually she said she would remember, 'lying on the floor being dead'. There was a long silence, then Mum went over to Jenny and held her hand. Jenny looked at her as Mum said, 'I know you feel all alone sometimes. I want to help you.' After a short pause, the family packed up and left for the day. However, Marty rushed back almost immediately, asking whether he could take the baby bottle home with him. It was handed to his parents, with the request that they should return it the next day.

THURSDAY

On their arrival the family recounted that the previous evening had been better, largely because everyone was so emotionally exhausted and had gone to bed early. For the first hour of their session, Jean and Jack discussed the previous day's events with two team members. Concurrently the children had a combined sibling session.

In their session, Jean and Jack considered the previous evening in more detail. Jean recounted that Marty had had both cuddles and the bottle at bedtime. As predicted, he had asked to hold the bottle himself but Jean had explained that she needed to hold it for him. Marty had slept well that night and in the morning, for the first time, had climbed into their bed for cuddles. His parents stressed that Marty was still his usual busy and demanding self, only now he seemed able to be closer to Jean. Although they felt the family cradling had been upsetting, the end result was well worth it. They also commented that Marty frequently had tantrums at home that were much worse than yesterday's. This way of handling his tantrums clearly appealed to both of them, as until now the approaches they had tried had been unsuccessful and had just left them feeling failures. They both felt that during the past few days Marty had shown he could be calmer and closer to Jean than he had managed previously.

However, both parents were deeply worried about Jenny. They were alarmed by her story, when she chose to be dead because her fear of the witch was so strong. In fact the child about whom they had *not* been worrying, largely because Marty took up so much time, actually appeared far more worrying. They were very distressed and tearful to realise that Jenny was not attaching to them but still wanted to go back to the birth mother who had abused her. The two therapists explained that the next session would focus on this issue for both children, but perhaps for Jenny in particular. The parents were informed that Jenny and Marty were currently in another room, working on creating a life-size model of their birth mother, Paula, to whom they were going to be asked to write letters. Jean and Jack were also asked to write letters to Paula, saying how they felt about what had happened to the children. They found this very difficult because they thought that if they said what they really felt it could upset the children. When the children were placed, Jean and Jack had been told by social workers that it was essential that Paula was portrayed positively, to enhance Jenny and Marty's self-esteem. As a result they had always told both children that their 'tummy-mummy' loved them but could not look after them. Some time was spent exploring the ambiguity of this statement, particularly in terms of the meaning of 'love' for Jenny and Marty. Jean and Jack grasped this readily and were delighted to receive permission to write what they wanted to Paula about how she had let the children down.

Jenny and Marty had co-operated well together to create the model of their birth mother; they particularly enjoyed going out to get clothes from the local charity shop to dress her in. They asked for their life storybooks, to make sure that the model they made looked just right. It was noticeable how easy it was for them to collaborate on this task, when in other more mundane tasks it seemed almost impossible for them to do so. Their model looked strikingly like their birth mother and both children were delighted with the results of their hard work. Jenny worked very intently on making the face, and in particular the eyes, right, whilst Marty had been keen to get the body stuffed with newspaper. Subsequently, each child was given 20 minutes to work separately with their therapist, to write a letter telling Paula how they felt and asking anything else they wanted to know. It was explained to both children that these letters would be shared with their adoptive parents. Jenny struggled to write anything, needing a good deal of support from the therapist to express herself; Marty also struggled to write but was very clear about what he wanted to say.

Finally it was suggested that everyone took an early lunch, so that there would be a longer session for the family to share their letters; the family was again reminded that these letters were not actually going to be sent to Paula. The children were keen to keep their model hidden until after lunch; there was an air of excitement and anticipation as they all went out. The model looked strikingly real and made other members of the team flinch when they entered the room, having forgotten it was there.

The family arrived back early from lunch, keen to start the next session. The children were very excited as they led their parents in to see the model of their birth mother. Everyone sat on cushions on the floor facing the model, which was placed on a chair centrally. Each member of the family had their letters with them. The therapists placed the children on either side of their parents, with Marty near Jean and Jenny beside Jack. The lights were dimmed and 'Paula' was introduced to everyone.

Mr and Mrs Saunders were asked to read their letters first. They had chosen to write a letter together, which Jack elected to read:

> To Paula,
>
> We cannot believe you could hurt Jenny and Marty in the way you did. It's dreadful to think about how scared they must have both been. We are so angry with you for doing this to them. We are sure you had a very difficult childhood of your own but this does not make it okay for you to have hurt your children and not care for them properly.
>
> Jenny and Marty are our children now and we promise to take care of them and love them always. It has been very difficult for our family in the last couple of years because you did not teach Jenny and Marty how to be a part of a loving family. We are now getting some help as a family and we hope that we can all learn to trust and love one another. We know that it is going to be very difficult at times but we desperately want to be their Mum and Dad and to show them what a good family can be like. We love them as if they had been born to us.
>
> We hope that you are managing your life a bit better now and have maybe found some happiness for yourself,
>
> Mr and Mrs Saunders

Jack began to cry when he read out how much he wanted to be a dad; Jean put her hand on his and started to cry too. The children looked at them and seemed surprised by their tears. One of the therapy team said quietly, 'It's all right to cry. Take your time. Go on when you are ready.' After a while Jack finished reading the letter in a broken voice. A long silence followed. Jean and Jack held tightly to each other, pulling the children in towards them. Marty collapsed onto Mum, she pulled him on to her lap and he reached up and stroked her face. Jenny remained rigid and looked panic-stricken. Eventually, Jenny was asked by one of the therapy team to read her letter. Jenny read:

Dear Mummy,

I miss you very much. I think about you all the time and wonder how you are. I hope that you are happy. I hope you are thinking about me. Do you still love me? Do you remember the time we went to the park and found that lost cat? You said we could take him home. I called him Sooty and put a bit of string round its neck. I wonder where Sooty is now. Do you know?

Let me know where you are and then I can come and see you.

Lots of love

Your daughter Jenny

Jean leant over, looked at Jenny and smiled kindly at her. Jenny seemed very worried and gave a sheepish smile back. The therapist then encouraged Marty to read his letter. He read from Jean's lap:

Dear Mummy Paula,

How are you? I hope you're well. Sometimes I feel sad when I think about you. I try to think about happy things and play with toys because then it is alright. I have a new mummy now who is very nice.

Goodbye.

Love Marty XXX

There was an extremely awkward atmosphere after everyone had finished their letter. Jenny looked furious, yet when asked said she was fine. Jean and Jack repeated that they had not realised how much Jenny missed her birth mother and how much time she spent thinking about her. Jack agreed, saying it was good that they both now knew how Jenny felt. However, it did not really sound like either parent felt good about this, which was acknowledged sensitively by one of the team. Jenny then shouted, 'We *are* going back. She said she was going to get us back!' Marty seemed very scared, so his parents reassured him that this would not happen. He emphasised that he wanted to stay with them and his pet hamster, Weeble. Immediately Jenny stood over Marty, who was still on Jean's lap, and cried, 'Marty you promised Mum! We said we'd wait for her until she came to get us back. You promised. I knew I could never trust you, you little bastard!' Marty began to cry, muttering 'sorry' over and over again to himself. Jean and Jack looked shocked and confused. Jenny's therapist came over and said, 'Why don't you ask Paula yourself, Jenny?' She replied that that would be silly but looked intrigued. One of team went over and stood behind the model, acting as Paula's voice. The conversation went like this:

Jenny: How are you, mum?

Paula: Oh, I'm alright love, getting by.

Jenny: Do you miss me?

Paula: 'Course I do, you're my daughter. 'Course I miss you.

Jenny: Can I come home?

Paula: Well, it'd be a bit difficult right now. Got a few problems at the moment. We'll see how it goes, alright?

Jenny: Mum, I want to come home. I don't want to stay here with these people.

Paula: Why? Are they hurting you, love?

Jenny: (long pause)

Paula: I'll bloody have the bastards if they are!

Jenny: No, Mum. Did you push Marty?

Paula: Now why would you think that? You know what he's like, all over the place. He just got in the way and sort of fell.

Jenny: Mum, I got blood all over me. I thought he was going to die.

Paula: Well, he didn't, did he?

This conversation continued for some time; after a while Marty and his parents joined in. Marty needed their support to ask his questions and he remained very close to Jean during this session. Jenny was alert and interested throughout the role-play. Finally, one of the team asked Jenny if the way Paula was portrayed was right. She replied, 'It was just like her. I'd forgotten what she could be like. She *did* say at our last contact that she would come and get us. She said I was just to wait and then she'd come and collect us outside school. She said she knew where we was going and she'd sort herself out and then come for us.' Jean enquired, 'But I thought Stephen, the social worker, was supervising that contact the whole time.' Jenny replied that they had talked when they went to the toilet together. When a team member asked Jenny if she had been waiting all this time for Paula, Jenny confirmed that she had. Jack went over to Jenny, bent down and looked into her face, saying, 'Jenny, she isn't going to come. She doesn't really know where we live or where you go to school. Even if she did, social services would not let her take you to live with her again. I want you to stay with us. Do you believe that she hurt you and Marty?' Jenny responded, 'I remember lots of things she and her friends did to us but I still love her. She's my Mum.' To this Jean replied, 'I know, Jenny. She'll always be your Mum but somehow we have to find ways of you being happy with us, not spending your whole life waiting.'

The family was then made a cup of tea. Marty, who had become very noisy and agitated, began running round the room. Jean was encouraged to take hold of him, put him on her lap, and reassure him. At first Marty struggled, then he began to cry. Jean just held him and rocked him while he cried; Jenny sat at a slight distance and watched; Jack sat between the rocking mother and child and the distant Jenny. The day closed with a family game of 'hide and seek', in which both children readily joined. Their parents were astonished at how well they were able to hide together. On the other hand, when it came to their turn, Jean and Jack were nowhere near as good at hiding. It was agreed that they needed to practise this skill!

FRIDAY

The family arrived slightly early and seemed in a good mood. Jean and Jack explained that they had played 'hide and seek' at home the previous night: this time the children had struggled to find their parents. Everyone joked about how the week's therapy had improved their 'hide and seek' skills tremendously, before discussing the fact that this was their last day; in effect only a half day. They were reminded that the Follow Up plan would consist of monthly, full day sessions and telephone support. The children seemed pleased to learn that they would be returning. One final task remained for the children before the week's closing ceremony: to pack up the model they had made of their birth mother. Jenny and Marty located the room where the model was stored, with two therapists from the team. Together they began to decorate a box in which it could be kept; again they co-operated well. The children decided to write a message on the box to Paula. It read:

Dear Paula, see you soon, love Jenny and Marty XX

Concurrently, Jean and Jack spent time talking through the Follow Up plan with the remaining team members. The idea of facilitated contact (see Chapter 11) with Paula, for both Jenny and Marty, was discussed as a means of helping them let go, so that they could settle better in their adoptive family. It was agreed that this would go ahead only if it were felt that Paula would be able to give the children positive messages. The parents were then invited to join Jenny and Marty as they completed the packing away of their model; Jenny looked extremely sad; Marty was clearly very agitated. The children agreed that their model should be kept at Family Futures, in case it was needed in later sessions. The family was then asked to make a five-day plan of the Intensive Week, writing down how they felt about each day. They were reminded that members of the family might have different feelings about different days. They set about sticking together five large pieces of different coloured paper and Jenny offered to list the days of the week at the top of each. Marty volunteered to write 'The Saunders Family' as a title.

All the family worked conscientiously at this. For Jenny, the most important day had been when she had had the chance to 'talk' to her birth mother again and had told everyone she was waiting for her mum's return. Marty said that the best and most difficult bit for him was when he had pretended to be born to his adoptive parents. He said he loved having the bottle of warm milk and asked could he have one now. Jean said she found it very painful writing the letter to Paula, admitting how difficult things had been, and how much she wanted to be a mum. Jack concurred but added that he would always remember the 'hide and seek' game they had played at home on Thursday evening, and how much they had all laughed. He commented that this had felt like the first time they had all laughed together.

It was agreed that the day should end with a final 'tea ceremony'; the team had a small gift for everyone. Once the tea and 'farewell' cake had been laid out, four small, wrapped packages were produced. There were large mugs for Jean and Jack, one inscribed 'MUM' and the other inscribed 'DAD'.

For the children there were teddy bears: one large and one small. Finally there were 'goodbye' hugs all round, for family and team members alike.

Summary

This is an example of an Intensive Week, showing one way in which such a week might be structured. We continue to explore the story of the Saunders family's Follow Up Programme in Chapter 10.

The Drama Unfolds

Jay Vaughan

Introduction

The Intensive Week forms the first part of our Intensive Attachment Programme. We think of it as a kick-start to the essential, ongoing process of attachment and healing. It provides a starting point, from which themes and issues can be seen more clearly; it also establishes a strong bond between the family and the therapy team, forming essential foundations for the Follow Up Programme. The Intensive Week provides families with emotionally intense, shared experiences, some difficult, some joyful, both as a family unit and as an integral part of the therapeutic team. It also provides a frame of reference for future work. The Follow Up Programme is equally challenging; this is stressed to families from the outset. There is no quick 'cure': it is hard work over a minimum of two years, sometimes much longer. However, it is a 'journey' which is not undertaken alone but with the therapy team firmly alongside. The Follow Up Programme consists of some, or all, of the following:

- **Fortnightly, or monthly, half or full day family sessions**

  Ideally these sessions are for all family members and the time is used in similar ways to the Intensive Week: there is time for parents to be seen separately from children, individual time for children, sibling sessions and family group sessions. Immediately following an Intensive Week, sessions are usually arranged fortnightly, then extended to monthly. Frequency of sessions is based upon both the therapy team's recommendations about the family's needs and the feasibility of frequent attendance for the family. Occasionally, family sessions may be arranged on a weekly basis.

- **Regular telephone support**

  Telephone support provides regular, systematic support to families and a forum for exploring parenting strategies on an 'as needed' basis. It is seen as essential 'life support' and not as crisis intervention. A designated member of the therapy team provides the service, which is carefully integrated with overall therapeutic aims.

- **Emergency telephone support**

  In addition, every family has access to the Family Futures' emergency 'bleep' number in the event of a crisis, or the need to talk to someone urgently out of hours.

- **Home visits**

  We provide home visits to families, either as part of the Hands on Help Programme, or as an integral part of the Follow Up Programme. These visits provide support particularly to parents unable to reach the therapy space regularly. Families find that a visit from one of the therapy team at home helps to connect what happens in therapy with what is happening at home. It can also provide the therapy team with additional insights into the precise difficulties that families are experiencing at home but have not been apparent in therapy sessions.

- **Hands on Help**

  This is Family Futures' Parenting Strategies and Parent Support Programme and is discussed in more detail in Chapter 13. Every family that participates in the Family Futures' Attachment Programme is offered the parenting strategies element of the Follow Up Programme. For some this represents a major component of their ongoing support.

- **School visits**

  Liaison with a child's school often forms part of the Follow Up Programme. This may occur later in the Programme, when it is felt that an educational assessment would be helpful and the original educational appraisal of the child is reviewed (see Chapter 14).

- **Facilitated contact**

   The complex issue of contact, current or historical, is inevitably a core issue for all adopted children and a major element of the therapy programme. Contact may be arranged as part of the Intensive Week or as part of the Follow Up Programme. The concept of facilitated, therapeutic contact is discussed in Chapter 11.

Follow Up Programme Year One – The Saunders Family

Following the Saunders family's Intensive Week it was agreed that the Follow Up Programme would initially consist of the following elements:

- Fortnightly family sessions for the first six months, subsequently extending to monthly intervals.

- Daily telephone support for the first month, gradually reducing to weekly, and then monthly, telephone support. Access to emergency telephone support available at all times.

- Hands on Help Programme to focus on Marty's need to regress and become closer to his adoptive mother. Home visits and some sessions at the therapy space to support the parents in implementing the developmental reparenting programme. Telephone support also to focus on supporting this programme of work.

- Individual facilitated contact to be arranged for both children with their birth mother, to try and untangle the ambiguous messages from their previous 'farewell' contact. Also to enlist her support in encouraging them to settle with their adoptive family.

Although Jean and Jack had initially been shocked by what they had discovered about Jenny during the Intensive Week, they were not surprised when they considered the issues in subsequent therapy sessions. They felt that all the signs had actually been there but, due to Marty's more overtly difficult behaviour, they had been unable to recognise them clearly. They felt that Jenny's feelings were inevitable and very understandable, considering how long she had been with her birth mother and her experiences there. A well-prepared facilitated contact session (see Chapter 11) was proposed for Jenny and her birth mother so that many of these issues could be addressed as part of the healing process.

It was agreed that whilst facilitated contact was being set up primarily for Jenny, Marty would participate on a separate occasion. The main aim of contact for Jenny was to resolve issues of separation and loss, whilst the therapeutic focus for Marty was to consolidate his progress in developing attachments, begun during the Intensive Week. During therapeutic sessions Jenny continued to participate in family sessions but was also given individual therapy time. The content of her sessions was, as always, fed back to her parents. This individual work was taken very slowly and gently. On the other hand, Marty worked more exclusively with his parents, to encourage early parent-child interactions and attachment behaviours. At times Marty struggled with these sessions; at other times he clearly delighted in them. At home Jean was encouraged to keep Marty with her as much as possible, as would be appropriate for a much younger child. Most of the work with Marty focused on helping him practise being close to Mum. Marty was told clearly in the therapy sessions that his homework was to continue to practise this closeness: he helped Mum load and unload the washing machine, roll out pastry and plant flowers in the garden. Sometimes Marty refused, saying, 'I don't want to! Why should I? This is boring.' Then Jean might grab him saying, 'Ten tickles and squeezes say I want you to', until Marty beamed.

It was not always that easy, however. Sometimes, for no apparent reason, Marty woke in a bad mood and no amount of playfulness seemed to help. On these occasions Marty might throw a tantrum and try to hit and bite Jean. She would then take him on her lap and cradle him gently but firmly until he was calmer. Initially Marty would become enraged at not being allowed to do what he wanted, becoming increasingly angry, until both he and Mum were exhausted. Then he would collapse into floods of tears and allow himself to be stroked. Only after this would he be able to snuggle into Mum, gulping out in little pants, 'Hug me, Mummy. Hug me. Don't let go, Mummy!' This would sometimes take several hours. Jean soon realised that if she was exhausted and stressed herself she was much less able to help Marty recover from one of his moods. It seemed that her good humour and strength were essential to keeping Marty on an even keel. If Mum could maintain the balanced emotional tone of her interactions and encourage Marty to attune to her, then they could pretty much survive all his moods. However, Marty was very skilled at noticing when Mum was not feeling good and would always take this opportunity to play up. In therapy sessions Marty began to talk about feeling sad about his birth mother. On one occasion he talked about feeling guilty that he was now having more fun with his adoptive mother.

An important factor here was Jenny's reaction to the developing relationship between Jean and Marty. Jenny made it clear she did not like all the tender, playful stuff between them: in fact she hated it. She would slam out of the room when she saw Jean and Marty getting physically close. Sometimes she would try to encourage Marty to disobey Jean. On several occasions she joined in the playfulness only to start whispering to Marty, 'Tickle her back, Marty.' Consequently, Jenny began spending increasing amounts of time alone in her room, although she did accept Jack's offers of trips out, from time to time. Her parents felt that Jenny wished she could have this kind of relationship herself but was absolutely unable to acknowledge this.

Six months into the Follow Up Programme Marty seemed to be settling more at home. He was still having tantrums but they occurred less often and did not seem to last as long. Jean commented that she now felt she had a son, or rather a baby, and that at last they were having fun together. On the other hand, Jenny seemed sad, lost and alone. Her parents reported that, on the whole, she was not a problem. However, they were worried about how disconnected she seemed from everyone both at home and at school. The facilitated contact with their birth mother seemed to be very necessary for both Marty and Jenny at this point. (See Chapter 11 for a detailed description of the facilitated contact from Jenny's perspective.)

The therapy team discussed, with Jean and Jack, Jenny's strong connection with her birth mother, distorting her perceptions of the world and altering her behaviour towards other people. They also explained that Jenny had not internalised a positive mother figure that would help her make sense of her frequently terrifying, early world. Jenny therefore continued to lack any real sense of herself or of relationships. Trying to make sense of her present world would, in itself, be highly stressful and confusing: she would probably fall back on earlier dissociative ways of coping. No doubt Jenny became adept at dissociating when she was traumatised as a young child. However, what had been an extremely useful survival skill was now interfering with Jenny's healing.

Following facilitated contact both children seemed more settled at home and Jean and Jack were really pleased. However, their pleasure was short-lived. At the children's school parents' evening they suddenly realised that neither child was coping well in school, yet as parents they felt that both were bright and extremely verbal at home. According to her class teacher, Jenny was not coping at all with her schoolwork and did not come across as able or bright. She also commented that Jenny spent most of her playtimes alone and had no friends. Jean and Jack were shocked because, although few friends had been invited for tea (and never the same one twice), Jenny talked readily about all her friends at school. It seemed that this was not the case: the children at school avoided her and complained that she smelled. Certainly Jenny tended to wet or soil herself under stress, Jean encouraging her to shower when she arrived home. Both parents were very concerned and terribly sad for Jenny.

Marty was also reported to be having problems: his behaviour in the classroom was very disruptive; he frequently had to be sent to another classroom. The class teacher was particularly despairing of Marty's insistence on crawling around underneath the tables whilst other children were working. Marty had barely completed any class work during the past couple of years and often destroyed what he had done, especially if the teacher praised his work. Jean and Jack were distressed that they had not realised how difficult things had been at school. The deputy head explained that the staff had all been aware of how much stress the parents had been under at home and felt that the children needed time to settle into their new family. On reflection, staff felt that keeping quiet about the children's problems had not necessarily been the best thing, since now their problems seemed to have become exacerbated and entrenched. There was concern that Jenny was approaching her last year at primary school and would have difficulty managing the transition to secondary level. Staff also wondered how much longer they could contain Marty within the school.

During the next therapy session it was suggested that both children would benefit from educational appraisals and assessments from an educational psychologist. Jenny's issues around friendships would be considered as part of her therapeutic work. In general it was felt that Jenny's academic issues needed to be considered separately from her emotional issues: as Jenny was still trying to develop her relationships within the Saunders family, it seemed unlikely that she could yet manage extended friendships (Southgate 1996; Archer 2001b). It was agreed that a member of the team, experienced in working with schools, should collaborate with staff to find ways of helping Marty manage better in school, as part of the Hands on Help Programme (see Chapter 13). (For a more detailed exploration of these educational interventions, see Chapter 14.)

By the end of the first year of the Follow Up Programme some serious school concerns remained, although life at home seemed to have settled down. Marty now trailed Mum around the house and did not want to be parted from her. At times this drove Jean mad and she complained, like all mothers of toddlers, that she could not even go to the toilet alone. The therapy team reassured her that this was a positive step forward, since Marty had progressed developmentally from baby to toddler. His tantrums no longer seemed random and unconnected but now largely concerned separation from Mum. Although Jean felt relieved about this development she remained frustrated by Marty's clinging. Jenny was also beginning to make some tentative steps forward. She still struggled to be close to Mum, generally finding closeness easier with Dad. However, she did allow Jean to do her hair and file her nails. On one occasion during a therapy session Jenny told Jean how much she would have liked to have been her baby, saying it was not fair. Subsequently, a single tear rolled down her cheek and she allowed Mum to take her hand and kiss it. For some time Jenny sat absolutely still, while Jean held her hand and looked terribly sad. It was moments like these that gave both parents hope that things with Jenny could improve and that perhaps one day she might love them.

Follow Up Programme – Year Two

The following Christmas was marked by the death of Jean's father, Jenny and Marty's grandfather. Both children were openly upset by his death and cried a great deal. Jean was in shock for a while, as his death from a heart attack had been sudden, but soon recovered enough to focus her attention on the distressed children. For several months subsequently, family therapy sessions focused on this loss for everyone. The theme of loss was intentionally made overt to the children and connected to all the other losses they had experienced in their lives. Marty talked about not having ever known his birth father; Jenny frowned, said little at first but eventually spoke of wanting to be the same as all the other girls at school.

Jenny still struggled with peer relationships at school and had absolutely no friends: perhaps the only difference being that she was now able to acknowledge this to her parents. Staff seemed less concerned by this issue, until Jenny punched another, smaller girl in the stomach after a row at school. Everyone was surprised, as Jenny was not known as a bully. At first Jenny denied the whole thing but eventually acknowledged that she had hit her 'but not that hard – only a tap'. Jean and Jack were shocked but intrigued to hear of another side of Jenny they rarely saw at home. In her next individual therapy session Jenny admitted being teased at school for being smelly and for touching herself. When the therapist asked her where exactly she was touching, Jenny did not answer. In the feedback session Jean and Jack wondered whether she had been masturbating, saying that she did this sometimes at home, in front of the television, when she forgot where she was. Jenny was furious and extremely embarrassed. This was the first time that this issue had been raised.

The subject of sexual abuse became a major feature of future sessions for Jenny, who fluctuated between being extremely angry and extremely distressed. After outbursts of anger she began to talk about people coming into her bed at night, when she was living with her birth mother. She cried, commenting that the women were 'okay' but the men hurt. She said that she told Paula but nothing had changed. With encouragement, Jenny decided to write and send a letter to her birth mother: unlike the letter referred to in Chapter 9, which was not intended for posting. In the next session Jenny wrote:

Dear Mum,

I've been feeling very sad and missing you. I have terrible nightmares sometimes and I'm scared. I remember these nightmares of scary men from when I was little. Do you remember them? Please help me by telling me if you do too!

Everyone here is very kind but I need you to help me.

Lots of love, your sad and scared little daughter.

Jenny

XXXXXXXXXXXXXXXXXXXXXXXXXXXXXXXXXXXXXXXXXXXXX

Jenny cried and cried after writing the letter and again after reading it aloud to her parents, who also cried. Marty said he remembered being scared and Jenny said she used to cuddle him when he was scared and push him under the bed when the people came. Jean and Jack were distraught and held the children close to them, saying they were so sorry they had not been there to help them. Jenny allowed Mum to hold her and stroke her hair. This extremely sad and distressing time seemed to bring the family closer than ever before.

Jenny received a reply from Paula, consisting of a short note and a photograph of Paula with her new baby, Jennifer. The note said:

Dear Jenny,

Here's a picture of me with your new sister Jennifer. Isn't she lovely? She looks just like you. Don't worry about me, I'm doing fine.

Love,

Mum X

Jenny was very quiet as she read this and looked at the photograph in the family session. Marty became very worried about whether the baby would be fed properly. The therapy team promised to obtain updated information about the birth family from social services.

That night Jenny deliberately cut her arm with a piece of glass taken from a picture frame she broke. The frame contained a photograph of Paula. Jean heard Jenny crying, went to find out why she was upset and discovered her lying on the bed covered in blood. After Jean and Jack had cleaned her up and decided that a hospital visit was not necessary, they all sat together and drank warm milk. Jenny cuddled up and fell asleep on Jean's lap. After they had tucked her into bed, Jean and Jack rang the Family Futures' emergency number and spoke to a member of the team. They were praised for their calmness and reassured that they had done the right thing. It was agreed that this was a potentially serious situation, most likely a desperate cry for help, to which they had responded well. Jean kept Jenny off school the next day and they spent the day together, cuddled up on the sofa watching daytime television. In the next session Jenny chose to sit next to Mum and Marty was furious. As a consequence the next therapy session focused on 'how to share a mum'.

The summer holidays were now approaching and the Saunders family had a trip planned. They were going camping in France with two other adoptive families they knew. They were all excited about this, even Jenny. In the September session immediately following, they all talked about their holiday and celebrated, as a family, their most successful holiday together. Marty had had no tantrums whatsoever and Jenny had made a whole group of friends. Their parents were delighted. Cries of 'Three cheers for the Saunders family!' and 'Hooray' came up from everyone. The therapy team acknowledged that this was an amazing and wonderful step forward and certainly one to be celebrated.

It was decided that the remainder of the session should be spent creating a drama story as a family: 'The Mountain Climb'. The Saunders family embarked upon this task enthusiastically and co-operatively: still an unusual feat for both children. They were asked to create a story, as a family, about four people who go on a mountain climb together. They had to agree the five scenes that took place, including the trials and tribulations they would face. They decided on their characters, who was to be leader, who the helpers, the nature of their costumes and their experiences on their journey. The family was also told that whatever happened, they must all return: no one must die. The children had wanted a journey full of adventures, monsters, magic, death and disaster. Throughout the planning stage there was a great deal of laughter. Finally, collapsed in giggles, they sat together on four chairs wearing their costumes and carrying essential props such as biscuits, toilet paper and an umbrella.

The family was then interviewed by 'the press' (therapy team members), about their hopes and fears for the journey. They were united in their optimism, enthusiasm and idealism; then they set off. Disaster struck immediately as Marty, in an over-enthusiastic bounce, pushed Jenny off the mountain in Scene One. Jenny let out a blood-curdling scream and Jack jumped over the edge to rescue her. Jean administered first aid and luckily Jenny survived, but only just. Marty danced for joy and ate all the biscuits. Fortunately Mum had a secret extra supply, so Jenny had some too. Dad then had to carry Jenny, who was still hurting, while Mum tried to control Marty, as they crossed the 'shark-infested river' (a large piece of blue material). Jenny clung to Jack and, when he pretended to slip, squealed with delight. Marty tiptoed across the 'stepping stones' (small cushions), holding Mum's hand tightly. However, the horrors were not over. A very large, hairy monster (one of the therapy team's coats) attacked them. Mum sprang into action and wrestled the 'monster' to the ground, to the cheers of all the family and therapy team.

Several times during this journey, the therapy team 'froze the action', to ask questions of the family about what was happening. Marty was not sure if he had pushed Jenny in the river and why he did, if he did. Did she fall or was she pushed? Jenny was not sure how she became unable to walk at all and had to be carried for the whole journey: she was meant to have made a full recovery with the help of a magic potion. Jean said that she somehow knew she would need extra, secret supplies of biscuits and that she discovered bravery she did not know she had, tackling the hairy monster. Jack commented that he was unsure whether he was strong enough to carry Jenny, but somehow he managed it, and that it was good to see Marty trusting Mum to help him over the river.

Finally they made it back to 'base camp' to be welcomed by 'the press', who enquired whether the journey had lived up to their expectations. Jack replied immediately: 'It started out like a lovely bright sunny day and I hoped we would have a lovely picnic. Then look what happened. If I'd known at the beginning of the journey what it would be like I'm not sure I'd have gone.' Jean commented: 'I didn't know what I would have to face and how strong I would have to be but somehow we all pulled through. It was worth it in the end.' Marty said, 'I loved the bit when I got the biscuits…and I love my Mum!' Jenny looked at Marty and paused: the silence seemed to go on forever, then she said thoughtfully, 'It was terrible when I fell off the mountain but luckily I had my family. I had my Mum and my Dad and they rescued me. I wasn't sure at first if I wanted to be rescued but then I did. It all turned out okay in the end.' In a whisper she added, 'I love you.'

Summary

The 'drama' for this family is not over. There is still so much they will have to face in the coming years, of which adolescence will form a major part. However, we would argue that there is now a foundation of attachment between parents and children from which they can continue to grow. Jenny and Marty still have lots of work to do learning what being part of a family is like and they both have many ghosts from their past to face. However, importantly, they have taken crucial first steps in allowing themselves to become vulnerable and dependent on their adoptive parents. They have also begun to know the joys of being a family: sharing, being playful and laughing together.

Family Futures' role during the two-year programme has been to provide a framework in which the family could make sense of the children's past experiences and current behaviours. The family was able to use therapy sessions to explore issues from daily life, as well making connections with the past. The primary focus of therapy was to help the children attach to their parents and provide a 'stage' on which the children could play out their feelings and be understood. Regular family sessions were crucial in this, alongside the Hands on Help Programme. Sometimes practical work, such as letters to and from birth parents, formed part of these sessions. Sometimes painful connections between behaviours such as Jenny's masturbation and her being teased in school could be made. The aim of each session was to consider difficult issues sensitively, whilst balancing the family's need to experience increasing intimacy. Our goal is to weave these strands together so that there is a flow from one to the other and they become almost inextricably linked. For example, the child might move from discussing painful material in a session to being enjoyed by his parents, delighting in the freckles on his face. The dance in the sessions is the symbolised dance of attachment (Hughes 2002), as the therapy team encourages the whole family to move closer to each other: becoming more familiar with, and responding to, cues for intimacy. For the parents it is, simultaneously, an educative process. They are being asked to help their child attune, albeit belatedly, to his inner sensori-emotional cues, make sense of them, express them safely and get his real needs met by his parents.

In this work there is no one right way of working as a therapist: it is about collaborating as a team to do one's best. At times it is about risking staying with such pain and despair as feels unbearable, when one's heart and soul cries out to change the pace, move away from the pain: then staying a little longer. It is only by bearing the unbearable, and helping the family bear it too, that the hurt can be worked through and transformed (Hughes 2002). As a therapist one needs to be open and responsive oneself: so that one can go with the flow, following the child's cues to what they need and balancing this with the pace that parents need. The therapist is in many ways the director of this process, shaping the movement of the dance: keeping the balance between safety, containment and the exploration of painful material. Moreover, it is not just children and parents who are touched by this process. There is so much pain, love and laughter that everyone cries a little. When one has witnessed a child like Jenny repeatedly pushing away love and then one day looking at her adoptive mother with tears in her eyes, one recognises that something truly amazing has taken place: the first tentative steps in the lifelong dance of attachment are really being taken.

CHAPTER 11

Contact as Therapy
Alan Burnell

A Snapshot of a Birth Parent Contact: From Jenny's Perspective

I spent ages that morning getting ready. I must have changed my outfit six times. The black skirt with the new red top looked too smart. I tried my faded embroidered jeans on with a belly top but it looked too trendy. And Mum hates it when I look tarty. I wasn't sure how I wanted to look. I just wanted to look right. I hadn't slept for the past few nights, well not properly anyway. Jean came in, fussing as usual. Trying to be nice I suppose. Pain. Told her to go away. Put my music up loud. That'll tell her. I can't wait to see my Mum. I keep going over in my head how good it will feel. She will hug me and it will all be alright. Thought perhaps I should pack my bags ready, you know, for when they sort it out and we get to go home. Marty says he doesn't want to come. Well, I'll go without him. I've been waiting for so long. He's not going to spoil it now. What does he know? Nothing. Absolutely nothing. Decided on the black skirt, with the sweatshirt top. I love that top. 'No I don't want any breakfast!' Don't they understand I can't eat anything? How can they be so thick? And now it's time to go.

I feel all sweaty on the journey to Family Futures in the car. I wonder if they'll let me see her on my own? Probably got to see her with everyone there. Still it'll all be fine after today when I go home with her. Shit! Who do I call mum? Jean'll expect me to call her mum. Mum'll expect me to call her mum. Maybe I won't say mum to anyone. Yes, that's it! But what if she doesn't come? What if he won't let her? What if she turns up drunk again? No. No. She wouldn't do that. Not after so long. What did they say she was alright for, if she's still drinking? I wonder what the baby will be like? Smelly probably. Maybe she won't bring the baby. Maybe she'll leave the baby with someone else. I mean, she is coming to see me. It is special. Why do I feel so scared? Mustn't show how scared I feel.

'No. I don't want a drink.' Here we go: 'individual time to think about how I feel.' I tell the therapist I want to see my Mum on my own. I don't want my adoptive parents there. It'll be too difficult. Who will I call mum? The therapist wants me to think of questions I want to ask Mum. I know how I feel but there's nothing I want to ask. I just want to go home. I want my Mum. Took them bloody ages to get her here but I suppose they managed it in the end. 'I don't want to talk. I just want to see her. Could I make a mask?' While I make the mask we think of questions together. Good questions. Just too difficult to ask:

- *Do you think I could ever come back and live with you?*
- *If you kept the baby, why didn't you keep me?*
- *Why did you let me get hurt?*
- *Did you know what the men did to me?*
- *Why did you leave me?*
- *Why didn't you look after me?*
- *Don't you love me?*
- *Can I come home now?*
- *Do you remember the cat we rescued?*

I'm going to make this really beautiful to show my Mum. A beautiful mask with glitter and stars and sparkly bits hanging down. Really special. A gift for her. Yes, I'll give it to her. A present. A special present from me to her. Could put a small black cat on the side, like a tattoo. The black cat we found. That's special between us, that cat. 'You can ask the questions I can't.'

I am so scared. She's here. I heard the door. Is that a baby? No, probably just Marty acting babyish again. Silly kid he is now. I am so scared. I don't want to leave this room. Perhaps I can just wait here and she'll come to me. Maybe I can just stay here forever knowing she is just outside. If I breathe deeply maybe I'll be able to smell her. Mummy. Mummy!

Here we go! I'll breathe deeply and think of something else. I'll think of what colour to paint my fingernails. Oh, no! The door is opening and there she is. They are. She brought the baby! Why? I can't speak. I can't look at her. I'll just sit where they put me. This is awful. I thought she would hug me. I know, I'll put on the mask then no one can see me. I want to scream, cry out 'Mummy' but I can't. I don't want to cry. I won't cry. Please don't let me cry! Mummy. Where are you, Mummy? Why didn't you come back? Oh no! I can feel the tears. Perhaps the mask will cover them and no one will see. I think they're asking me questions but all I want is for her to put down that smelly, horrible baby and come to me. I hear my questions get asked but I can't bear to hear the answers. I shut my eyes and my mind. I hear nothing. I focus hard. I pray. I never normally pray: what can God do? Where was he when I needed him? But now I pray: 'hug me, cuddle me!' Why doesn't she? Mummy, why? I am lost. My tears streaming down my face so that they can all see. Someone touches my arms, at last. Thank you. But when I turn to look it is Jean. She is crying. I can see my tears in her eyes. I try to speak but I can't. I let her hand rest on my arm. She asks me to take off the mask but I shake my head. I know they can see my tears, my snot pouring through the eyes and nose of the mask. But they can't see me. Not the real me underneath. I feel safe behind the mask.

> *Mum says I should be happy with my new Mum and Dad.*
>
> *Happy, how can I be happy?*
>
> *Mum says I should not think about her.*
>
> *What does she know?*
>
> *Mum says I can't come home.*
>
> *But why? Why?*
>
> *Mum says he won't want us.*
>
> She *doesn't want us.*
>
> *She has a new baby.*
>
> She never *wanted us.*
>
> *But why? Why?*
>
> *Smiling mask on the outside.*
>
> *Happy to cry and smother my fears.*

And then she strokes my arm again and all the hairs stand on end. This other Mum. It tickles, it almost hurts, but I need someone. I can't say 'no, don't touch' but I can't say 'do it more'. So I say nothing and allow the tingle to run up and down my whole body. This other Mum gently removes my mask and I see that everyone is looking at me and trying not to show they are. My tears. This other Mum leads me over to my Mum and puts my hand in her hand. I look up and catch her eyes. The eyes look back but don't see me. I look and see her tears and she sees mine but she's looking somewhere else. Always those eyes have been looking somewhere else. She says she has to go and I mouth goodbye. 'Goodbye Mummy, Goodbye!'

The other Mum puts her arms around me and holds me, while I cry and cry. I feel weak and my legs start to shake. The tears roll down and soak my sweatshirt top. I love this top. I love this top. She rocks me back and forth and hums little soft words to me. I can smell her perfume and she smells nice and sweet and kind. It would be so easy to push her away. I hate mums. But for now I need that rock, that hum, that smell. I'll push her away another time but not now. Now I have no choice really: I need her.

(*Jenny and Marty's story by Jay Vaughan*)

The dramatised account above is intended to highlight some of the feelings and thoughts an adopted child may experience when making renewed contact with a birth parent. Contact can be a very painful process for everybody, yet it can also have a very positive, therapeutic impact if managed well. Below I explore contact issues, including facilitated contact such as this, in more theoretical and practical terms.

Contact in Context

Contact has been one of the most contentious issues for looked after children. Since the passing of the 1989 Children Act, there has been the 'presumption' of contact continuing. In my experience more hours have been spent in court discussing contact issues than threshold criteria. In many cases outcomes have been determined more by legal process than by the child's needs: frequency of contact often decided by compromise in courtroom corridors rather than by realism.

The presumption of contact laid down by the Children Act strongly influenced the evolution of adoption and fostering practice arising from the emergence of post adoption services during the 1990s. Whilst working as a counsellor at the Post Adoption Centre in London I counselled adults who were adopted as babies and 'voluntarily relinquishing' birth mothers. The prevailing culture of silence and secrecy was beginning to be brought into question. The lack of any mechanism for birth parents to gain information about their relinquished babies, or for those 'babies' to have easy access to information about their birth parents, seemed a glaring anomaly at a time when openness was very much a contemporary cultural attribute. Both the

Post Adoption Centre itself and prominent self-help groups for adopted adults, birth parents, and adoptive parents were advocating more openness. Increasingly my colleagues and I felt it appropriate to suggest to adoptive parents that some form of contact for their child, with his birth family, might be an appropriate way of allaying his fears and fantasies and answering the questions he would have as he grew towards adulthood. This innovative practice has now become an accepted feature of contemporary adoption work, with most local authorities and adoption agencies developing at least a 'letterbox' service. Some have even advocated open adoption as part of the progressive future for adoption services (Fratter 1996).

In time, these practice changes regarding openness, evolving out of an era of baby placements, began to be applied to contemporary adoptions, where the majority of children being placed were older and had been traumatised, if not always intentionally, by their birth parents. There is now a presumption of contact for these dysfunctional birth families. From my current perspective, as part of a post adoption service endeavouring to support adoptive families for the duration of the adoptee's childhood, this development presents something of a paradox. Working with many families where children have had direct or indirect contact, I am acutely conscious that, in the majority of contemporary adoption situations, direct contact represents contamination and retraumatisation, unlike baby adoptions where contact represents continuity and the building blocks of future identity. Unless some degree of reparation is facilitated this relationship pathology continues as part of the child's inner representations, distorting his self-perceptions and current interactions.

A further dimension to direct contact is its complexity in relation to sibling groups. Where non-biological siblings are placed together there may be disparities in the levels, and desirability, of contact. Amongst sibling groups placed apart, differing contact arrangements between siblings and their birth parents can lead to direct contact, as it were, by the back door. Where children have letterbox contact, adoptive parents are able to exercise some control over the content of communications. In direct contact, even when supervised, it is far harder to manage communication and interaction. In our experience, what seems to have been lost in this whole debate, and in the specific arrangements made for children, is the subjective meaning of contact for the child: not just in terms of their understanding of what is said and done but also symbolically by the very act of contact.

The Meaning of Contact

- For the parentified child, contact can perpetuate his parental role, or provide reassurance that his parent no longer requires his care and attention.

- For the sexually, physically or emotionally abused child, contact can jeopardise the safety and security that his new family offers.

- Explicit or implicit messages from birth family members can confuse the child about the permanence of his 'forever' home.

- For siblings, contact can perpetuate dysfunctional birth family roles and relationships: perpetuating the preferred child in his role or endorsing the neglected child in his.

- For siblings placed apart, contact can reawaken dysfunctional interaction patterns: often undermining adoptive parents' efforts to provide healthier relationship models and threatening to retraumatise siblings themselves.

If this appears a rather negative portrayal of contact this may be because the complexities of contact can be so overwhelming, not only for the child but also for his new parents, siblings, and birth relatives, that it can become distressing or unmanageable. Conversely, for some children the absence of contact remains problematic. For children whose 'farewell contacts' occurred when they were two, three, or four years old, important messages may be forgotten by the time they reach eight, nine, ten years and are passing through a period of 'adaptive grieving'. It is also clear that children can be selective in their recall and, in particular, may 'forget' the finality of previous connections for which they are still likely to be yearning unconsciously. Conversely, 'messages' may be remembered that are inappropriate yet remain, fossilised, within the child's belief system. In all cases the major issue for practitioners may be an in-depth evaluation of renewed contact. Many 'farewell' contacts not only occur when children are relatively young, they also are often experienced by them, and no doubt their birth parents, as traumatic events. As anyone will know who has ever been present at one, they are laden with emotion; many confusing and conflicting messages are conveyed. For such children it is sometimes helpful to say 'hello' again in order to say 'goodbye' more meaningfully. If contact takes place in the context of some form of therapeutic process, when the child is older and better supported, then he is likely to be able to make sense of the event in ways that were impossible originally.

The Long Goodbye

It could be argued that there is no final 'goodbye', just a continuing 'long goodbye', since integrating early experience and memories of birth families and birth family life is an ongoing task for the child as he matures (Siegel 1999). Here, contact can help or hinder the process, depending upon whether it reinforces the reality or the fantasy of life in the child's birth family. For children going through middle childhood, their understanding of the meaning of separation, loss and adoption adapts as their cognitive development progresses. Brodzinsky and colleagues (1998), from their research in respect of baby adoptions, suggest that children experience periods of adaptive grieving and will naturally be curious about what has happened to birth parents, siblings, and other significant others at certain developmental stages. Children who experience traumatic relationships or maltreatment learn to cope through dissociation and idealisation. Once again contact can perform a helpful function in confirming or confronting the remembered realities of childhood. It is particularly in this context that we began to consider contact as a therapeutic intervention and a responsibility rather than a 'right'. In assessing children who are clearly disturbed, distressed and failing to form attachments in their permanent families we have recognised a 'golden rule of contact': that children are either having too much contact or too little. Another profound conclusion we have reached is that there can be both 'good' contact and 'bad' contact. Regarding the latter, I would differentiate between the two in terms of whether contact confirms the child's place in the world in the present and leaves him feeling secure, or perpetuates his confusion and distress.

There is much research, and many reviews of research (e.g. Thoburn and Sellick 1997), that suggests contact is a protective factor for children in care and that open adoption can be a positive experience for youngsters (Fratter 1996). As with all research, one must view these findings with caution. Many of the studies were conducted over quite different 'eras' in child care practice. They cover a very varied sample population of children in short-term care, long-term care, and in adoptive families. They also include children of very differing age groups. The population of children that Family Futures has dealt with over the past few years is fairly specific; the average

age of children with whom we have worked has been approximately eight years of age. This is a post Children Act population that, as a consequence, has typically experienced multiple placements and rehabilitation attempts. The stringent criteria for permanent removal of children following the implementation of this Act also means that children being placed in permanent families are likely to have suffered serious neglect, physical, sexual or emotional abuse: often experiencing all three forms of trauma. All these factors predispose them to exhibiting severe attachment difficulties when placed in substitute families. I believe that this group of children are, sadly, not untypical of many children in the care system today who require permanent family placement. It is for this group of children in particular that we should reconsider the meaning of contact.

Facilitating Contact

'Supervised' contact for children in care, based on accounts from children and their parents, tends to be rather chaotic. Birth parents and siblings, some of whom may be placed separately, are often brought together for an hour or so of rather frantic activity, present sharing and trips to the toilet for secret conversations. Typically there are no meaningful communications and what seems to occur is a ritualised re-enactment of life in the birth family. In fairness to both birth parents and their children, contact can be an overwhelming experience due to the multiplicity of expectations that all parties bring and the maelstrom of emotions that are rarely acknowledged, let alone processed, at any stage.

The facilitated contact protocol developed at Family Futures represents the converse of this rather stereotyped contact. It is our belief that contact for parents is a responsibility not a right. It should only happen if, for the duration of contact, however short or long, the birth parent is able to act as a good enough parent, doing and saying things that are in the best interests of the child. Frequent face-to-face contact with birth parents should be the exception rather than the rule. In our view, the role of contact is to help the child resolve unanswered questions, convey the messages they wish to convey and strengthen their perceptions as to who their psychological parents really are. Frequent face-to-face contact, particularly when it is unstructured, can leave children re-traumatised, fearful and uncertain about their future, with their attachments emotionally frozen.

As a precondition of any form of contact we arrange one or two pre-meetings with participating birth relatives, to discuss with them the purpose of the contact, their role and our mutual expectations. In all cases the aim is to provide opportunities for the birth relatives to convey:

- their ongoing concern for the child's welfare

- parental acknowledgement that they were unable to parent the children well enough to ensure their safety and future growth and development

- in the case of birth relatives, acknowledgement that the children were not sufficiently well cared for

- remorse and responsibility for events that occurred within the birth family

- acknowledgement that the adoptive parents are their children's permanent parents with whom they will live until they are grown up.

If parents or relatives are prepared to make a commitment to these aims then we regard them as acting in an appropriate parental way. We acknowledge and discuss with birth relatives just how difficult a task is being asked of them, because of the range of emotions that such an undertaking will evoke. For birth parents who often feel very powerless during our sessions with them, in particular, we try to reframe their perceptions and help them to see that even though it may not feel that way, they are probably the most powerful and important persons in the room during contact. As anyone who has cared for children separated from their birth parents for whatever reason knows, the power of the absent parent can be more intense than the power of the parent who is present. Many birth parents understandably feel diminished and degraded by the experience of care proceedings and the permanent removal of their children, even if they have consented to this. We see contact as offering positive therapeutic experiences for birth parents, from which their perception of themselves and their significance to their children may be positively enhanced.

Having considered these issues with the birth relatives, the next aim of the preparatory session would be to help them decide what 'messages' they wish to convey to their child and the easiest way to do this. We have, on occasion, suggested to birth parents that we write out the statements for them that they wish to make and offered to verbalise these for them during the contact session. Occasionally, we suggest that birth relatives draw a picture that they then share with the child. The counsellor conducting the preparatory session with birth relatives is there throughout the contact process, as their identified counsellor, to ensure that they are supported and have opportunities to process their feelings about the contact. We believe that this has a containing effect, limiting the amount of 'emotional spillage' that can occur during unsupported contact.

The child and his adoptive parents have similar, preparatory sessions before contact. It is a central principle of our work that adoptive parents are present with their child throughout contact. For all children, contact will provoke high anxiety, evoking strong feelings from the past. It is therefore crucial that it is the current caregivers who help the child manage his feelings and provide him with a source of comfort. This should never be an experience that a child undertakes on his own, or with the support of strangers, since this would represent a painful re-enactment of the child's early experiences of emotional abandonment. The adoptive parents must model a positive parental role and show the child that there is sufficient alliance between them and the birth relatives to survive the contact experience. Without such an alliance, it is highly questionable whether children should be placed in the invidious position of having to mediate between two worlds, two families, even with the help and comfort offered by professionals. It is also worth repeating here that we would only envisage facilitating contact for one child and their birth relative(s) at a time. This acknowledges that every child's relationships with his family are unique and different; the therapeutic use of contact is primarily an individual and deeply personal experience, not a family get-together.

Preparation of the child for contact effectively begins during the Intensive Programme week, with detailed disclosure of birth family history and the 'birth parent psychodrama' (see chapters 9 and 10). The latter, which involves the child making a life-sized model of their birth parent and reading a letter to them, is very much a rehearsal for face-to-face contact. The psychodrama provides opportunities for the child to say things that they would like to but would not necessarily say at the contact meeting. The exercise allows the child to express his deeply felt ambivalence towards his past caregivers. During the course of the facilitated contact it may become the role of the child's designated counsellor to express that ambivalence for the child, since it can be very liberating for him to witness that his birth parent can tolerate his anger and ambivalence and accept it. As part of the ongoing therapy programme we may also arrange a role-playing re-enactment of contact or 'farewell contact'. The preparation sessions leading up to contact aim to identify the messages that the child wishes to convey at the meeting. As with the birth parent messages, we often introduce elements of creative expression for the child, for example through the use of mask making or painting.

The outcome of these preparations is shared with the child's adoptive parents, as a way of informing them of the concerns and issues for their child and reinforcing their parental role, as primary caregivers. The experience of sharing by the child can provide further rehearsal of the process and more soundly embed it in his personal narrative (Hughes 2002). For the adoptive parents, their child's messages, and their own emotional responses to them, are explored separately during their personal preparation session.

The adoptive parents' participation throughout their child's preparation for contact provides opportunities for them to explore the meaning and significance of contact to him. In parallel with the child's preparation session the adoptive parents will also have opportunities to explore their own feelings about birth relatives. Many adoptive parents find this experience quite liberating. As part of their parenting preparation by adoption agencies they have usually been encouraged to think and talk positively about birth family members. However, we believe that this puts the adoptive parents in a 'Catch 22' situation: if one is to love, bond and care for an adoptive child one will inevitably have intense feelings for them and about what has happened to them. In this context it would be strange if adoptive parents did not feel angry, jealous or upset when thinking about the child's birth family and his early life experiences with his birth parents.

Many adoptive parents have told us that they feel guilty about having such feelings. Our preparation for contact therefore provides opportunities for them to express these feelings and for them to be acknowledged and validated as an integral part of the essential attachment process. When these feelings are not acknowledged they can cloud and distort the adoptive parents' attitude to contact and may hamper their ability to speak freely and honestly about the child's birth family. The information disclosure exercise, carried out during the Intensive Programme, where distressing details of the child's early trauma are shared with the adoptive family, often provides the catalyst for adoptive parents to express their feelings towards the birth parents. The importance of this exercise is not just that these parents are better informed about their child's past but also that they emotionally 'own' their child's past. The child's history moves from being an intellectualised chronology to become a very real part of the shared emotional connection between parent and adoptive child.

Contact Day

Immediately prior to contact itself the birth relative(s) and the child, accompanied by his adoptive parents, are seen in separate areas. They are helped to go over, once again, the messages they wish to convey. The birth relative(s) are also given the opportunity to prepare for the questions and messages that their child will wish to convey. In our experience this reduces the 'shock and surprise' element, giving the counsellor an opportunity to contextualise what the child is saying for the birth relative(s).

The facilitated contact then takes place in a separate, neutral space. Participants will be the birth relative(s), the child and his adoptive parents, the birth relatives' counsellor, the child's counsellor and the adoptive parents' counsellor. Although this may seem a large number of adults, the effect is to make all parties feel more secure and better supported; everyone in the room is seen as part of the team aiming to make this a positive experience for all concerned. The setting is informal, with refreshments offered to all parties; there is a selection of toys, art materials and props available. After an initial settling-in phase, one of the counsellors takes the role of contact facilitator and formalises the meeting by reiterating the purpose of the contact, its agenda and timescale. Part of the facilitation process is to ensure that the respective parties are positioned 'in the right place': that is, the adoptive parents are seated next to their child, so that they can touch them, and that the child faces the birth relative(s). It is also important that the respective counsellors are positioned so that they have eye contact with the person they are supporting. We find it is often important for the counsellor supporting birth relatives to sit beside them, so that they can make physical contact with them, where necessary, during the contact. This issue would have been discussed with the birth relatives prior to the contact: this negotiation is vital because of the number of birth relatives who have experienced sexual or physical abuse in their own childhoods.

Aspects of Good Contact

- Contact must involve the foster or adoptive parents. It is essential that they should be present to perform parental tasks of reassurance and protection that cannot be performed by professionals or third parties. Contact should be a shared experience and as such one that enhances attachments between the child and his adoptive parents.

- Close collaboration with participating birth relatives is essential. For the duration of contact, birth relatives must behave as responsible and good enough parents, to meet the needs of the child. If they are unable to do so then it is clearly questionable whether direct contact should take place. To achieve this, many birth relatives will require considerable preparation, support, and counselling, to help them realise that they can still make a positive contribution to the futures of their children and remain a powerful force in their children's lives.

- In many cases face-to-face contact with birth parents will not be ongoing, although indirect contact and direct contact with other birth relatives may be incorporated into the plan.

- It is essential that the meaning of renewed contact is made clear to children, since in their eyes, contact is frequently associated with rehabilitation, removal, or return home. It is also important that the child understands that direct contact will not lead to unsolicited contact in the future.

- Contact should be part of an integrated therapeutic process. Prior to direct contact, considerable preparatory work will need to be done with the child and his past and current caregivers, exploring their expectations for contact. For contact to be a truly positive experience for children, their feelings, both in the present and from the past, must be acknowledged and validated by their birth relatives, particularly birth parents.

- Validation can take the form of a simple acknowledgement that what happened did happen. Children who have been maltreated have often been forced to distort their view of reality and maintain secrets (Mollon 1998; Ross 1997). They often find it problematic, as well as painful, to remember events clearly and coherently (Mollon 1998; Waites 1997). Part of the therapeutic task with children is to go beyond life story work, as it is commonly practised, to develop a coherent and authentic narrative – sensori-affective warts and all. As discussed in chapters 2 and 15, a coherent narrative is an essential prerequisite for adult mental health.

- Contact should be a form of empowerment for children. Often children's experience of contact is of something that is done to them, not something that they do: the court, the social worker, the parent, decides what should happen and when. Children are left to mediate contact as best they can, often despite 'supervision'. They tend to fall back on the psychological defences, along the helpless-hostile dynamic (Lyons-Ruth, Bronfman and Atwood 1999) upon which they relied to survive within their birth families: either through superficial compliance, caregiving and dissociation or hyperactivity, oppositional, controlling and superficially charming behaviour.

- As part of the therapeutic preparation for contact, children should be helped to rehearse what they want to say, how they want to say it and how they would like contact to be conducted. This provides children with some sense of control over their lives.

- Contact should always be for an individual child and not a sibling gathering where the individuality of the child's communication is lost in the chaos of the communal.

- Contact will inevitably lead to some degree of distress before, during, and after the event. With proper support and preparation, this can provide caregivers with vital opportunities to reparent 'the hurt child within' and to acknowledge, with and for the child, how sad, angry, and scared they feel. In this way, contact can become an integrative experience for both parents and children, during which caregivers can help their youngsters develop and explore their autobiographical narrative, not just on a chronological level but, more importantly, on emotional and relationship levels.

- Experience of supervising sibling group contact has led us to conclude that, in many situations, it is better for siblings to have individual contact with each other, in or around the vicinity of their new family home. This can emphasise the separateness of their new lives and that they are now in new and different, permanent families. However distressing this process may be initially, it tends to validate and strengthen new attachment relationships.

- One-to-one sibling contact provides opportunities for both adoptive family groups to discuss the children's shared past experiences, as a further form of narrative validation. It is also very important, where there is an intention to consolidate and develop sibling relationships in the future, that 'he knows what she knows and she knows that he knows'. The coherent narrative has to be one that is shared by all.

- Where sibling groups have contact, what often emerges is a re-enactment of role relationships, frequently of a pathological nature, that occurred within the birth family. In our view, such regression is neither helpful nor healthy, since it undermines the child's newly emerging sense of self. In such circumstances we recommend that the children's current caregivers limit face-to-face contact between separately placed siblings for some time, until they are more securely attached.

Facilitated Contact Protocol

The protocol we have established for facilitated contact is set out below:

- The child's messages and questions are conveyed first, either by the child himself or by his counsellor, in whatever form has previously been agreed.

- The birth relative(s) then respond, having prepared their response in advance; they then convey their own messages and questions. Depending upon how comfortable the parties are, this may lead into a more free-flowing exchange.

- If the interaction appears stilted and difficult the facilitator may lead the conversation, introducing elements they know from previous explorations are especially relevant.

- If the discussion is seen to be wandering from the central issues, the facilitator's role is to be directive and to refocus the conversation.

- On the vexed question of gifts we explain to the child and their birth relative(s), prior to contact, that the contact meeting is not a forum for exchanging gifts.

- However, with the permission of the adoptive parents, we take a group photograph, copies of which are presented to the birth relatives and the child. This is intended to demystify the 'mother-child reunion' fantasy and provide a tangible reminder of the occasion.

- We also ensure that both birth relatives and child have written copies of the messages and questions they have prepared and received from the other party. This provides everyone with a further permanent memento.

- The birth parents' responses frequently provide a reference point for the child in subsequent therapy sessions.

- Orchestrating closure is a very important task for the facilitator, since there is often a history of bad endings in the lives of both children and birth parents. If the issue arises, it is made clear that discussions about the possibility of future meetings will not take place during the contact meeting, since it is not a decision making meeting, but may occur at a future date.

- The facilitator articulates how emotive the contact experience is for all parties, alluding to feelings expressed both overtly and covertly by participants. She also congratulates each of the parties for their positive contribution to the meeting.

- The physical act of separation and leaving the room is also acknowledged to be difficult. Our protocol is that the birth relatives leave first, saying 'goodbye' and then returning to their preparation room with their counsellor.

- Physical contact between child and birth relative is limited to a hug since, for many children, their abusive history would make kissing inappropriate. It can also be a negation of their naturally ambivalent feelings.

- Understandably, it is not unusual for one or all parties to become distressed or upset, during or following contact. In our view this is an appropriate expression of the inherent sadness of the occasion. Immediately following contact, all parties are therefore offered opportunities to process their feelings separately. All parties are encouraged to stay until they have reached a state of composure.

- Typically such meetings last only half an hour in all, sometimes less.

Messages from Jenny's Facilitated Contact

Jenny:

- I think about you a lot.

- Do you think I could ever come back and live with you?

- If you kept the baby, why didn't you keep me?

- Why did you let me get hurt?

- Do you remember the cat we rescued?

Birth Mother:

- I think about you a lot too.

- You can't come back and live with me. I wouldn't be able to look after you and the baby. I have a new boyfriend now who doesn't know you.

- I am going to keep the baby.

- You have a new Mummy and Daddy now who I know love you and will look after you.

- I feel bad about what happened when you were little and I am sorry I could not keep you safe and you got hurt.

- This won't happen to my new baby.

- Maybe I will get another cat. I like cats. He was so sweet.

Although such communications may seem rather stylised and the contact contrived, as you can see from the interactions of Jenny and her birth mother they can also be very direct and hit upon central themes. During the processing of contact, the sadness, the longing, the guilt and the anger can more easily be explored because the parent-child communications are not clouded by the static, interference and chaos that typifies traditional contact. Our therapeutic aim is to make as many of the central issues as starkly clear as possible, so that neither the child nor the birth parent can have doubts about the other's position. In Jenny's case, she left the contact session knowing that her birth mother could not, and would not, take her back. This focused Jenny's sadness and anger on her birth mother: feelings that previously have often been directed at social workers, for not letting her go home, or her adoptive parents, for taking her away. In addition, Jenny was also reassured that her birth mother still thinks and cares about her and that she has formed an alliance with Jenny's adoptive parents: demonstrating that she believes that this is where Jenny belongs. The intensity of the emotions surrounding the contact, and the shared nature of the experience for Jenny and her adoptive mother, became the basis of a growing bond between them, as for the first time she allowed Jean to comfort her. Paradoxically, by bringing Jenny in contact with her birth mother it drew her closer to her adoptive mother. Jean and the therapy team will continue to build on this in future sessions.

Summary

This is a broad impression of the way of working we have developed over the past few years. The outline set out here is intended as a framework, not a prescription. Our overarching concern regarding contact is that if it is to happen at all it should lead to positive therapeutic outcomes for the child and possess healing potential for all parties. Contact must always be seen in terms of what it means to the child; how it affects his inner world and the new and fragile attachments he is forming with his adoptive parents. Although even the best managed or facilitated contact may not always go according to plan or have a happy ending, in our experience, well supported and well managed contacts can provide a 'win-win' experience for the child. If all goes to plan, they enable the child to move on and enhance the attachments in his adoptive family. If facilitated contacts do not go to plan, and birth relatives deny past events, fail to accept responsibility, become angry and out of control, or attempt to reclaim their child, then the child is reminded of his vulnerability and the unsafe nature of further contact or care from them. Although such contacts may initially be distressing, they can be used positively by the child to gain a realistic sense of his past relationships with birth relatives and an awareness of the importance of his newly-formed attachment to his adoptive family. Inevitably, given the emotive nature of contact, there will be some rough edges and 'emotional spillage': these can form the basis for further, sensitive therapeutic exploration.

CHAPTER 12

Holding the Fort

Christine Gordon

Introduction

'Holding the fort' at home is not easy. Traumatised children often feel that their safest course of action is to 'close the drawbridge' and ensure their 'fort' is enclosed by 'shark-infested waters'. Our job at Family Futures is to work with parents to keep these bridges open and make their homes comfortable and secure. This chapter and the following describe the way in which Family Futures works with parents. Christine Gordon, Family Futures' parent support co-ordinator and an adoptive parent, developed the parenting programme from her personal experiences and the shared experiences of those families with whom she has worked. The parenting programme recognises:

- the fundamental role of parents in helping their adopted children recover from their early traumatic experiences

- that parenting a traumatised child is a very different task from that of parenting a securely attached child

- that parents need to understand and make sense of children's behaviours if they are to adopt appropriate developmental reparenting strategies

- to fulfil this essential role, parents need support, empathy and validation. Many also need encouragement to take greater care of themselves.

The parenting programme starts 'where parents are at', by accepting that parents are experts on their child and giving them confidence to use their natural expertise to meet their child's needs.

Expectations of Family Life

Prior to Jenny and Marty's placement, Jean and Jack Saunders had been assessed as a loving and stable couple with a good deal to offer. It was felt they had a great deal of patience and would approach parenting as a shared task. Their social worker was impressed by their 'laid-back' attitude, their willingness to listen to children and their capacity for putting the children's needs at the forefront of family decisions. The couple had emphasised how important it was to them to take the views of everyone into consideration when making family decisions. The couple's referees had also commented on how thoughtful Jean and Jack were; one referee mentioned how much their children looked forward to seeing 'Aunt Jean' and 'Uncle Jack' and the fun-loving way they interacted with their children.

Jean and Jack began the task of reparenting Jenny and Marty with the firm intention of providing the children with stability, love and security. They knew that it would take some time before the children learned to trust them but were convinced that, with the patience and love they were offering, the children would eventually flourish. They had visualised seeing the children blossoming at home and school; they had imagined them making friends at school and inviting these children home for supper; they had talked with enthusiasm about how much they were looking forward to the children's first birthdays and Christmas with them. Although Jean and Jack recognised that the task of parenting would be a difficult one they thought that the difficulties would be interspersed with fun and laughter and they expected to share the tasks of parenting as equal partners. They had actually decided to adopt two children because they felt that this would provide a balanced family experience both for themselves and the children. They also believed that the children would have a positive relationship with each other and would be able to play together. In fact the description of Jenny and Marty's 'close and caring relationship', supplied by the placing agency, had been one of the things that had initially attracted Jean and Jack.

The Realities of Family Life

Two years down the line Jean and Jack are distressed by the lack of progress made by their children. Even more, they feel they have failed as parents. They had wanted to offer Jenny and Marty security, stability, love, understanding and patience. Instead they frequently find themselves shouting at the children, even telling them how bad they are, or arguing with each other about how best to parent them. They often wonder if they will ever have any fun with the children. Before the children were placed with them Jean and Jack had a wide circle of friends, many of whom had children of their own. Now few of their friends visit and those who do comment that Jean and Jack seem to have little control over their children. Friends' advice to the couple has included suggestions that they should take a firm line with them, that they are too strict and controlling and should 'lighten up', and hints that they are exaggerating the children's difficulties ('all children act like that'). While well intentioned, this last remark can be one of the most disempowering for adoptive parents who are struggling, since it can make them feel even more isolated and misunderstood, and increase their sense of self-blame.

Expectations of Adopters

By the time they seek help, adoptive parents are likely to feel a sense of failure. There are a number of reasons for this:

- Unlike birth parents, adoptive parents are 'assessed' and 'approved' before they have children placed with them. This can lead to problems in being able to acknowledge or articulate very real parenting difficulties (Archer and Swanton 2000). They may, therefore, seek support only as a last resort, or in crisis, and are likely to view seeking support in terms of personal failure.

- Placing social workers are very strongly committed to making the placements of 'their' children work: this may interfere with their ability to 'hear' the family's difficulties readily. Inadvertently, they too may imply that parents are failing (Furedi 2002).

- These issues may have particular relevance for baby adopters who are unlikely to have been prepared for the difficulties they may face, or alerted to the fact that their baby has suffered early trauma. Hence they are more likely to feel personally responsible for their youngsters' difficulties (Verrier 1993).

- For potential adopters, the assessment and approval phase is one during which they consider, among other things, their expectations of themselves as parents and the impact they might have on their children. Most anticipate difficulties and are keen to help their children settle. They expect that love will make the crucial difference to their child's lives. When they find that love is not enough it can be a devastating blow to parents' confidence in themselves (Howe 1996).

- The assessment process can lead to parents developing expectations of themselves as 'superhuman': parents who would always be calm and understanding and never respond to their children with anger. These altruistic expectations can lead to parents feeling guilty when they find themselves becoming angry and frustrated with their children. We must remind ourselves, and parents, that anger and frustration go with the job and are vital tools in helping parents begin to tune into, and understand what is going on for, their child (Archer 1999b).

- Adoptive parents may have been compared unfavourably by the children for whom they care with birth parents or previous foster parents. Many adoptive children repeatedly proclaim: 'I don't have to do what you say. You're not my *real* mother.' The inference here is that the adopters are not doing a good enough job as parents. Repeated often enough, they may begin to believe this (Howe 1996).

- Other family members or friends may imply that the adopters are not acting in a good enough manner in suggesting they are too strict, too lenient or exaggerating their child's difficulties (Archer 1999b).

- The child may behave differently with social workers or teachers. He may be able to 'hold it together' in school or during supervisory visits but may act quite differently in the privacy of his own home (Keck and Kupecky 1995). In these circumstances parents may be incorrectly perceived as the cause of their child's difficulties, reinforcing self-doubts.

- Children are more likely to act out their early history with mother figures and present different behaviours with fathers, especially if Mum is the primary caregiver. Moreover, mothers are often the first to recognise the extent of their children's difficulties. In these circumstances couples may have contradictory perspectives of the child, leading to the mother figure experiencing an even greater sense of failure and isolation (Levy and Orlans 2000).

- Child care professionals may give adoptive parents conflicting advice. For example, suggesting that adoptive parents should always present the birth family in a positive light, to help the child feel good about himself, denies them the right to be angry on behalf of their child for the hurts he has suffered. This may reduce parents' capacity to become fully engaged with their child at an emotional level and contribute to a reduced sense of 'entitlement' to him (Archer 2000a).

- This message is also confusing and misleading to children, potentially leading them to feel that their experiences in their birth family were acceptable, grossly exaggerated or occurred because they themselves were 'bad'. This adds to the ambivalence and confusion that many 'transplanted' children already feel (Delaney and Kunstal 1993).

What Parents Need

As a result of their unique pathway to parenting, adopters may be highly sensitive to any implied criticism of them as parents and see potentially 'helpful' suggestions as further indications that they are not doing a good enough job. At Family Futures we have found that it is vital to convey our trust in parents' ability as parents: that they *are* 'good enough' parents doing a very difficult job. Our work hinges on the premise that adoptive parents are doing their best to understand, love and parent their child. We have found that most of the difficulties in the home relate to children's early traumatic experiences and the way in which these continue to impact in the present. We blame neither children nor parents; instead we try to work with adoptive parents to help them gain confidence in themselves as good enough. We work hard to get alongside parents, to respect their knowledge of their child and to build a therapeutic alliance with them (see Chapter 8). Integral to our team approach to working with families, is our emphasis on parents being the experts on *their* child: since they live with them 24 hours a day, they know them and understand them very much better than anyone else. Our work is aimed at empowering parents to believe in themselves. This is often the first step in facilitating the attachment process between parents and children.

Many parents who come to Family Futures have lost confidence in their ability to do a good job and admit to feeling angrier with their child than they had anticipated. Some say that they are not able to love, or even like, their child. Typically they feel that they were inadequately prepared for the child and were given inadequate information to allow them to understand what is going on for them. Sometimes parents feel like giving up and may have been encouraged to think this way by well intentioned friends or relatives ('after all they are not really your *own* children'). Another initial task at Family Futures is, therefore, to provide parents with space to explore their own feelings about their child. We acknowledge parents' right to have a whole range of feelings about their child, accepting that these may be the result of years of antagonism and rejection by the child. We give parents permission to feel and express the anger this may bring up, encouraging them to do this when the child is not present, and suggesting a range of useful strategies. For example, we might encourage parents to write a letter to their child about how they feel. The letter is not seen by the child and is ceremonially torn up by the parents when they feel able to do so.

Our main reason for encouraging parents to explore their feelings is that acknowledging and dealing with feelings appropriately can help discharge the frustration, sadness and anger which could otherwise be directed at the child (Archer 1999b); this makes it less likely that parents will act in hurtful ways towards him. Freed from these understandable but distressing emotions, parents are then able to access more positive feelings towards their child. In this way we can help to promote healthier attachments to, and empathy for, the child (Gordon 1999).

We give parents opportunities to consider the impact that caring for a traumatised child has had on themselves as people and as partners. We encourage parents to reclaim their lives by looking after themselves; as Steinberg (2002) contends: 'we have not paid enough attention to the mental health and psychological needs of parents' (pp.4–5). We urge parents to take up an activity unrelated to their child and to make time on a daily, or at least weekly, basis for themselves. We explore ways they can spend time together as a couple, without their children. This can seem like an insurmountable task to parents who have spent months caring for a child who consumes their entire waking (and sometimes sleeping) hours.

It can be very revealing to ask parents to talk about their own skills and interests. I am frequently saddened that parents have become so disempowered that it seems almost impossible for them to think of even one thing they believe they do well. Child care and mental health professionals or friends, who emphasise the need to put the child's interest first and who value caregivers who are self-sacrificing and child centred, can compound these difficulties. The implication here is that people who prioritise looking after themselves are 'selfish' and lacking in the necessary qualities to be good parents. 'Selfishness' is not seen as a virtue in our society, yet this is an essential prerequisite for developing the self-knowledge and self-renewal that is both a tool for survival and a positive role model for the traumatised child (Archer 1999a, 1999b; Hughes 1997).

Living with a child who challenges every parental request, however reasonable or minor, can lead to parents lowering their expectations of their child or conceding to unreasonable demands from him, to minimise potential conflicts. While this is understandable it gives the child messages that his parents are not worthy of consideration or respect, or capable of taking the safe control so challenged, but so desperately needed, by the child. At the very least this puts the child in the driving seat in the family. Given the fact that this is a frequently favoured (although unhealthy) *modus operandi* it seriously inhibits the child's capacity for change. We therefore emphasise to parents that an essential step in their child's healing is to find ways to love and respect themselves (Thomas 2000; Hage 1995) and to work towards putting themselves in charge of 'holding the fort' within their families.

Life with Marty and Jenny

Jean and Jack's experiences typify these dynamics. By the time they came to consult us they had not been out as a couple for six months. Both said they found it difficult to obtain childminders who could cope with the children's difficulties. They also felt too exhausted caring for the children to plan a night out and the aftermath of their last evening without the children had negated any positive impact for them.

Jean had the major role in caring for the children. Jack left for work early in the morning and did not arrive home until after six in the evening. Jean was therefore responsible for getting the children out to school and occupying them for several hours after they returned home. Jack conceded that he enjoyed his job, that it gave him a much-needed break from the difficulties at home. He often dreaded going home and would sometimes look for tasks at the office to delay the litany of misdemeanours that Jean wanted to share on his return home. Jack acknowledged that he sometimes found it difficult to be empathetic when Jean was describing her day. The children, while difficult at times, generally behaved reasonably well when he was around. Jenny in particular always looked forward to seeing him and would rush up for a cuddle. Jack sometimes felt that Jean was too strict with the children and that their behaviour might improve if she could be more positive. Jean described feeling isolated and alone; she said that the children refused to obey even her simplest requests.

Marty's defiance was more overtly hostile than Jenny's: he often responded to simple requests (for example, to wash his hands before meals) with tantrums and screaming. Jenny's non-compliance was more passive: she would appear not to have heard or understood what had been asked of her, or would say 'I'll do it in a minute'. However, the end result was the same: parental requests were ignored or dismissed. The children were often late for school and Jean arrived there feeling frazzled. She felt that the children's teachers believed she was incompetent and blamed her for the children's late arrival. At times she felt that Jack, too, questioned her competence as a parent.

Our initial meeting with Jean and Jack clearly highlighted their differing perspectives on the children. Jean accepted that she was often tired and angry with the children and that she sometimes felt that she had failed as a parent. Jean acknowledged that Jenny was cuddlier with Jack; however, she also felt that Jenny frequently did this in a calculated way, without any depth of emotion. She had noticed that Jenny was most affectionate with Jack when she had been most rejecting of Jean. Jean felt that the cuddles and smiles were a way of trying to isolate her, rather than genuine attempts to get closer to Jack. In addition she had become aware of how Jenny seemed to smile with some satisfaction when she and Jack argued about how to parent the children.

Helping Parents Take Care of Themselves

Jean and Jack's differences of opinion about the children are not uncommon. As discussed in Chapter 3, it is the mother to whom the child has most difficulty attaching and who often experiences the child's most profound difficulties. This is likely to leave her feeling isolated and alone. Parental anger and disagreements are also common features in adoptive families with traumatised and controlling children. An excellent strategy for the child hell-bent on maintaining control at home is to work towards isolating mum and to 'engineer' situations where his parents are arguing. This was patently the case in Jean and Jack's family.

Jean clearly looked surprised when we acknowledged that she was probably correct in her perception of the situation: perhaps an indication of her loss of self-esteem over the preceding months. She was even more astonished when we asked her what she did for herself. She said that she used to enjoy swimming but had long given this up. She used to meet friends for coffee every week but this, too, was something she had not done for months. She said that she felt too tired to consider reinstating these activities and, furthermore, was not certain that it would do any good. Both children had an uncanny knack of knowing when she had been out with her friends and this led to an escalation of their difficult behaviours. As we felt that a vital first step in helping the family was to address issues of self-care for both Jean and Jack we began by talking to them about the importance of taking care of themselves. We emphasised that they needed to do this to be fit and well to manage the task of reparenting Jenny and Marty and to provide an essential role model for them.

After some discussion both parents agreed that they would try to do *one* thing for themselves each week during the next month. Jean proposed to meet a friend for coffee, whilst Jack planned to spend half an hour each evening reading a novel. At our next meeting both Jean and Jack said that they were feeling more relaxed and less exasperated with the children. Jean had decided to return to swimming and had booked herself into an aqua-aerobics class, which she could fit in while the children were at school. Jack had made arrangements to play a round of golf. He recounted that on the previous day Marty had sworn at him three times, had refused to sit still in the car and had screamed all the way to school. Jack laughed as he told us that he intended to use his game of golf to deal with the anger he still felt over these behaviours by thinking about Marty as he swung his golf clubs. One valuable way of reducing the likelihood of parents acting out their angry feelings towards their child is to ask them to imagine the worst things they could do to their child, when the child is not there. This makes it very much easier to let go of understandable but unhelpful feelings and replace them with the empathetic approach so vital to the reparenting task.

Taking Care of Family Relationships

Having made this progress, we decided to move on to look at the couple's relationship with each other, in particular the fact that they had not been out as a couple for several months. Jean and Jack agreed that they used to enjoy going out for a meal together but had stopped doing this when their sitter would no longer look after the children. With encouragement, Jean and Jack decided that their 'homework' for the subsequent week was to invite Jack's mother to mind the children so that they could go out for a meal. Jack's mother agreed to this and even indicated that she would be happy to do so on a fortnightly basis. This took Jack and Jean by surprise. Early in the placement Mrs Saunders looked after the children on several occasions but, after one particularly difficult night when the children had been rude and refused to go to bed, Jean and Jack had sensed her reluctance and felt that it would be unfair to ask her again.

On their first evening out Jack and Jean found it difficult to enjoy themselves. They worried about how the children were behaving in their absence and felt guilty about enjoying themselves. Furthermore they spent the entire evening talking about Jenny and Marty and when they tried to change the subject they had been at a loss to know what to say. They agreed that some preparation was needed before their next evening out. We explored possible ways forward and Jean and Jack eventually elected to talk about the children only until they reached the restaurant. After this they would talk about Jean's aqua-aerobics and Jack's golf. It was wryly suggested that a forfeit should be paid by the first person who mentioned the children after they had arrived at the restaurant!

This plan worked well. Jack and Jean enjoyed their evening and were looking forward to a night at the cinema. They were both relieved that the children had behaved well with their Gran, although they had been particularly difficult both before and after the outing. Consequently Jean was unsure if the pleasure of the break was worth the increase in family stress. She felt guilty about leaving them and wondered if she might be adding to their feelings of insecurity. We acknowledged these very natural feelings and accepted that the children's behaviour indicated that they were, indeed, having some difficulty adjusting to changes in their usual routine. Looking at the children's early history we recognised that their parents' absence could trigger feelings of abandonment from the past (Archer 1999a, 1999b; Hughes 1997). It was felt that the children would benefit from some help to deal with their feelings. Once we had explored ways in which Jack and Jean might do this with the children, they felt more comfortable about talking to the children about their feelings and whence they originated.

Before their next evening out Jean and Jack sat down with the children and talked about their intentions. They told the children that they understood it was difficult for them to trust they would return: this was understandable in view of their experiences of other adults who had abandoned them. Jean and Jack knew that whatever they said the children would not really believe that they were different from these other adults; they might need practice before they could really begin to accept this. To help them, Jean gave the children a photograph of themselves to remind them that they would be coming home. Jean and Jack also prepared an audio-tape in which they talked to the children about some of the good times they had had as a family, reminding them that they were safe and that they would not abandon or hurt them. In addition, Jean lent the children toys from her own childhood, as meaningful transitional objects. Finally, they let the children know that they planned to take them to the park the next day, to spend some time together as a family.

This conversation certainly seemed to reassure Jenny and she said that she would try to behave well for Gran. Perhaps more typically, Marty told Jack and Jean that he did not care if they went out or indeed came back. He said that he would not miss them and that, as Gran let them stay up later, he did not mind at all if they went away for the entire weekend. He barely looked at the photograph when his parents gave it to him. However, after Jack and Jean returned from their night out Mrs Saunders told them that she had heard Marty playing the tape Jean had made and that Jenny had fallen asleep cuddling her mother's old teddy. It seemed obvious that both children had taken comfort from their parents' sensitive understanding of their worries (albeit unconscious). This gave Jack and Jean encouragement that they were on the right track in the task of reparenting their children; they decided to look for further opportunities to empathise with the children over their difficulties with separation and loss.

Fun and Effective Parenting

When Jenny and Marty arose the following morning they were especially difficult. Jean and Jack were expecting this response and were not surprised when Marty reacted badly to being reminded that they were going to the park, saying that he did not want to go, as he would miss his favourite television programme. In stark contrast, Jenny smiled sweetly at Jack and asked him if he had had a good evening out with Mummy. She said she had missed him and hoped she could hold his hand all the way to the park. At the same time she ignored Jean when asked if she had slept well. Jean and Jack, recalling previous discussions at Family Futures, realised that this behaviour was likely to be a result of feelings of abandonment: rather than risk feeling 'rejected' the children were 'rejecting' their parents first.

Reminding themselves of the maxim, 'fear can stop you loving', the parents recalled strategies we had explored to deal with Jenny's distancing behaviours and the need to support each other. Jack told Jenny he was glad that she had missed him and that he would happily hold her hand on the way *back* from the park. However, he had noticed she was having difficulty hearing what Mummy said, so to help her practise being close to Mummy he would really enjoy seeing Jenny hold Mummy's hand on the way *to* the park. Meanwhile Jean began helping Marty become more aware of his difficult feelings. She told Marty she could see that he was angry and wondered if this was about her going out with Daddy last night. She hoped he might get rid of his angry feelings while they were at the park and, in a reassuring tone, she said she was sad that he would miss his favourite television programme. Finally she gave him a hug and suggested that, next time he was going to miss a programme, he might figure out how to ask in an acceptable way for it to be videoed.

On the way to the park, Jenny scowled as she held Jean's hand and Marty continued to complain about his missed television programme. Jack congratulated Jenny warmly on her practising and wondered with good humour whether she might be able to scowl just as well on the return journey. Jean continued to empathise with Marty about his 'problem' and expressed genuine interest in helping him to find a solution in future. As they approached the park the children were becoming argumentative, so Jack and Jean decided to stage a pre-emptive 'argument' about whose turn it was for the swing and about the unfairness of the roundabout being only for children. This reflected their previous visit to the park, when the children had spent the first half-hour arguing. Initially, Jenny and Marty looked on amazed, then they rushed off to play on the roundabout together. Meanwhile Jean and Jack were feeling much happier than they usually did on family trips. They were actually having fun with the children *and* they felt more in control. While this was not the way they had envisaged acting as parents it was certainly more pleasant than constant arguments with the children.

Summary

This vignette highlights a number of key elements of the Family Futures philosophy. First, it demonstrates the need to develop strategies that place parents safely back in the driving seat in the family; this may mean introducing seemingly bizarre humour into family life (Archer 1999b; Delaney 1991; Keck and Kupecky 1995, 2002). It also means tempering parental containment with empathy for the child and the difficulties he is making for himself (Cline 1992; Hughes 1997, 1998; Levy and Orlans 1998). This is not an easy task. It can mean turning traditional parenting approaches on their head, by acting in ways that initially seem strange or nonsensical. To be able to do this genuinely, and with confidence, parents need to feel supported and validated; we therefore offer them high levels of affirmation. At times this may mean telephoning them daily, if we anticipate they may be feeling stressed. When parents speak of occasions when they have 'lost it' with their child we look at the reasons for this, in a spirit not of blame but of working together to identify the problem and considering alternative responses. We see occasions when parents have 'lost it' as opportunities to work towards more effective solutions, not to focus on 'failures'.

Simultaneously, we need to give parents opportunities to express just how 'bad' they feel about how they have interacted with their children and to explore feelings of failure. We help parents consider situations with which they are having especial difficulty and to recognise why these particular circumstances trigger negative responses. Sometimes the child may be setting off feelings from the parent's own past. If this is the case we offer individual counselling time for parents to explore these issues. Often the parent is acting as a 'sponge' for their child's difficult feelings: we then encourage parents to recognise where these feelings belong, with their child, and to respond in a calm and accepting manner. When parents do this they remain connected to their child, while encouraging him to 'own' and manage his feelings. This allows the child opportunities to 'practise' feelings in a safe and nurturing environment (Archer 1999b). Parents can be helped to acknowledge they are doing a great job of getting close to, and tuning into, their child: turning potentially negative experiences into positive ones (Archer 1999b).

Finally, at Family Futures we recognise that reparenting traumatised children is a challenging job requiring long-term commitment; we acknowledge that the road is likely to be a bumpy one. We see our work as being part of an ongoing, reciprocal learning process requiring regular reviews, updates and changes of emphasis in response to the changing needs and feelings of families and children. In this way we aim to provide a 'safe container' for parents, so that they in their turn may 'hold the fort', offering safety and containment to their children (Winnicott 1971).

CHAPTER 13

Hands on Help

Christine Gordon

Hands on Help, our parenting strategies and developmental reparenting programme, forms an integral part of our therapeutic work at Family Futures. We offer this service directly to families, although more usually it forms a significant part of our Intensive Attachment and Follow Up programmes, reflecting our philosophy that parents are essential members of the therapeutic team. Providing effective stategies for managing behaviour is fundamental to the survival of adoptive families and to the provision of repeated, everyday opportunities for healthy change for traumatised children. Behaviour forms the major means of communicating the child's perspective to those closest to them. Viewed in this way, children's behaviour can never be seen as 'bad', merely as a direct expression of their 'inner world', since it understands their current behaviours as representing 'ghosts from the nursery' (Karr-Morse and Wiley 1997), rather than arising from current interpersonal relationships. This approach provides the springboard from which change within adoptive families can occur; it also forms an understanding from which parents and therapists can begin to work together in a real therapeutic partnership to help children heal (Hart and Thomas 2000). From here we can begin to help children recognise parallels between their current behaviour and past, traumatic experiences.

Part of the philosophy of Family Futures is to use our knowledge of children's backgrounds to consider how their behaviours may have helped to keep them safe in unpredictable and chaotic environments. We explain this to children simply, congratulating them on being able to do so and expressing wonder at how such young children could have been so successful in keeping themselves safe. We go on to discuss whether these behaviours are still relevant, when children are not currently being hurt, abandoned or rejected, while acknowledging to them that it may still feel that way. In suggesting alternative ways of acting in current situations we often propose that youngsters 'practise' new behaviours, to test out whether these might be more helpful now. We might suggest, with his agreement, that a child has at least six hugs per day from his parents. We would not insist that he receive the hugs with enjoyment or meaning, initially; rather we tell him that genuine feelings may follow, when he has practised the new behaviour sufficiently for him to assess whether it is more helpful than, for example, tantrums or pushing Mum away.

We feel that it is important to be as frank as possible with children about their difficulties. We talk openly and honestly about difficult behaviours and of how sad we feel about children's stealing, lying, aggression, eating, relationship and friendship problems. This approach is neither punitive nor shaming if done with genuine empathy. Instead it brings issues into the open, making the unspeakable speakable and, with loving encouragement and support, offers the child opportunities to consider alternatives. This in turn challenges children's current cognitive distortions (Siegel 1999) and can eventually lead to alterations in their internal working models and patterns of relating (Schore 1994; Siegel 1999). These issues are explored further in chapters 3 and 4. With Marty we discussed the value of his taking food to reduce his hunger when his birth mother had no money to feed him. We went on to say that we would work with him and his adoptive parents to help him practise getting 'filled up' in more acceptable ways. We considered aloud what Marty might be trying to tell us: for example, that he feels alone and empty. We then wondered if it would be possible to practise letting Mummy give him cuddles to 'fill him up' instead.

Our work takes into consideration that many traumatised children have overwhelming feelings of shame, triggered by abusive and neglectful parenting (Schore 1994, 2001a; Hughes 1997, 2002). During the toddler years, youngsters begin to be socialised by their caregivers. However, to be effective and non-shaming this limit-setting process must quickly be followed by positive engagement, to reassure the child that it is his behaviour and not his being that is inappropriate or unacceptable. Children who have been abused may both have been socialised too severely and not have received corrective positive engagement (Hughes 1997). This impacts on the child at fundamental neurobiological and existential levels (Schore 1994,

2001b). It is essential that we remain aware of this in all our work with children and find ways of communicating with them positively, at non-verbal levels, in order to keep them engaged. This could include reaching out and taking a child's hand or exaggerating facial expressions of sincere concern.

We need to be highly sensitive in our communications with children, and work toward reducing their feelings of shame to less overwhelming levels. Suggesting that Marty continued to take food because he frequently went hungry in his birth family, often not knowing when he would be fed, gently acknowledges and accepts his past. It also enables him to recognise the underlying reasons for his current behaviour and to explore ways of getting his needs met more appropriately. Encouraging his adoptive parents to talk sensitively to Marty about how these feelings still persist, although he now has enough food and regular meal times, promotes positive engagement and healthy attachments (Hughes 1997, 2002) and enhances reflective functioning (Fonagy 1999). We might agree that Jean helps Marty to remember that he no longer needs to take food surreptitiously by providing him with a daily menu and a personal supply of staple food items and by reminding him that he can ask for food at any time. These simple interactions provide opportunities for Marty to feel cared for and special, remind him that he can talk to Mum any time he feels like taking food, and that Mum understands and is actively helping him to alter his behaviour. These are just a few examples of the many, varied strategies we might propose to deal with a particular issue, since we encourage parents to select the most appropriate approach for their child, based on their 'insider knowledge' of his individual needs.

Outlining our Approach

At Family Futures we believe that parents are central to helping children heal the hurts of their early experiences. Hence we place parents at the heart of all of our therapeutic processes. Developing effective parenting strategies forms a key element of our work. Taking as read that adoptive parents have the commitment and skills necessary to be good enough parents, we acknowledge that they may need ongoing help to develop their expertise in ways that allow their child to make best use of the opportunities in his new family. To do this, parents may need to adjust their parenting approach to take into consideration their child's distorted, or disorganised, attachment patterns. They need help to understand that the parenting styles they acquired as securely attached children may not initially be most effective with children with insecure attachment patterns (see also chapters 2, 3 and 4). Conversely, parents whose early attachment experiences were less than optimal may need reassurance that they are unlikely to repeat the cycle of maltreatment, and encouragement to recognise the additional strengths they may have evolved over time (Levy and Orlans 2000).

Clearly, we need to begin from 'where the parents are at', then validate the key role they play in the process of change for their child. To do this we must value and 'hold' parents emotionally (Archer 1999b). We recognise that the journey we want them to take may be difficult; we provide the support and containment to give them courage to begin. In devising individual parenting programmes we also start 'where the children are at', by looking at their early lives and current behaviours: using these to inform our understanding of current functioning. In so doing we acknowledge 'the fear that stops them loving' and then help them move gradually towards accepting 'the love that will stop them fearing'. Therapists and parents work together in seeking to contain and transform overwhelming negative feelings, replicating the transformative parent-infant interactions observed by Target and Fonagy (1996).

Initially, traumatised children are unlikely to understand the origins of their behaviours. In practice they are more likely either to blame their adoptive parents (or others) for their behaviours, or to view them as a confirmation that they are indeed bad and unworthy (Hughes 2002). It is *essential* for parents to recognise this as they begin the task of reparenting their child. It is also vital that parents are given as much information as possible about their child's early experiences and are helped to interpret their meaning for the child in terms of relationships, inner 'road maps' and general developmental processes (see also chapters 3 and 4). This information gives them the building blocks from which to make sense of their child's behaviour and allows them to relate to him with greater understanding and sensitivity. It also reduces the likelihood that parents will blame themselves, or the child, for his difficulties and lessens the chances of parents acting punitively towards him. We saw earlier how Jean and Jack were able to respond to their children's feelings of abandonment and loss appropriately by making connections with their early life experiences. We also saw how they were able to empathise with the children's expression of these feelings in their difficult behaviour, such as Jenny's rejection of Jean and Marty's anger following their parents' first night out together for several months (see previous chapter).

The capacity for empathy lies at the heart of our approach. We emphasise the need to convey this in the way we 'speak' to children through our words and actions – through both verbal and non-verbal communications. We do this primarily through tone of voice and body language, in the subtle ways we act to convey that we are there to help children manage their lives in better ways. On the other hand it is vital that parents should not accept, make excuses for, or condone unacceptable behaviours. Although we try to understand children's behaviours in terms of dealing with past traumas, our aim is to help them develop new patterns of behaviour that open them up to the loving commitment of their adoptive parents. Hence parents are encouraged to let their children learn gently from experience about the consequences of their actions. Children can then be helped to feel comfortable with the loving control of parents whom they can trust will be there for them, and to develop behaviours that make sense in this context.

In summary, our parenting programme aims to:

- heighten parents' awareness of the historical antecedents of children's behaviour

- provide a framework that gives parents opportunities to foster positive relationships, appropriate to their child, using their unique insights into the child's difficulties

- help parents feel that they are supported and contained in the battle *for* their child rather than a battle *with* their child

- put parents in **safe** charge in families

- limit the number of control battles

- give children opportunities to learn from mistakes, by experiencing the consequences of their actions

- provide opportunities for traumatic neurological responses to be replaced by ones that help the child to feel safe, contained and loved (Bernhardt 1992)

- reduce angry or confrontational interactions

- make family life more comfortable and enjoyable for everyone.

We achieve this by helping parents understand where their children are 'coming from' through:

- Informing them about the impact of early experience on the child's understanding of the world. This information needs to include the impact of trauma on the child's psychological, neurological and biological development.

- Providing the fullest possible information about children's early experiences and helping parents make sense of their child's current behaviours.

- Introducing concepts around 'developmental reparenting' and 'thinking toddler'.

- Modelling effective communication strategies in the therapy setting and at home.

- Encouraging parents to 'practise' these approaches and gradually introduce them at home.

- Seeking feedback and adapting strategies, in the light of parents' experience, and providing ongoing support.

Areas explored would include:

- Responding to children with empathy.

- Giving children choices and helping them manage the consequences of their choices.

- Expressing sadness, not anger, when a child makes an inappropriate choice (Cline 1992).

- Positive reframing of negative behaviour by interpreting the behaviour in the light of a child's history and by providing an alternative meaning for it. For example, we might talk to Marty about where his anger has come from, congratulate him on beginning to share these feelings with his parents and marvel at the trust he has that they will be able to help him with his difficult feelings.

- Using developmental reparenting strategies to promote positive interactions. These would include exploring ways of interacting with children at sensory, emotional and interpersonal levels

(Archer 1999b, 1999c; Hughes 1997). For example, a parent may elect to wash a child's hair, if they are reluctant to do it for themselves, thus allowing the child to experience an essential, sensory, attachment experience (Archer 2001a).

- Reducing the number of control battles by having a range of strategies and finding 'win/win' situations (Fearnley and Howe 1999), where parents are in charge no matter what their child does.

Theory and Practice

Current research (Fonagy 1999; Schore 1994, 2001a, 2001b; Siegel 1999) corroborates the pioneering work of John Bowlby (1988) in emphasising that secure attachments and the capacity for learning begin in the first few months of life, through repeated parent-infant interactions. Positive interactions help children feel comfortable with dependence, accept they are loveable and can influence what happens in their world. Sadly, traumatised children internalise a very different set of beliefs about themselves and the world around them: that dependence is unsafe, that they are not loveable and that they have only a limited capacity to impact on their world. Through our developmental reparenting programme we encourage parents to provide children with repeated early nurturing experiences. These help youngsters distinguish between positive parenting and abusive and neglectful parenting: gradually remodelling their inner 'road maps' (see Chapter 4), the neural pathways that form the neurobiological basis for their 'internal working models' (Bowlby 1979). It can be a great relief for children to learn that their behaviours are not about *being* 'bad' and that they are capable of change. It is an equal relief to parents to recognise that these behaviours are expressions of past maltreatment and not an indication that they are doing a bad job as parents.

We do not give children timescales for how long this learning process might take. Instead we tell them that we are happy for them to go on practising for as long as they need. Frequently children will respond well to their 'homework' and are keen to let us know the outcome. They will often remind parents that their 'hugging homework' has not been done and will spontaneously seek cuddles. However, sometimes children respond by withdrawing further; these are frequently the children who have been most controlling and most resistant to parents' attempts at closeness. Here a different and more flexible approach may be more appropriate, although empathy still remains an essential component of our work with these children. We model our sadness that they do not yet feel safe enough to let go of their controlling behaviours and acknowledge how scary and difficult this must be for them. We encourage parents to give similar messages in their day-to-day interactions with their child.

We express sadness about the wonderful opportunities youngsters may be missing and hope it will not be too long before they are able to begin doing things differently. We wonder out loud how much more energy they will have to put to other uses, when they figure out they no longer need to continue struggling for control. We discuss the relief the child will feel when they are truly comfortable with being dependent on parents who can help them to feel secure, and well cared for. We also continue to work with the parents on ways that they might help their child at home, emphasising that, as experts in their child, we should collaborate on approaches that are sensitive to his particular needs. Since the child's difficulties with trust and control stem from disrupted primary attachment relationships, it is vital that adoptive parents are enabled to provide very secure boundaries for their children (Archer 1999b; Thomas 2000).

While it is essential that all children are treated with empathy, it is even more vital for children who continue to challenge, despite parents' best efforts to provide love and security. These children are likely to have had early, distressing experiences, which led them to develop a deep-seated feeling of worthlessness. They are often particularly sensitive to expressions of anger and disapproval, which further undermine their fragile sense of identity and self-worth. We therefore work hard to help parents maintain positive connections with their children. For example, we encourage parents to follow a brief expression of disapproval of their child's behaviour with a quick hug, providing 'interactive repair' of the attachment relationship temporarily broken by the disapproval, or socialisation, phase (Hughes 1997, 2002; Schore 1994).

Parents need to be encouraged to follow disapproval with expressions that confirm their child's essential self-worth and their love and commitment. In this way the child is more able to receive the message that his behaviour is unacceptable yet his parents continue to love him. This approach mirrors the way good enough parents socialise their toddlers: serving to remind us that traumatised children who have missed positive early parenting experiences may need to 'go back and do it again', this time in the context of a positive, loving parent-child relationship (Archer 2001a). In this way children are able to resolve early traumas through repeated opportunities to experience, at a deep body level, that others can be there for them and help them (Bernhardt 1992).

Principles into Practice

Before we begin, I ask parents to prepare a diary of life with their child. I ask them to make this as detailed as possible and to include all areas where there are difficulties. It is then my task to devise an individual parenting programme that addresses issues identified by parents. I try to give a number of different suggestions for each issue, recommending that these suggestions be used flexibly, since many traumatised children are highly skilled at sabotaging strategies designed to help them, but which they may perceive as threatening (Keck and Kupecky 2002). To be effective these strategies depend very much on parents being able to remain sensitive and loving with their children: without significant support this can be very difficult. This underlies my previous emphasis (Chapter 12) on the need to provide long-term support, alongside encouragement to parents to take care of themselves.

From Jean and Jack's diary, and from subsequent conversations with them without the children present, the following appeared to be the major issues for the family:

- temper tantrums
- trust and control
- cause and effect thinking
- stealing
- school/peer relationships
- negative interactions
- rejection of parents' love
- lack of fun in their lives.

Jean, Jack and I explored these issues in various ways.

Creating Winning Situations

We looked at strategies that create 'win-win' situations: considering those where they could thank their children, regardless of what they actually did. For example, we discussed this concept in relation to Marty's tantrums. Although Jean and Jack were becoming confident in cradling Marty through his tantrums, there would be times when this was just not feasible. As an alternative, we discussed encouraging Marty to scream louder, or longer, to express his feelings. If Marty continued to scream Jean could thank him, sincerely, for doing as she had asked, or for letting her know how angry he felt. If, on the other hand, Marty were able to communicate his distress in more acceptable ways, Jean would then congratulate him on coping well with his feelings. Jean might choose to thank Marty for having enough trust in her to show his most difficult feelings. Again, if Marty stopped screaming, he could be congratulated for figuring out that he no longer needed to scream to be heard in this family. Either way, Marty would feel more contained and Jean would be in safe charge.

Jean and Jack, by conveying their messages with empathetic and encouraging body language and voice modulation, could also help Marty to consider different, more positive, responses to situations and to begin to alter the 'road maps' and neurological connections that maintained his negative behaviours. Traumatised children often demonstrate poor cause and effect thinking (Cline 1992; Levy and Orlans 1998), their early lives having provided them with limited experiences of predictability or self-agency. Marty's tantrums often appeared to be triggered by frustration or change. Understanding this, his parents' tolerance and gentle explanations could go some way towards altering his perceptions of the world. Providing Marty with controlled experiences of accepting responsibility could both pre-empt tantrums and reinforce neural and cognitive connections between actions and outcomes, enhancing his self-esteem and self-agency.

Trust and Control Issues

Our strategies take into account the fundamental nature of children's difficulties, their need to be in control and their difficulties with trust. We aim to offer children real opportunities to experience parents being in charge and for this to feel safe. For example, Jean taking charge, either through verbal or physical containment, during Marty's tantrum allowed him to experience safe parental control. In time, Marty began to feel more comfortable with himself, as he became less overwhelmed by his feelings and increasingly saw his parents as a reliable source of comfort. Gently cradling a child through a tantrum and encouraging him to express his feelings provides him with opportunities to experience control as safe, and thereby establishes trust (Welch 1988; Archer 1999c). This process is explored in more detail in *Introduction* (see also *Developmental Reparenting* below).

Consequences of Actions

Children must be given ample opportunities to discover that their behaviours have real consequences. This is often very difficult for caring parents like Jean and Jack, who naturally wish to be protective and ameliorate the negative outcomes of their children's behaviours. Here again we lead parents towards a greater understanding of their child's need for improved self-agency; this can only be learned through trial and error. We encourage parents to give children choices, while bearing in mind safety issues and their child's individual capabilities: this allows children opportunities to face, and learn to deal with, real-life consequences of their behaviour. Thus, when Marty next stole from Jack, he had either to repay the money stolen with interest (similar to adults who steal and are fined, or people who borrow money), or repay the worth of stolen goods by washing the car for a specified period (similar to Community Service). As the adult, Jack, rather than Marty, decided on the nature of the consequence and the relevant 'interest' or 'Community Service'.

It is in a child's best interests to learn the lessons of real life sooner rather than later, when these behaviours have become entrenched and they have to deal with the much tougher consequences of the adult world (Cline 1992). We encouraged Jack to express sadness rather than anger when Marty had to wash the car. Jack also reminded Marty that he would have further opportunities to make more helpful choices in the future, if he were tempted to steal again. Jack expressed genuine hope that Marty would make a more helpful choice next time. A 'win-win' situation is maintained if, when Marty continues to steal, Jean and Jack are genuinely able to thank him for being helpful around the house, or for letting them know he is still struggling with his feelings.

Selective Strategies

It is important that parents work only on issues with which they feel comfortable and which they can realistically and successfully tackle. For example, school can be a contentious area and parents often try to help their child with the difficulties they have with schoolwork, peers and teachers. Unfortunately these are areas where parents have little direct influence and where strategies to help are unlikely to succeed. We therefore suggest that most school issues are best left to teachers and other educational professionals and explored during therapeutic sessions. Network meetings with relevant lay and professional participants would also be considered. Parents are also advised to approach one area of concern at a time at home: perhaps starting with an 'easy' option, one that they feel comfortable about tackling and winning. An example might be asking the child to tidy his bedroom, since this is not immediately crucial to the comfort of other family members. Removing pressures to conform, both in terms of time and safe outcomes, gives parents and children time to consider and adjust to this new 'house rule': giving them confidence in their new found skills and enabling them to see that change is indeed possible.

Promoting Positives

Underpinning all our strategies is the philosophy of promoting positive interactions between parents and children. Parenting children who challenge every decision, no matter how trivial, is no fun and parents often respond to these challenges with understandable anger. Earlier I described how we encourage parents to create opportunities to have fun with their children and to deal with their own inevitable anger in ways that do not impact negatively upon them. However, avoiding negative interactions is not in itself enough. Having fun with children, especially 'rough-and-tumble', has been shown to have a positive psychobiological impact (Panksepp 1998, 2001); Holden (1993) explores the health-enhancing properties of laughter in *Laughter is the Best Medicine*. Enjoyment can also lead to the development of healthier patterns of behaviour, improve self-esteem and develop a sense of belonging (Hage 1995). Furthermore, from recent research (Schore 1994, 2001a, 2001b; Siegel 1999), we know that helping children develop healthier attachment patterns can have reciprocal effects on their neurological development, by helping them develop increased sensory, emotional, bodily and cognitive awareness and integration (see also chapters

3 and 4). Thus, providing strategies that are both fun and effective can have significant impacts at somato-sensory, behavioural, and neurobiological organisational levels: it helps children replace the language of fear with the language of love.

Developmental Reparenting

Many children who have experienced early abuse, neglect or abandonment fear and reject parents' attempts at closeness. Like Marty, they may have developed 'hostile' disorganised attachment patterns (Lyons-Ruth, Bronfman and Atwood 1999), using anger, aggression and hyperactivity as a way of trying to keep parents at bay. Alternatively they may have developed more withdrawing, 'helpless' patterns (Lyons-Ruth *et al.* 1999), typified by Jenny's rejection of Jean. While the underlying feelings informing these behavioural choices are understandable in terms of their disorganised mental representations, they are neither healthy for children nor conducive to the development of healthier parent-child relationships. Giving children copious opportunities for 'good baby experiences' is an effective way of helping youngsters, who are understandably wary of touch, become comfortable with intimacy and safe containment. 'Good baby experiences' allow parents to nurture their child in ways that go back to early mother-infant interactions. We would, for example, encourage regular night time 'cuddles' with rocking, stroking, singing and comforting physical closeness.

Part of our work with parents is educational. Helping them understand the impact of early trauma and loss of early nurturing experiences can allow adopters to recognise the need to help their children 'go back and do the baby stage again': this time in the context of a loving and nurturing family environment. Developmental reparenting (Archer 1999c) is a very potent way to help children gain these reparative nurturing experiences (see also *Introduction*). In the early stages of our work with the Saunders family, Jean and Jack expressed reservations about using family cradling as part of the developmental reparenting approach at home. They were concerned that they did not have the necessary skills and that they would, in fact, make things worse for the children: pointing to Marty's aggression and Jenny's avoidance to justify these fears. While respecting their point of view, work during the Intensive Week (see Chapter 9) helped Jean and Jack feel more comfortable with family cradling and the concepts of 'reparenting the baby within' and 'thinking toddler' (Archer 2001a) that underlie developmental reparenting.

It was agreed that Jenny would benefit from some intense nurturing sessions and that these would be carried out at home, as part of the daily routine. We introduced Jenny to the idea of having regular times during the day when she could practise being close to her parents. She was asked to sit between her adoptive parents, as they spoke of their sadness that she still found it so difficult to accept cuddles from them. She was then invited to practise being close by being held on Jean's lap, with her legs across Jack's, whilst Jack supported Jean with an encouraging arm across her shoulder. At first Jenny had some difficulty establishing and maintaining eye contact with her parents. Jean and Jack continued to talk to Jenny about their love for her, and their commitment to helping her feel more comfortable with closeness, with warmth, patience and empathy. Her parents were gradually able to help Jenny feel more comfortable with closeness, express her feelings and experience their ability to respond to them sensitively.

Marty originally experienced family cradling during therapeutic sessions in the Intensive Week. He also benefited from being held at home, when he had tantrums and there was no other way to keep him safely contained. His parents demonstrated that they were able to contain his strong feelings and keep everybody safe. His anger soon gave way to sadness as he sobbed, telling his parents how scared he was that they would 'give him away, just like everyone else'. Prior to this Jean and Jack had often resorted to shouting at Marty, or sending him to his room. Neither of these strategies was effective in helping Marty. Shouting seemed to trigger terrifying feelings from the past; 'time out' in his room left him feeling rejected and abandoned (see also *Introduction*). These feelings inevitably resulted in a worsening of his behaviour. Conversely, gentle cradling helped Marty feel safe and demonstrated clearly that his parents could be there for him and contain even his worst feelings and behaviour. Gradually Marty's need for tantrums lessened, as he began to believe that this time he had parents who could continue to love him and would not 'give him away'.

The Saunders – Their Journey to Become a Family

When Jean and Jack Saunders were referred to Family Futures their children had a range of behaviour problems that were causing difficulties. We asked them to complete our 'Day in the Life' diary (see also Chapter 7). We then devised an individual parenting programme based on the principles discussed, employing a variety of strategies designed to put Jean and Jack in loving charge within their family. We supported them with regular telephone calls as well as regular therapeutic updates: thus the programme was integrated within our ongoing, therapeutic work with the family. It was also supplemented by 'networking' with people who played a significant part in their family life. For example, we arranged a meeting to discuss strategies with Jack's mother, to cover occasions when she was caring for the children, embracing the notion that childraising is a global, rather than an individual, family responsibility (Freeman 2002). In this way we could continue to develop the consistent approach to parenting Marty and Jenny that is so vital to the process of change. The journey that the Saunders family was embarking upon had had a very bumpy start. They were aware that the path would continue to be difficult and that, at times, they would feel that they had been cast ashore on foreign, or dangerous, soil. However, we hoped that we had provided some signposts that would help them find their way toward calmer waters.

Our parenting programme, intensive therapy and ongoing support package generally forms a two-year programme that aims to provide families with the basic elements for establishing the foundations of secure attachments. We are aware that this is not the whole story and that children will continue to experience difficulties, especially at crucial stages in their lives, such as during adolescence. Adoption, and supporting a family's healing process, is truly a lifetime commitment.

CHAPTER 14

Difficulty with Learning or Learning to be Difficult?

Griselda Kellie-Smith

Introduction

How we learn, and particularly how children learn, fascinates most of us. Why do some children learn so easily and others find learning so difficult? As a child and young adult I had great difficulty learning to read and to spell. This eventually led me to teach children who struggle: some because of dyslexia, dyspraxia, autism or attention deficit hyperactive disorder (ADHD), many because they were traumatised, had attachment difficulties and no secure base from which to explore. This profoundly affected their learning. When nothing quite fits or makes sense, trying to sequence ideas to follow a 'thinking map' feels terrifying. Terror causes mental shut-down: so here too 'fear can stop you loving' to learn. When it seems as if everyone else can read, gather their thoughts, and explain what they mean in short sentences that make sense, children who cannot do so start to think there is something wrong with them: they feel ashamed.

Given empathy, understanding and time, traumatised children and adults can learn. It certainly took empathic, interested, patient tutors and colleagues to help me fight my shame and boost my confidence sufficiently to complete degrees and diplomas that have supported my own curiosity about learning. As we explore together the puzzle of attachment and developmental learning, children are our best teachers. Traumatised children teach us what they had to do in order to survive. They often behave in ways that are difficult, and in ways that make learning difficult. As we work with them, their adoptive parents and their teachers, we try to understand their individual, developmental, learning maps. We look for therapeutic and practical routes to help their journey feel safer.

Learning to Live Together

Learning was at the heart of what the Saunders family was doing together. Until Jean and Jack got to know their children, they had no idea they were severely traumatised, so their plans to learn to love them, care for them and teach them seemed straightforward. By the time they met Family Futures they were aware this was not so. They knew how difficult it was for Jenny and Marty to learn to trust them, and recognised the difficulties they were having as parents in coming to terms with that. They were beginning to wonder if the children would ever learn to accept their support, their help and their love – and what about school?

Jean and Jack had investigated schools so they would be well prepared for the child they hoped to adopt. When social services told them that Jenny and Marty could be placed with them, they felt pleased they had done their homework. They were confident Collett Wood Primary School fitted their philosophy about children and education. The children could start school as soon as they had settled at home. Jean and Jack knew they would have a lot of work to do learning about each other, but felt it would be best for the children to be in school where they would start to make friends. As Jackson points out (2001) education has often been disrupted for children in care, and is often not seen as a priority. Jenny and Marty had missed out on schooling because of their numerous moves, so getting started at Collett Wood seemed important.

Jenny was quiet the day they went to buy lunch boxes, bags, and new shoes. Marty could hardly contain his excitement, making decisions and changing his mind quicker than Jean could believe possible. Jenny seemed 'away in a dream' for much of the morning but was firm about what she wanted, giving Jean a frighteningly intense stare when she suggested the shoes Jenny had chosen might not be good in the rain. Jenny swung her bag triumphantly as they walked back to the car. While Marty chattered to Jean, Jenny walked alone but within earshot. Jean was surprised how tired the expedition had left her, and later was puzzled by feeling terribly sad, when she had expected to feel excited about the children going to their carefully chosen school. Jenny was more distant than usual at bedtime and was bad-tempered with Marty as he danced about, chattering incessantly about his lunch box being the best and asking repeatedly whether there would be animals at school. Jack asked Jenny if she was feeling worried about starting at a new school. 'No!' she said with a brittle smile, 'I'm going to make friends.'

Learning to Live at School

When the children were finally in bed, Jean and Jack collapsed. Coping with the children's intense, undigested emotions was exhausting but they continued to think about school. Collett Wood had a good reputation and good SATS results, so the teaching must be good. They liked its atmosphere and teaching style, with children working in small, co-operative groups. The lunch-time staff seemed friendly. They wondered about collecting the children from the playground: the headteacher told them it was calmer for everyone if parents did not come into school. Instead they should make an appointment to talk to their child's teacher. They realised they were feeling quite nervous, as if they would be starting school on Monday! Jean hoped she would be able to get enough idea of how the children were settling from talking to them on the way home.

Initially the children said nothing about school. After half-term Jean made appointments to see their teachers. Both gave similar messages. They commented that it was early days; Jenny and Marty were learning routines, getting to know the other children and the teachers. Marty, in particular, was finding it difficult to sit still and concentrate. His teacher felt he was an energetic boy but would settle as he got to know them better. Jenny's teacher sometimes wondered what was behind that 'far-away' look. After each meeting Jean came home feeling on edge but she brushed that aside as the children again demanded her attention. Their behaviour at home was definitely becoming more difficult.

Traumatised children struggle with the intimacy of becoming part of a new family, yet paradoxically they also struggle with being at school, alone. At school it is easier to look as if they are 'fine', so teachers can easily miss the struggle they are having. Teachers are trained to see the positive in their pupils, to 'catch them being good', so children can struggle for a while before any alarm bells sound. Parents are children's best barometers. They are very sensitive to their children's anxieties and stresses and it is often a relief to them when the team asks 'Is Marty struggling at school? It must be so hard for him given his difficulty with allowing adults to be in charge.'

Learning and Getting to Know

Adoptive parents think a lot about their children. As they come to understand that their difficult behaviour is a consequence of their efforts to survive, they begin to understand how hard it is for their children to take in the good things they are trying to teach them. The dictionary defines 'learning' as 'getting to know', which is what families are busy with: learning about each other. It can be a task that feels too difficult to do alone. Adoptive parents need support to enable them to reach their traumatised children in ways that are different from conventional parenting; they negotiate steep learning curves (see chapters 12 and 13). If the strategies start to work at home, what about school? Teachers know a great deal about learning but to make sense of helping traumatised children to learn, they need to know a child has experienced acute, developmental distress and what triggers are most provocative. Adoptive parents quickly become experts on their damaged children but everyone involved needs to think collaboratively in order to support each child as effectively as possible.

The Legacy of Trauma

Chamberlain (1987) explains that babies in the womb build up behavioural memories, held in their bodies. Janus (1997) stresses the importance of early experiences, including the neonatal period, in establishing foundations for an individual's relationship with the world. Karr-Morse and Wiley (1997) remind us that 'all our senses are fully installed and are being test driven pre-natally' (p.51), including primitive emotional memories directly linked to the mother's emotions. *In utero,* babies learn a great deal about how safe their world is through their mother's emotional state and at birth they recognise her heartbeat, smell and voice tone (Brazelton 1992). Babies are designed to recognise these familiar characteristics as a source of safety when distressed. If a mother cannot protect her baby or, worse still, is the source of his terror, the infant faces a terrible dilemma; he is left with intense feelings that are neither contained nor digested; he remains 'dysregulated' (Hughes 2002). In order to survive, the baby has to find ways of dealing with these dysregulated feelings. This is where he may learn the beginnings of being 'difficult'. Drawing on the work of Damasio, Schore, Siegel and others, Robin Balbernie (2001) states that 'when the caregiving relationship is persistently compromised so too is the future life of the child' (p.247). Even at this very young age he is learning not to trust but to be either hypervigilant or shut down (Karr-Morse and Wiley 1997); very often these distressed children feel intense shame. This is a truly damaging legacy.

When we are distressed we have three options: to fight, flee or freeze. Little children in the care of terrifying parents cannot win a fight; they have no one to run to, so they flee to their lonely inner world, where they remain aroused and hypersensitive; or else they freeze. In these states, they have little hope of real learning. As Perry (1999) contends:

> This is particularly true when considering the learning experiences of the traumatized child, who may be sitting in a classroom in a persistent state of arousal and anxiety, or dissociated. In either case, the child is essentially unavailable to process efficiently the complex cognitive information being conveyed by the teacher. This principle, of course, extends to other kinds of learning, social and emotional. (p.23)

To learn we need the 'secure base' of which Bowlby (1988) talked, from which to venture out into the world with curiosity and interest. Hughes (2002) tells us that a child will do his best but

> not having a caregiver to serve as a 'safe haven', he tries to rely on his own poorly developed capacities for regulation. When these capacities fail, symptoms of post-traumatic stress disorder ensue. (p.1)

Perry (1999) helps us to understand that although traumatised children often seem bright and 'street-wise', they have great difficulty making sense of new information for which a state of attentive calm is needed:

> Children in a state of fear retrieve information differently than children who feel calm. We are all familiar with test anxiety. Imagine what life would be like if all experiences evoked the persisting emotion of anxiety. If a child in the specific moment is very fearful, whatever information is stored in cortical areas is inaccessible. (p.24)

We now know how important attuned interactions between baby and mother are for the maturation of the emotional and social brain (Siegel 1999). In the interactive 'dance', the mother attunes to the baby's strong and often frightening feelings and processes them before offering them back, digested, understood and safe. This attuned interaction of affect is filled with eye contact, laughter, touch, understanding and joy and is a vital ingredient in a baby's development (Stern 1985). Neither Jenny nor Marty were taught that 'dance'. Neither of them knew the security of what Siegel (1999) describes as 'feeling felt', being deeply understood. They both had to put their creative energy into surviving. Their legacy of trauma taught them ways of behaving that made intimacy and trust impossible. Did they have to learn to be difficult in order to survive? Winnicott (1984) identified that acting out could be a good sign, indicating children fighting for their sanity and not giving up. However, it takes very special parenting skills to keep everyone safe and sane!

Although Jean and Jack had nagging doubts about how things were going at school, they were still shocked to hear, at the school open evening, that Jenny's teachers did not think she was very bright or able. They had wondered about Marty, with his short attention span, but Jenny was reading well and bringing homework back regularly. She did not like help with her work but that was how she was with everything; she appeared fiercely independent. Jean and Jack were worried to hear the school was sometimes barely coping with Marty's behaviour and very sad to hear Jenny had no friends. They felt angry. Why had the teachers not told them sooner? They felt frightened. Would they be able to help these difficult children they were learning to care about so deeply? They felt sad. They felt exhausted and defeated.

Working Together

The next day Jean discussed the open evening with the Family Futures team. Jenny and Marty were probably testing their teachers. Marty was behaving aggressively while Jenny was 'switching out'. They were probably both reacting to triggers from their histories that teachers had no way of recognising. Jean and Jack felt a mixture of anger and sadness that their children had had to learn such negative behaviours in order to survive. It was agreed to focus on school during the next follow-up session and that both children would have a brief educational evaluation to obtain a clearer picture of their strengths, struggles and learning styles. The next therapy day began with a discussion with the whole family about school difficulties. The team leader told the children their parents were pleased they had been getting to school every day but thought they were finding some things at school really difficult: today the job was to talk about that. Parents and children would start off separately, then everyone would get together to think about what might help the children with learning, with expressing anger and with making friends.

Jean and Jack were reminded that they were key players in their children's drama. They were encouraged to acknowledge their support of the children as they began to glimpse their terror and rage about their early history. They made a list of the positive changes they had helped to make happen, and another about their school concerns. It was agreed a team member should ask to observe the children in school and meet with their teachers to hear their concerns and explain the rationale for the strategies Family Futures was suggesting. This would involve an explanation of disordered attachment and some information about specific triggers for Marty and Jenny. The next step would be a meeting for parents, teachers and Family Futures to share concerns and strategies and decide whether a full educational assessment by an educational psychologist would be needed.

Educational Evaluation

We had agreed to look at Jenny and Marty's learning styles. How would they cope with testing using the Aston Index (a test for diagnosing written language difficulties)? Jenny went first; she looked anxious as she wrote her name and started to decorate it; she avoided eye contact and seemed remote. She relaxed a little as she tackled the practical tasks: she even managed eye contact and laughed when she found she was playing 'peepo' through a hole in her paper. However, her anxiety shot up again when asked to write a short story. Jenny had written an imaginative story about 'Bruise' during the Intensive Week, but now she was being tested she felt paralysed. She had 'no idea what to write' about. When it was suggested she could draw first, this did not help. When the therapist suggested they draw together on a big sheet of paper, Jenny sat, watching. At last, seeing a hedgehog appear and start 'walking' across the page towards her she said, 'I know!' and was off. She wrote a quirky, dark tale about a hedgehog who would not come out of his hiding place until he thought of ways to camouflage himself. When he did come out, he was not recognised by another hedgehog because his camouflage was so good, but he was sad. Jenny worked really hard at her writing; by the time she had completed half the remaining sub-tests, she had run out of energy. Far from appearing 'not very bright', Jenny had high scores on the tests giving measures of general intelligence. What were striking were her anxiety level, her moments of 'floating off' and her lack of stamina. She was pleased to receive feedback that she had written a really interesting story that seemed to say a lot about feelings. The therapist noted how pictures in her head seemed to help with story writing and Jenny smiled.

While Jenny had a session playing with puppets and thinking about friendship, Marty tackled the Aston Index. He enjoyed drawing a man, but rushed, so omitted details he might have represented if not so keen to see what else was on offer. He enjoyed 'games', but his attention span was short, reducing his score. He found the early spellings 'easy', but quickly struggled, became angry and wanted to stop. He got off his chair and rolled around the floor. He demanded the fighting sand-tray men when faced with the prospect of writing a story, or even a few sentences. Ball-catching, telescope-making and bead-threading focused him enough to attempt to write. He did this in collaboration with the therapist. They took turns to write sentences. This gave him the opportunity to copy words he noticed the therapist had used. His story remained concrete, short and ended abruptly with the death of one of the fighting men. Marty's results indicated how difficult he would find sitting still when tackling formal schoolwork. Given practical tasks he could follow instructions accurately and his anxiety level lowered dramatically. His scores were uniformly low for his age, suggesting it was Marty, not Jenny, who was not so bright. Marty's learning difficulties could be the result of the defensive processes he needed to use as a young child (see Chapter 4). This would certainly explain some of his aggressive behaviour and his tendency to crawl under desks. These behaviours could also be due to hyperarousal and hypervigilance for current, environmental triggers, or the activation of painful or frightening memories (see below and Chapter 4).

After lunch Jean and Jack heard how the children had fared. Jenny did not want to talk but clutched her hedgehog story. Marty rushed to show Jean his picture of a man but pulled it back to add a sword 'so he can fight'. Jenny was congratulated on finding how to get started with her writing and for being able to say how scared she felt in the playground without a friend. She gave her story to Jack. She looked puzzled when told the tests showed she was good at thinking but nodded at the suggestion that she found it difficult to think at school. Marty was praised for being able to slow down and have another go at copying shapes and for noticing words to copy from the therapist's sentences that helped him to write. They were told about the plan for a Family Futures visit to their teachers, to think about ways to help with their learning, with difficult-to-manage feelings and with making friends.

The team discussed together why Marty and Jenny were finding school and learning difficult. Marty's anger might be erupting when he sensed work was getting too difficult to understand. Jenny might be closing down her feelings when anxious about not coping with work or with making contact with other children. This had resulted in her teachers' assessment of her as 'not very bright': she had persuaded them to accept, unchallenged, her evaluation of herself. In addition, both children were struggling to learn that Jean and Jack are not like their birth parents: they would help them with whatever they did not understand, at home and at school. They were having the greatest difficulty learning to trust and some difficulty with school learning. Were they also in the process of learning to be difficult? The school seemed to be suggesting there were real problems brewing.

Sometimes we need a more detailed and focused educational assessment. When we do we ask our educational psychologist, Richard Lansdown, to see children to help us obtain a clearer understanding of how they are learning, what makes sense and what is causing anxiety. The more information that can be gathered from school, doctor, parents and the team, the better the assessment will be. The educational psychologist can refine his choice of tests to focus on what the blocks to learning may be. For instance, many children have poor memories. Traumatised children may not want to remember (Mollon 1998). They have often learned to survive by remaining in a constant state of 'red alert' which takes up large amounts of attention capacity (Perry 1999). They may also find sequencing instinctively hard due to their early chaotic experiences in birth families. Far too often these children are overwhelmed by the legacies of their early trauma. Somehow they have managed their anxieties well enough to be able to survive. To become creative thinkers, and effective learners, they now need sensitive, informed help from deeply committed parents and teachers. A full educational assessment can help draw a clearer map.

Overlapping Learning Difficulties

Getting a clearer idea of children's strengths and difficulties is invaluable when planning how best to encourage and support them. We are becoming increasingly aware that many of the difficulties that traumatised, insecurely attached children have with learning overlap with the difficulties most commonly experienced by children with learning disabilities such as dyslexia, dyspraxia, ADHD and mild autism. These include processing problems, difficulties with memory and concentration, poor sense of self, difficulty with social skills, fear of failure and disabling shame. For instance, Marty and Jenny shared many underlying difficulties from the long list below:

- shame
- fear of failure
- hypervigilance
- hypersensitivity
- dissociation
- lack of trust
- inability to reflect
- impulsivity
- need to control
- focusing and concentration
- short attention span
- distractibility (of self and others)
- sitting still
- understanding boundaries
- making transitions
- cause and effect
- learning from mistakes
- learning by imitation
- coping with intense feelings
- following instructions
- dealing with authority
- learning to read
- spelling

- sequencing
- learning mathematical tables.

A Visit to School

The Collett Wood teachers welcomed a visit from one of the Family Futures therapists. They found the Aston results helpful. Jenny's teacher was interested in her story about the hedgehog but checked if she had had help because it was better than anything produced at school. At Family Futures Jenny had the undivided attention of an adult and time to explore what would release her from her shut-down state and get her started: impossible in a large class. We thought about what might help her manage her flagging energy and bring her gently back when she 'floats off'. Because Jenny had issues around being abandoned and ignored, it was agreed that 'time-out' would not be helpful (see *Introduction*). Instead 'time-in', close to the teacher, doing something useful and focused would be a supportive way of keeping her engaged. Because of her difficulties with friendship, Jenny would be asked to do those tasks with Alex, a friendly, easy-going girl, likely to help Jenny learn some of the friendship skills she needs. It was agreed to stay in touch so that these suggestions could be monitored, adjusted and celebrated. Marty's teacher had recognised he was struggling with some things but not across the board. She would observe him carefully to see if his anger was directly linked to his capacity to cope with the task in hand. She found it helpful to have more information about his lack of trust. She wondered if he would find learning any easier as he began to find a more secure base in his life.

Having observed Jenny and Marty in school and talked to their teachers, a list of proposed strategies was sent to Jean, Jack and the school. After discussing it together, the whole team felt the following would best support the children in their learning:

- a full educational assessment for both Jenny and Marty by the Family Futures educational psychologist, since there was very little information about the children's development, and the initial, brief evaluations had surprised their teachers

- a diary to go between school and home, to record any concerns, together with something specific, clear and positive about each child, each day

- Jean to telephone the teachers once a week to check in

- a list of 'Strategies to Try' (see below)

- 'time-in' for Jenny, as described

- 'time-in' for Marty to include achievable, useful tasks close to his teacher's desk

- feedback for both children on what is working and what needs to change: Marty's feedback to focus on anger management and Jenny's on friendship.

Strategies to Try – In Collaboration with Teachers

Sometimes children's behaviour is so challenging that the adults caring for them use up all their energy just trying to manage them. It can be easy to miss their struggles with learning, yet when these struggles are not recognised, behaviour can further deteriorate. Having a child who is not coping with school is an isolating experience, and often parents feel inadequate; children frequently echo these feelings. Beneath the defiant bravado, the clowning, the bullying or the timid, anxious, over-sensitive 'mouse', there is an isolated, hurting child. Hence we need to bring teachers, parents and children together in our search for effective ways of teaching children who find learning difficult and for whom learning to be difficult has become a necessary defence. In particular, children need help to fill the gaps in their global developmental learning and to utilise their strengths to support their difficulties. Some of the most useful strategies we use are:

- humour and kindness

- staying connected, genuinely curious

- challenging children to do well – with encouragement

- giving unconventional rewards for staying on task for specified length of time

- creating opportunities for movement, such as taking a message to another class or making time to stretch, swing or roll. A short exercise break can be helpful for the whole class, not just the struggling child (Panksepp 1999)

- offering two choices, both of which are acceptable to the adult, to help with cause and effect and boundary setting

- being clear about consequences: keeping them contingent, not punitive

- giving occasional unexpected rewards, to keep the child thinking

- using paradoxical logic to keep the child thinking and out of habit-forming mode

- providing help with learning about boundaries

- giving feedback to support learning

- encouraging the child to think of ways to support his learning

- multi-sensory teaching to encourage all possible learning routes and interconnections

- modelling making mistakes as a vital piece of learning

- using 'Circle Time' to encourage thoughtful peer-interaction

- using specific encouragement – 'I like the bit when the hedgehog realised...' and following up with a question like 'What do you think he wants to do next?'

- 'time in' rather than 'time out' – keeping the child connected, not isolated

- checking with the child that he understands what he is being asked to do, why and for how long

- being clear about the timetable and the next half-hour. Help child make personalised timetable

- giving ten minute, then five minute, warnings before transitions: offering short, supportive commentary on what is going to happen

- giving choice time at the end of the day as reward for achieving personal target

- offering 'time allowed to move about' as a reward for a task well done

- posting a sheet of 'ways to deal more effectively with anger' and encouraging the child to add his own ideas

- helping the child identify what he is most hypersensitive about and supporting his efforts to protect himself

- giving sensitive feedback when child dissociates, helping him know when he 'goes' and encouraging him to make choices about reconnecting. Encouraging use of body awareness to support choices about reconnecting and to help him feel anchored

- creating ten minutes of reflection time at the end of the day for the class to connect with the teacher and each other.

Transition to Secondary School

For Jenny the next step will be from primary to secondary school. Most children find this stressful: there are massive changes to be negotiated, all needing flexible thinking. For those children lacking the cognitive and behavioural organisation conferred by early secure attachments (Solomon and George 1999a), the lack of a 'secure home base' in secondary school as they move from classroom to classroom, and teacher to teacher, can be overwhelming. As well as fear of the unknown (common to all), for adopted children, moving can frequently trigger all the old terrifying memories, beginning a destructive negative spiral. Hence the last 18 months of primary school are an enormously important time to undertake as much repair work as is realistic. Children need as solid a belief in themselves as possible; they need to believe in themselves as learners; to believe themselves valuable in their own right is even more important.

Early in the summer term, before Jenny moves to her secondary school, Jean and Jack will visit and talk to the head of Year 7, Jenny's tutor and the special needs co-ordinator to discuss Jenny's needs and what is likely to support her. This visit will give them an opportunity to get a clearer picture of what life will be like for Jenny, what extra activities will be on offer and how the lines of communication work, so they can feel able to contact teachers quickly if necessary. It will also help them feel more secure in supporting Jenny as she explores her anxieties.

'Homework' and Fun

While school is important, home is even more so. Traumatised, insecurely attached children have missed out on so much safe, playful interactive learning with their parents. Gradually, as Jenny and Marty begin to trust some of the attunement between themselves and their adoptive parents, so they can begin to take the risk of engaging in games that help to develop emotional communication. Many of the gently physical games that we play naturally with young children can be enjoyed at several levels of intimacy. Most children love hide-and-seek, and being found has a powerful message for an abandoned child. Rocking games, rolling, wriggling, face-pulling, 'Grandmother's footsteps' and 'Simon says' help with co-ordination, balance and following instructions (Archer 1999a, 1999b). They also help children catch up on the eye contact, touch, joy and laughter they missed as babies and thus provide essential affect modulation experiences (Buckwalter and Schneider 2002). Thus, 'developmental reparenting' (Archer 1999c) is essential, interactive 'repair work' for traumatised children within adoptive families.

Music is also enormously supportive to many children: from creating a rap that communicates difficult feelings, to exploring how many different sounds can be made without getting up. Banging drums, or coaxing the softest sound from the same instrument can encourage connections and memories that were buried in a deep, safe place. The musical 'conversations' children have with their parents are fun and can be a subtle, moving experience, as both parents and children take in the attunement the children missed as babies. Music is healing and a powerful transmitter of feelings and ideas (James 1989; Siegel 1999; Smith and Pennells 1995).

Fine Tuning

Sally Goddard (1996) and Peter Blythe, at the Institute for Neuro-Physiological Psychology (INPP), describe very focused remedial work based on infantile reflexes that have either failed to switch off after birth or have not fully matured. These can result in subtle neuro-developmental delays that leave children vulnerable to under-responsiveness or, at the other extreme, over-arousal and stimulus overload. Parental involvement in the INPP remedial exercise programme is essential and playful. HANDLE (UK) also designs playful exercises, tailored exactly to a particular child's needs, which are intended to correct what is out of balance and may be causing blocks to learning. Parents take their child for an assessment and then spend time each day working directly with him on a programme of exercises.

Neuro-feedback is another avenue of exploration; however, it is currently relatively expensive and not widely available. Using specially designed computer games, the child learns to reprogramme his brain waves, reducing the power of some and raising the power of others to achieve more balanced neurological activity. According to Ladnier and Massanari (2000) this technique has been successful with a number of ADHD children. They report that educational kinesiology ('brain gym') is also helpful in balancing right and left brain functions in children with specific learning difficulties. This can become a shared project between parent and child, enhancing intimacy as it simultaneously facilitates integration.

With the exception of neuro-feedback, these are all playful, strategic interventions that engage children closely with their parents. Being in a supportive relationship with parents who are genuinely interested and have their child's best interests at heart has been conspicuously absent from these children's damaged lives. Engaging in the joyful 'right brain to right brain' contingent communications typical of early childhood provides them with the best opportunities for essential 'interactive repair' (Schore 2001a). We believe that in helping them develop basic trust in their adoptive parents we are leading them towards more secure, reciprocal attachments that are the best learning supports available.

Summary

We continue to ask questions and to build on our skills and knowledge about what makes learning so difficult for damaged and traumatised children. It is good to have the opportunity to try out ideas with the courageous children with whom we work. The support their parents give them is exceptional. Their determination to stay connected, despite devastatingly difficult behaviour, is heartwarming. Without any doubt these remarkable parents are the solution, not the problem. They become the experts on their children, sharing with them the painful, difficult memories that sometimes get acted out in ways that challenge the most resilient and committed adopters.

Robertson (2000) contends that love can grow connections in the brain, just as cruelty can dissolve them. Working with families we see this miracle of love occurring, not always, but enough to be sure it is possible. We are all becoming aware, through the writings of Schore, Siegel, Perry and many others, and research involving the use of sophisticated brain-scanning equipment, that the miracle of repaired neural connections does actually occur. Alongside parents, we feel some of the pain and anguish, anger and despair that sometimes seem too hard to bear when much-loved adopted children are unable to accept the gifts of learning they are being offered. Then we see the joy, the laughter, the surprise and the delight when emotional connections are felt, a breakthrough happens in thinking or behaviour, or a mother realises she has spent a whole hour relaxed with her child.

All these are moments of joy underpinned by a special kind of love that only parents can know. They are the ones who best understand the difficulties with learning their children struggle with and how these can, in turn, lead to 'learning to be difficult', but they are also the ones who are fully part of the repair that grows new connections. These parents draw their family's map as they make the difficult journey together, and as they learn, the way becomes clearer. For some children the journey is particularly difficult and learning remains a struggle, but with their story a little clearer and a map with some landmarks on it, they have a better chance of making some sense of where they are.

Some brave and fortunate children are able to learn that they do not have to stay in the terrifying place into which they came, where 'fear can stop you loving'. They learn – through committed teaching, from people who are genuinely interested in them, who are curious about them, who want to help them work out the sometimes very frightening but always interesting puzzle of their lives – that love can help with the fear and allow them to learn. They do that in relationship with the most important people in their lives, a relationship that parents and children deserve. The dance of learning to love has the dance of loving to learn woven into it. Together they support each other and grow.

Part III

State, Community and Family

The Future

CHAPTER 15

Weaving Together the Threads
Families with Futures

Caroline Archer

Achieving the Right Balance

As we approach the end of our first, collaborative literary work at Family Futures it is time to reflect on its often dramatic structure, form and content. In his Foreword, Dan Hughes makes the essential distinction between state of the art in attachment theory and in practice: echoing the bi-partite approach we have taken in structuring this book. For many years, within the fields of adoption and child mental health, theory and practice seem to have existed as 'segregated systems' in the United Kingdom, with very little integration. This has become more recognised over the past decade, as demands for 'evidence-based practice' have become increasingly voluble. Whilst these attempts to draw essential threads together are to be welcomed, some pitfalls remain.

As Alan Burnell points out (see chapters 3 and 11) research data being applied to today's difficulties often appear to belong to an earlier era and must therefore be treated with some circumspection. For example, findings that ongoing contact with birth family members was beneficial to adoptees (Fratter *et al.* 1991) was drawn from a time before contact was commonplace, when both families of origin and adoptive families were willing participants, committed to making this innovative process work. To generalise from these outcomes could be unsound, since many subsequent contact arrangements have been directed by the courts, or pressed upon anxious adopters by placing agencies keen to improve their outmoded practices. Hence, for 'evidence-based practice' to be optimised we need also to think in terms of 'practice-based evidence' and to view the two as reciprocally linked in a mutual 'intelligent information system', within which data feedback is recursive and immediate: open to 'bottom up' challenge, as well as from 'top down'.

Within the field of neurobiology this two-way paradigm is epitomised by recent challenges to 'top down' thinking. Where once philosophers were clear that the psyche, or mind, took ultimate charge, biological scientists contend that the brain – more specifically the neo-cortex – is the ultimate controller of our bodies, our minds and our emotions. However, an innovative branch of neuroscience is evolving under the title 'psychoneuro-immunology'. One of its pioneers, Dr Candace Pert, has demonstrated that there are as many, or more, specific receptors for neurotransmitter and neuropeptide 'messengers' in the body as in the brain itself. It is Pert's term 'intelligent information systems' (1999), coined to denote the highly complex interactions between body and mind, that I have borrowed in my discussion of research, theory and practice. I shall explore the neuropsychology of the immune system in more detail later, as from observation it plays a vital part in the lives of many traumatised children and their adoptive families. First, though, I would like to consider research, theory and practice in terms of the cerebral hemispheres themselves.

Proponents of the 'scientific method' of investigation pride themselves on the rigid framework and rational structure of their techniques: their objectivity is intended to eliminate the pitfalls of subjective theorising or tendentious claims. It seems an impossible task to achieve complete objectivity and, I would suggest, not a wholly welcome one. Even the most scrupulous researcher brings to his work a lifetime of previous experience, expectations and beliefs. Indeed it is one of the cornerstones of this volume, backed by clinical data, that to achieve mature, personal and social integration we need to formulate internal working models of the world and evolve a personal narrative that is coherent, allowing us to engage in realistic reflection. These inner models are said to evolve from right brain functions in the neo-cortex and limbic system (see Chapter 4), yet to achieve resolution and cognitive maturity an individual must achieve hemispheric balance.

My anxiety about the 'scientific method' lies not so much in its left hemispheric emphasis as in its potential for imbalance; I am concerned that in the search for 'veracity' the essential, right hemispheric, intuitive approach is being sidelined, although it may still exist in the belief systems, perceptions and expectations of 'the observer', underpinning interpretation of raw material and representation of research findings. Perhaps rather than trying to override our 'gut-feelings', in an attempt to avoid the 'taint' of subjectivity, we should make conscious, positive use of them, alongside the rational approach. Pert (1999), alluding to quantum mechanics, refers to the new dimension of understanding that can be achieved by deliberately including the observer in the equation. Without such holistic creativity I doubt whether Darwin or Bowlby would have evolved such highly influential theories.

The Lens of the Observer

Throughout this work contributors have discussed the current state of adoption: considering theory and practice alongside a brief exploration of hoped-for changes. Everywhere the 'lens of the observer' has been apparent, hopefully adding that extra dimension to our understanding of the 'drama of adoption'. From a dramatherapist's perspective, Jay Vaughan substantiates this point in discussing how the therapeutic team endeavours to join the adoptive family 'on stage' and interact with them directly. 'Off stage' persona, including 'the audience', may also be drawn into the action deliberately, to enhance overall performance. This is 'the difference that makes the difference' which Schore emphasises in his discussion of the nature of healing interventions (2001b).

Despite an orthodox psychoanalytical background, Schore advocates throwing away the traditional couch, so that patient and therapist can engage in meaningful interactions, through face-to-face dialogue, mediated by 'right brain to right brain' contingent communications. Without the 'observer' as active participant, Schore argues that the early forming disorders of attachment, which form the basis for lifelong psychiatric difficulties, cannot be realistically addressed. Just as the mind-body is conceived of as an intelligent information system, so the parent-child relationship, mirrored in the therapeutic relationship, should be considered an intelligent information system, providing essential two-way communications. Thus, by encouraging parents to create new 'feedback loops' we can begin to 'reprogramme' the distorted neural circuits of the traumatised child. These shared processes of containment, reflection and resolution will provide him with ongoing, internal feedback mechanisms to achieve greater reflection, resolution and internal coherence as he develops.

Attachment has been referred to as a psychological immune system (Bowlby 1973). Extending my 'interested observer' analogy, one can see just how much good enough parents are able to 'immunise' their children against trauma and how adoptive parents of traumatised children can provide them with increased immunity to vulnerability, through replicating the interactive tasks of infancy and early childhood. However, according to van der Kolk (1996d), attachment is also the child's primary source of resilience to physical disease. Thus 'breaking the affectional bonds' has major implications for acquisition of innate good health, far beyond the short-term immunity conferred on neonates. Van der Kolk explores the effects of stress on the immune system, particularly the hypothalamic-pituitary-adrenal (HPA) axis. Exposure to distress initially leads to flooding of stress hormones, notably cortisol, and eventually to long-term exhaustion of immune functions. This gives rise to significantly increased risk of disease, particularly neuroimmunological and neuroendocrinological disorders (Perry 1994).

An apparent contradiction, from our observations at Family Futures, is the marked tendency, in a significant minority of traumatised children, not to display 'normal' childhood illness patterns. This seems a valid metaphor for the child's masked vulnerability and urge to be 'in control'. We have known adoptive mothers to wish fervently that their troubled children would become ill, because only then could they, as caregivers, have real opportunities to provide the early nurturing care their children resist. It has become an unofficial measure of therapeutic 'breakthrough' when children in families with whom we have been working begin to go down with the 'usual' coughs and colds. It is as if we have enabled parents to help their children find a greater measure of self-regulation, through actively promoting primary attachments, which in turn allows their bodies to 'return to normal' and deal with disease by throwing up expected symptoms. This is consistent with Pert's (1999) view of the emotional source of disease as the blocking (dissociation) of feedback loops within the body-mind system.

In dissociative terms, we might consider that these children are developing a more integrated sense of self, including the somatic self, alongside sufficient security to express somatic symptoms of distress without being overwhelmed: analogous to encouraging them to express their distressing emotions and find their voice, whilst being safely contained. Further research in this area would be welcomed, particularly with an awareness of the bimodality of neurobiological, sensori-affective, cognitive and behavioural expression which has resonated throughout this text. Since dissociative responses appear to be heavily implicated, one might reasonably speculate that disorganised attachment patterns play a very significant part here.

The Lens of Attachment

Attachment has been at the epicentre of our thinking and our work: its pre-eminence is marked by its primacy in our book title. Attachment weaves its way throughout this narrative. However, where once attachment was principally considered in psychosocial terms, recent integration of neurobiological strands has redefined attachment in terms of a biopsychosocial paradigm. As in the discussion of physical disease above, this more inclusive approach has helped us make sense of otherwise nonsensical observations. The challenge here crystallises the challenge we all face on a daily basis, of managing the fine balancing act between left- and right-brained approaches. In significant areas the reasoned observation and intuition of 'the father of attachment', Bowlby, has been underscored and given renewed validation by recent neurobiological and clinical research. Thus, Bowlby's conception of biologically-based internal working models (1988) and segregated systems (1979) have not only stood the test of time, they have actively informed recent scientific explorations, in the manner of the 'observer effect'. The works of Schore, Siegel, Spangler and Grossman, Lyons-Ruth, Bronfman and Atwood, Liotti, van der Kolk and Fonagy (see Chapter 4) resonate with references to original attachment concepts, as their authors take their findings in diverse directions.

Where the 1990s were denoted as 'the decade of the brain', I hope that the first decade of the 21st century will become known as 'the decade of increasingly joined-up research': providing a realistic and balanced evidence base for joined-up practice. By throwing ourselves wholeheartedly into the equation, we can bring added intelligence to bear on the complexities and perplexities of humanity: employing both brain hemispheres collaboratively to resolve an essential human paradigm. Family Futures values both the 'personal connections' and the 'joined-up thinking' approach, which is reflected in the wealth and diversity of experience and commitment that individual members of the team bring to the therapeutic process.

If anything, the consideration of attachment appears to have become more relevant with the passage of time. Weaving in newer strands of knowledge has certainly increased the enormity and complexity of the issues but, contrariwise, also contributes to simplifying and clarifying them. The *bio*psychosocial perspective then becomes 'an association of associations', where greater strength of connection, as for the neural networks themselves, allows greater clarity of 'thinking about thinking'. It can be no coincidence that a major area identified as crucial to the formation of the sense of self, autonoetic consciousness, and metacognition, or mindreading, forms a significant part of the 'association cortex' (Greenfield 1997). Since the capacity for 'thinking about thinking' is said to be a defining feature of our uniquely human condition, I would like to explore the orbito-prefrontal cortex in greater detail.

Social Chess Versus the Dance of Attachment

In his influential exploration of 'mindblindness', the inability to recognise or read the contents of other people's minds, Baron-Cohen (1999) discusses Humphrey's metaphor of 'social chess'. Humphrey (1984) suggests that the evolution of social intelligence functions enabled individuals living in groups to exist as mutually supportive communities. Beyond providing organisms with this social framework, 'social chess' is simultaneously proposed to promote the 'survival of the fittest': the individual who can best identify others' 'intentional stance' (Dennett 1987), attributing to them thoughts, feeling states, memories, hopes and plans. Thus the 'best' social chess player is said to be able to out-think and out-manoeuvre his companions in the 'game of life'. Baron-Cohen's essay is primarily concerned with the failure of development of 'theory of mind' in individuals with autism and he proposes a number of interlinked functional structures that facilitate mindreading. Since he identifies both the hippocampus and orbito-frontal cortex as major players in mindreading, a discussion of the 'social chess' analogy in relation to traumatised children is extremely relevant. As we have seen in chapters 3 and 4, developmental trauma has particularly damaging effects on these two areas of the infant brain.

Many of our contributors discuss ways in which parents and therapists can engage traumatised children in 'the dance of attunement and attachment'. We have seen how youngsters who have been traumatised tend to over-utilise 'fight, flight or freeze mode' and how these highly-charged behavioural states are strongly associated with socio-emotional isolation: a lack of connection with and trust in others, especially caregivers. In our experience these are children whose mindreading abilities are, in many cases, not lacking but heavily distorted into 'survival' mode: they have identified salient 'rules of the game' and are determined to use them unswervingly to attain the finite goal of the lonely 'victor's crown'. Their behaviours are predicated on the philosophy of 'win-lose' rather than 'win-win' (see also chapters 12 and 13). Children may attempt to eliminate the majority of the other players in their path (as Marty in our composite family, or the real-life Jason did) or use avoidance or pseudo-mature mechanisms to remain separate and 'safe', as our fictional Jenny did. It is heartbreaking to see just how hard children will struggle to 'win', little realising that they will be the ultimate losers. They may indeed appear extremely resilient yet in terms of survival 'there is a huge cost to soul and mind as important parts of one's self are buried' (Frazier-Yzaguirre 2000). Perhaps we need to rethink the twin terms of 'survival of the fittest' and 'the selfish gene' (Dawkins 1995) in terms of 'fitness for living' and 'the altruistic gene'.

The Dance of Attachment

This is the beauty of the 'dance of attachment' (see chapters 9 and 10): it invites traumatised youngsters to rethink their battle strategy across the board, in ways that allow them to rewrite the unwritten groundrules and experience the connections of the 'win-win' dance. Most of these children, given a choice, would elect to retain their survival strategies, using their distorted, yet surprisingly well honed, mindreading abilities to stay 'one jump ahead'. If direct tactics (fight or flight) are not effective they fall back on dissociative 'freeze' behaviours that can mentally 'get them out of a hole'. However, determined but empathetic adults can use appropriate, developmental, interactive sequences to 'redraw their mind maps', or 'rewrite the script'. Significantly, according to Panksepp (1998), the primary preoccupation of mothers with their newborn babies is mediated by oxytocin, which he terms 'the altruistic hormone'. By emphasising the fundamental interpersonal aspects of 'social chess' we provide children with a wider choice of behaviours, to ensure that they not only survive but also become part of a vital, thriving community. Re-emphasising the importance of individuals within a community striving together also highlights the collaborative social context within which we are all working to achieve these changes.

Labour of Love

For those of us lucky enough to be able to work together, it is a 'labour of love'; contributing to this volume has grown to be an equal labour of love. It has also been a learning process in itself: helping to throw the complex, interwoven themes into a tapestry in high relief. In my previous books (Archer 1999a, 1999b) I wrote primarily for fellow adoptive parents: since I could find no one willing to write the books I needed to make adoptive family life easier, I elected to undertake the task myself (with a lot of help from my friends at Adoption UK). That too formed part of my learning curve. In *Next Steps* I considered 'life on the front-line chess board' from my own experience and from that of many Adoption UK families. In trying to describe the sorts of children and challenges we faced I turned to hedgehogs: they represented the primal, maladaptive survival strategy I could see in traumatised children – and so much more. I identified these hedgehogs as predominantly 'Superkid' or 'Stuffedkid', both of whom carried a tiny 'Scaredkid' within. The distinction seemed clear enough: Superkid tended to 'act out' his inner hurts, be aggressively controlling and blame everyone else for his difficulties; Stuffedkid tended to withdraw from intimacy, shut off his feelings and blame himself. However, each hedgehog could, on occasion, play the opposite role with conviction. I made connections between these contrasting patterns and the contrasting patterns of the autonomic nervous system: most essentially between shame-rage (Schore 1994) where the child's overwhelming shame is overridden by 'acting out' anger, and debilitating, disempowering shame. My colleagues and I are now recognising just how far this bimodal response pattern extends (see chapters 3 and 4).

Lacking the integrating knowledge that caregivers 'download' from their mature right brains into the maturing right brains of their infants (Siegel 1999), there is fundamental disorganisation of regulation, compounded by the profoundly dysregulating effects of traumatic experience itself. Failure to 'join up' with an autonomous caregiver means that traumatised children remain 'poles apart', with segregated attachment systems and unintegrated internal working models (see Chapter 4). They tend to lurch dramatically from one feeling or behavioural state to another, since they have not acquired the means of integrating and making sense of their disparate part-selves (Putnam 1997). They tend also to act as if they are on stage, playing their assigned roles with a vehement and convincing intensity. Perhaps the saddest part of this metaphor is that they seem to lack any sense of themselves off stage: their philosophy appearing to be 'I act therefore I am'. One can think of famous but tragic actors who would fit this bill: Marilyn Monroe for example. Thinking, reasoning and mindreading, as for learning (Perry 1999), only become possible when physiological arousal levels are comfortably low. Traumatised children are 'neurophysiologically challenged' in all these areas, as we have seen (chapters 3 and 4).

Staying With the Body

From observation, many traumatised children have difficulty being in their bodies, or even recognising the somato-sensory communications emanating both externally or internally. Magagna (Chapter 5) begins to explore the psychological split between mind and body that can occur in maltreated youngsters. The dearth of experience-dependent associations in these children's early years also leaves them with dissociative gaps in their physical, as well as representational, sense of self. We have explored many creative ways of 'plugging' these gaps: all of which have a fundamental body focus. In the context of therapy (see Chapter 8), Jay Vaughan outlines bodywork therapies that provide many additional, innovative ways of addressing traumatic material; Kellie-Smith (see Chapter 14) examines body-focused approaches in terms of enhancing academic development. The work of Montagu (1986) and Field *et al.* (1996) has been influential in our approach to touch, whilst Panksepp's study of PLAY circuits (1998), Theraplay (Buckwalter and Schneider 2002; Jernberg 1990) and the contiguous fields of sensory integration (Ayres 1994) and developmental dyspraxia (Portwood 1999) have guided us with age-appropriate movement and play sequences. Collaboration with HANDLE (UK) and INPP (see also Chapter 14) has allowed us to begin to explore sophisticated, individually-tailored remedial interventions. We are fortunate to have obtained the consultancy services of Cris Nikolov, a neuro-developmental therapist with training and experience from both, to provide our families with additional body-centred support strategies.

Moreover, we find that complementary health care, in many shapes and forms, can significantly benefit traumatised children and their families. Nutritional supplementation can be of particular value here, given the degree of physical neglect that many of these children have experienced. In a recently reported piece of research with young offenders, Gesch (2002) demonstrated a significant reduction in aggression during a period of supplementation with vitamins, minerals and essential fatty acids. Amen (2002) also explores dietary interventions in terms of 'healing the hardware of the soul'. A good diet *per se* may be insufficient to remedy years of poor nutrition; attempting to alter early-acquired patterns of eating overnight is also likely to meet with strong resistance. Since food is so fundamental to the experience of nurturing this is a battleground best avoided (Archer 1999b). Moreover, experience-dependent development would leave many youngsters with a less than optimal digestive system, alongside a compromised nervous system. Pert's contention (1999) that adverse experience leads to poor development of neuropeptide receptor sites, many of which lie within the gut, implies that proportionately more of the 'good things' would be needed to make good longstanding deficiencies, in terms of a child's general well being.

At home the bodywork we advocate, in addition to regular, developmental exercise programmes, is equally eclectic and creative. We take on board the developmental vulnerability of many of the children with whom we work, and advocate large and regular doses of touch, rough and tumble play and rhythmic physical interactions, even for large, school age children (Archer 1999a, 1999b; Buckwalter and Schneider 2002). In developmental terms 'being a baby' is not just an emotional regression: it becomes a total body-mind experience. In insisting on plenty of 'practice' at 'good baby experiences', as part of developmental reparenting (see also chapters 8 and 13), we are taking advantage of the continuing plasticity of neural networks in order to establish newer, healthier associations. These are essential 'windows of opportunity' for all family members. Many adopters express genuine sadness at having missed out on their youngsters' infancy and early childhood. Suggesting that they can not only improve their child's physical and emotional well being but also 'fill some gaps' in their own parenting narrative can be quite empowering (Archer 2001a). Concerns about age-inappropriate behaviour can be dispelled by setting clear limits on time and place.

Furthermore, rather than creating further dissociative barriers, this clarity of approach seems to help children acknowledge and accept all parts of themselves: even the helpless, dependent, vulnerable parts they so fear. Having time to acknowledge and experience their infantile needs in very physical ways can actually free them up to be more grown up and independent with their friends, in school and within the wider community. There is, however, one overriding rule in our developmental reparenting approach: that parents and children must have as much fun as possible! Providing opportunities for heightened positive affect is essential (Hughes 2002). This is consistent with Pert's interpretation (1999) of the experience-dependent development of neuropeptide receptor sites: traumatised individuals require more positive inputs to produce 'normal' levels of joy and love.

'Shame About the Face'

There is a surprising lack of discussion of the nature and role of shame in developmental trauma literature, given its primacy in the generation of characterological disorders (Schore 1994). Schore attempts to address this issue comprehensively in his massive work on self development (1994); the theme is also taken up by Hughes (1997, 2002) and Siegel (1999), and applied by Archer (1999a, 1999b) to the developmental reparenting of traumatised children. The failure to integrate an understanding of shame into much of mainstream practice is astonishing, in light of the intrinsic links between trauma and attachment and neurobiological data relating to fight, flight and freeze responses. This might best be understood in the context of the extent to which many in the caring professions are themselves affected by shame. Significantly, shame is characterised, in neurophysiological terms, by 'conservation-withdrawal' and avoidance of interpersonal contact, or denied and projected outward in shame-rage (Schore 1994) and blaming others. Perhaps there are lessons for us here about repairing the stress fractures induced by shame in our own biographical narratives, if we are to be able, more fully, to address shame in others.

The prime importance of the human face in early attunement experiences is incontrovertible. In particular, the eyes are pinpointed as central to mother-infant dyadic communications (Baron-Cohen 1999). According to Schore, shame is experienced as the loss of positive regard, perceived in the eyes of the caregiver: it is, as discussed briefly in chapters 4 and 13, part of the developmental sequence of socialisation in toddlerhood. However, being exposed to persistent humiliation, rejection, abandonment or maltreatment leaves the child with overwhelming, and seemingly irresolvable, levels of shame. The classic shame reaction is observable as loss of eye contact, lowering of muscle tone, causing the typical 'hangdog' posture and reduced physical power, alongside the definitive 'blush of shame'. Deceleration of heart rate and lowering of blood pressure have also been observed (Schore 1994).

Physiologically shame results from a rapid behavioural state transition, involving a shift from sympathetic to parasympathetic autonomic nervous system (ANS) activity (Schore 1994). During the 'recovery period' the young child can be witnessed turning to his caregiver, seeking visual or tactile reconnection, which will restore him to sympathetic nervous system functioning. Repeated failure to effect this 'interactive repair', through sensitive co-regulation by the caregiver, prevents the youngster acquiring essential self-regulating skills and leaves him prone to dysregulated, disorganising, disempowering shame (Schore 1994). In such cases the child feels 'looked at', and appears 'turned in on himself' (Izard 1991); in addition, according to Powles (1992) he attempts to avoid attention and to render himself 'unseen'. His entire sense of being in the world appears to be challenged. This dysphoric cognitive-affective response pattern tends to colour 'all subjective experience' (Powles 1992) and is experienced as the helpless, hopelessness of despair, or transformed into unregulated shame-rage (Schore 1994).

A traumatised child has not had adequate opportunities to learn to manage shame reactions and is highly vulnerable to triggering of the shame response in non-threatening situations, particularly where adults engage in socialisation interactions. Conversely, offering unconditional praise can trigger the same response in maltreated children, since it conflicts with the child's perceptions of himself as intrinsically bad (Archer 1999b). He will then shut down neurophysiologically, appearing physically and emotionally to freeze, or conversely to utilise inappropriate fight or flight responses. In neither case will he be able to learn from the experience or re-engage in more appropriate activity. The direction of the bimodal response is determined by the dominance of extreme parasympathetic (low arousal) or sympathetic (high arousal) ANS activity and may be related to particular patterns of caregiving in infancy (Schore 1994, 2002). The similarities between these mutually exclusive shame states and those of traumatic fight, flight and freeze, as discussed in Chapter 4, deserve far more attention than I am able to provide here. I look forward to the emergence of a rich seam of relevant literature in the near future.

In the case of unregulated shame, the youngster is unable to achieve the transition to a more comfortable state himself, requiring the active intervention of the caregiver, usually through touch, to 'revitalise' him

(Schore 1994). Otherwise he remains in a 'closed feedback loop' of powerlessness or pseudo-powerfulness, typical of the helpess-versus-hostile diathesis discussed by Lyons-Ruth *et al.* (1999). It is therefore hardly surprising that shame reactions play a major role in the continuing misattunement between adoptive parent and child (or in therapy or educational settings) unless adults are sufficiently aware of the underlying, terrifying, desperate helplessness of shame. This poses the question that if 'fear can stop you loving' does shame, or the fear of shame, stop you feeling loved? It also leaves me with a final observation: that unless we are prepared to help children 'face up to shame' through 'right brain to right brain', face-to-face, and often hand-to-hand, communications we will be unable to provide them with more accurate and comforting 'road maps' and they will continue to 'act as if' rather than 'be' in this world.

Facing the Critics

Readers who have dipped into the varied chapters in this volume might question its fundamental coherence in terms of its patent eclecticism. Certainly we have endeavoured to draw many seemingly disparate strands of theory into our practice: yet we believe that we have also been successful in interweaving these threads so that they create a unified tapestry, rather than a hotchpotch of disconnected ideas. The extent to which we have succeeded in providing an integrated account of our philosophy may perhaps be measured by the degree to which you, the reader, feel connected to and inspired by our work. Our hope is that, as truly participant observers in what we believe is a vital, global enterprise, you will provide us with essential feedback on any aspect we have raised or omitted: setting us on course to establish an increasingly intelligent information system, a potentially 'worldwide web' of connections. To that end you may visit the Family Futures website at: www.familyfutures.co.uk

Perhaps one area where we might expect criticism is in relation to hard evidence for the value of the Family Futures approach. Given the rapidly changing population of children being placed for adoption over the past decades it is vital that we know what we are dealing with and identify 'what works'. This is a particularly challenging paradigm for us as practitioners. A significant point reiterated by several of our contributors has been that post adoption supports need to be not only broad but also long-term. The potential lifelong nature of post traumatic distress and of opportunities to repair attachments and 'rewire' brain circuitry offer continuing hope for traumatised children. The therapeutic work in which we engage at Family Futures may be considered long-term in that we provide direct input for at least two years and endeavour to establish community support systems that will endure. Moreover, we anticipate that difficulties may re-emerge at times of acute or chronic family distress, or as a response to developmental challenges, such as school transition, adolescence, or burgeoning sexual relationships. Preparing families for such crises and maintaining support links with them is vital if adopters are not to be thrown back into despair when things go awry. Taking the long view allows us all to weather these storms better and to remain confident of their resolution. A similar long-term perspective is invaluable in measuring the apparent 'success' of adoptive and foster placements (there is some discussion of this issue in Chapter 2).

Nevertheless, we have carried out a small-scale, internal evaluation of outcomes for the families with whom we have had the longest involvement. Using evaluation forms devised by Dr Phil Haynes and Dr Mick Cooper, senior lecturers in Applied Social Sciences at the University of Brighton, we asked user families and their children's social workers to respond to simple questionnaires relating to the 'assessment' and 'treatment' periods. Although we had few responses from the social workers, possibly because of their heavy and fluctuating caseloads, the responses from parents were very encouraging. In terms of the Assessment, the great majority of parents were clear about its purpose, felt that staff had a very good understanding of their families' needs and that discussions had been both relevant and helpful. However, parents demonstrated a marked lack of hope that local services would, as a result, be better able to help their child(ren). For all those families who participated in our treatment programme there were also marked improvements. Most indicated that the Attachment and Follow Up programmes had enhanced their children's well being and self-esteem considerably, had improved their children's ability to cope with stressful or difficult situations and increased their capacity to form appropriate attachments. In the area of mental health, improvement was less marked, supporting our view that therapeutic interventions must be long-term. A final question, relating to changes in school attendance and exclusion, indicated some ambivalence. This has informed Family Futures' approach to education services, including an increased emphasis on collaborative networking and the employment of a teacher as part of the team.

The service valuation was carried out in 2001: thus there were only a limited number of families available to be surveyed, many of whom had only recently completed the therapy programme. We plan to extend the evaluation to more participating families over an extended period. It is noticeable that there were no questions which directly measured improvements in parents' sense of well being, self-esteem or capacities for forming healthier attachments, although the generally optimistic nature of parents' responses would imply a good deal of personal satisfaction and enhanced confidence in their ability to be good enough parents. We recognise that these qualities are essential for the maintenance of placements and the long-term health of all family members. Clearly it will be difficult to evolve sensitive and sophisticated criteria to determine the relative 'success' of placements. However, the lack of a sound evidence base should not blind us to our inner, intuitive assessment capacities: using 'right brain to right brain' communications. The deep and enduring connections we, as a team, feel with the parents and children with whom we work must surely be some measure of positive outcomes.

We would not seek to gauge treatment success in terms of placement disruption, since we acknowledge that for some families to remain together they may need to make use of boarding schools, or therapeutic communities, over lengthy periods. Moreover, some young people who apparently 'vote with their feet' (prematurely moving out of the family home or returning to live with birth family members) demonstrate their enduring connection to their adoptive families only in the longer term. It is a measure of the commitment of many adopters that they continue to open their hearts and their homes to their children, despite very overt behaviours of rejection. In our experience their patience is enduring and often embraces premature grandparenthood. This interpretation is supported by Parker (1999).

We chose not to canvass the views of adopted and fostered children themselves for a number of reasons, not least because we recognise how distorted are the perceptions and inner worlds of traumatised children. Again, we would prefer to 'let time tell': as the youngsters' stories extend into adulthood. It is our belief that we will see their coherent narratives unfolding only as their lives untangle and they achieve greater self-awareness. For even the most untroubled individual this is a long-term process: for 'troubled transplants' it may take a lifetime. Thus an exploration of the expectations that all participants in the adoption process bring must include a realistic assessment of our expectations of 'outcomes'. Breaking the intergenerational transmission of trauma and disorganised attachments may well go beyond a single generation. For this first generation physical, emotional and social survival themselves may be fundamental criteria.

Critics might suppose that we have ignored the voice of the child. On the contrary; the very nature of the work at Family Futures enables children to find their real voice. Children who have been traumatised experience 'speechless terror'; they are unable to speak out about their experiences. Furthermore, in most cases, they have not acquired fundamental somato-sensory or affective literacy, since they have not experienced the dyadic non-verbal communications of the good enough attachment relationship that form the basis for self-awareness and verbal communication. Their cognitive representations remain disorganised (Lyons-Ruth, Bronfman and Atwood 1999); they have little true sense of self (Schore 1994, 2002). Through introducing developmental reparenting experiences we provide children with the foundations for self-literacy. In therapy and at home we provide them with opportunities and language to get to know and express themselves. By hearing their non-verbal voices we enable children to really speak for themselves.

Our focus on family dynamics and experiences, rather than exploring the feelings and thoughts of individual children, might appear to be out of synch with the current philosophy of respecting and validating minorities, whether defined by race, culture, religion, gender, sexuality, age or disability. If we have chosen to emphasise the universal over the individual here, that is because it seems to us that the principles underlying trauma and attachment are universal across the human race. Conversely, one could argue that it is precisely because these universals impinge on each of us as individuals that considering the broader picture can enable us to approach individual issues with more sensitivity and understanding. In terms of attachment formation, Southgate's conceptualisation of concentric attachment spaces may be highly pertinent (1996): enabling us to acknowledge just how fundamental the primary mother-child relationship is to an individual's ability to relate to, and identify himself with, broader bands of community.

Unless a youngster has acquired a clear, coherent and complete self-representation, initially through 'downloading' data from his mother's right orbito-frontal cortex (Siegel 1999), he is unlikely to be able to identify himself in any real and meaningful way with others of similar gender, race, religion or culture.

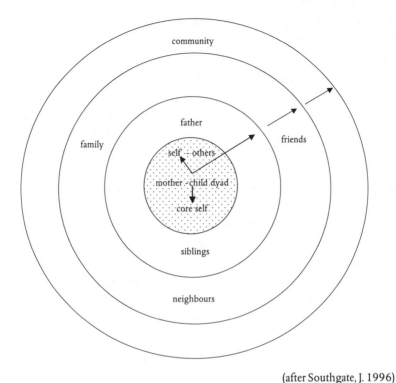

(after Southgate, J. 1996)

Figure 15.1 Development of Self within the attachment relationship: an 'inside-out' process

Maintaining segregated systems and multiple metacognitions may allow him to exist and interact within different environments, at the unacceptable price of belonging to none. This is borne out in studies of adults with dissociative identity disorder. Individuals frequently describe parts of self, or ego states, that are of different race, culture, religion, gender and sexuality and are expressed in different contexts (Ross 1997). Effective treatment programmes are based on clients acknowledging, accepting and engaging in inner dialogue with these segregated systems in order to achieve self-coherence (Goulding and Schwartz 1995; Watkins and Watkins 1997). However, it is essential not to deny the importance of addressing these concerns and the wider socio- political concerns they may raise in their own right. On the contrary, each may form an essential part of the integrative process of self-development and self-knowledge.

A Final Curtain Call

It has been a privilege for me to work with the small, energetic and dedicated team that is Family Futures. I have been able to witness first-hand the benefits of multidisciplinary input and creative thinking and the evolution of a coherent approach to the therapeutic treatment of traumatised children in adoptive families. It has been an equal privilege to be given the opportunity to help members of the team to express their philosophy in writing: an integrative learning experience in itself. It is the 'icing on the cake' to have the chance to draw these threads together, to tie up loose ends. I would like to thank Alan Burnell, Jay Vaughan and Paul Holmes for having the insight and inspiration to start us off on this literary voyage of discovery and for their individual and joint contributions. My thanks go also to Adrian Briggs, Elsie Price and Jeanne Magagna who have all become fully engaged in making Part I such a sound theoretical basis for our exploration of theory and practice. I am, as always, in awe of Christine Gordon's steadfast humour and practicality in approaching parenting issues and thankful to Griselda Kellie-Smith for her ability to transform problems into solutions. Finally, an especial vote of thanks must go to Lucy Greenmile, who has chosen to adopt a pseudonym to protect the privacy of her family but deserves much wider acclaim for her capacity to endure and remain sane in the face of great adversity. I admire them all for their tenacity in this 'labour of love', wrought alongside personal and work lives that were already full to overflowing. Last but not least, I must thank Lyn Vince and Olivia Wood, Family Futures' administrative staff, for their patience and quiet calmness in keeping us talking, thinking and sharing along the way.

In a literary 'positive paradox' this concluding chapter has provided me with space to begin to weave even newer strands into our evolving tapestry: as apparent endings are transformed into new beginnings. At times I have used this concluding chapter to be speculative, to introduce more innovative elements and to explore where they may fit in the scheme of things. I hope they will stimulate thought and reflective debate. I believe that the Family Futures' approach offers a constructive way forward for traumatised children and their substitute families and I trust that you, as committed observers, will accept and transform any inevitable weaknesses you perceive in our philosophy or practice to the benefit of your own.

Appendix

Family Futures Case Planning Matrix

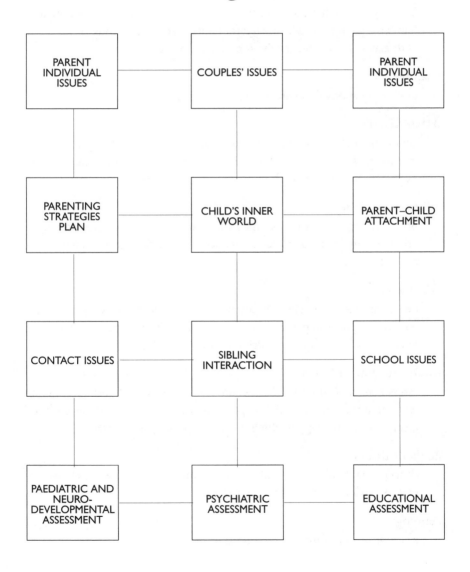

Glossary

A

abandonment

infants given up for adoption experience relinquishment as abandonment. Similarly, youngsters who are left for long or repeated periods, or socialised with excess shame, feel as though they have been abandoned.

adaptive

promoting survival, on an evolutionary or personal level.

ADD/ADHD

common medical terms for a cluster of symptoms, including poor attention, impulsive, and often hyperactive, behaviours. Diagnosis requires prior exclusion of disorders with traumatic aetiology (origins).

adhesive identification

primitive psychological process by which an individual clings to part of the self, the body or an object, to provide security and the illusion of temporary control.

adrenaline

neurotransmitter secreted by adrenal glands, whose release is associated with the response to perceived threat, raised respiration and heart rates, and reduced digestive processes. Primes for fight or flight.

Adult Attachment Interview

assessment tool, used to classify adult attachment: includes autonomous (secure) dismissing (avoidant), preoccupied (resistant) and unresolved/ disorganised insecure attachment patterns (George *et al.* 1985).

aesthetic distance

concept that helps define and maintain a fine balance between reality and fantasy within the dramatherapy process.

aetiology

cause or origin of disease or condition.

amygdala

> area of limbic system highly implicated in processing emotion: giving emotional valence to perceptions and memories. Involved in implicit and traumatic memory processing.

arousal

> body-mind responses to external and internal environment. Vital within normal 'comfort' limits; unhelpful when there is too little or too much.

Aston Index

> educational measurement tool administered by teachers. Consists of many sub-tests for screening and diagnosis of language difficulties.

attachment

> persisting, reciprocal relationship between two individuals. For an infant the attachment relationship initially involves complete dependency and facilitates survival at biological and psychological levels.

attachment – secure

> healthy pattern of relating, balancing dependence and independence needs. Leads to secure attachment organisation of both cognitions and behaviours.

attachment – insecure

> from 'strange situation' (Ainsworth *et al.* 1978) young children could be classified as insecure-avoidant or insecure-resistant. Later the disorganised/disorientated category was added (see below).

Attachment Disorder

> Both ICD 10 and DSM IV carry descriptions of reactive attachment disorders, with onset before five years of age due to gross maltreatment. Many adopted and fostered children develop distorted or disorganised patterns of attachment, as a result of early traumatic experiences that continue to influence their social and emotional relationships.

attachment disorganisation

> a child with disorganised attachments is said to display conflicting or 'freeze' behaviours in the 'strange situation'. Believed to derive from maltreatment in the primary attachment relationship, involving helpless or hostile caregiving (Main and Hesse 1990).

attunement

process of getting 'in tune' or 'in synch' with, another's somato-sensory or affective state, utilising mainly non-verbal communications. Attachment involves synchronic attunement, facilitates early co-regulation and promotes mature self-regulation.

autism/autistic spectrum disorder

characterised by a limited ability to form and use social relationships, weak psychological integration and poor mindreading (metacognitive) capacities. Defined by Williams (1999), an 'autistic' person, as 'an experience that describes a very complex interplay between identity, personality, environment, experience and the equipment with which to integrate and make sense of that experience' (p.9).

autobiographical memory

memory for personal history: constructed over time within social context. Available to verbal recall.

auto-immune disease

conditions such as rheumatoid arthritis, typified by the body 'attacking' itself. Frequently of traumatic aetiology (van der Kolk 1996; Perry 1999).

autonoetic consciousness

conscious self-knowledge and awareness.

autonomic nervous system

part of the nervous system responsible for involuntary responses. Includes network of glands and hormones mediating experience and behaviour. Characterised in traumatised individuals by sympathetic (high arousal) or parasympathetic (low arousal) patterns.

autonomous

adult attachment classification (AAI) equivalent to secure attachment in children. Having internalised secure attachments an individual can function responsibly and independently and provide appropriate caregiving to others.

avoidant

child attachment classification: tending to be fearful of close contact and relationships, stemming from early, traumatic experiences.

B

BASK

Braun (1988) introduced the BASK model to denote Behavioural, Affective, Sensory or Knowledge-based integration deficits in dissociative individuals.

behavioural states

infants come into the world with a small repertoire of response patterns. Gradually, within the co-regulatory attachment relationship, they extend their choice of behavioural states, learning to move between states readily and appropriately. In maltreated children these states remain unintegrated and state transitions problematic.

bimodal

having two alternative forms of expression. The autonomic nervous system (ANS) is a bimodal system, consisting of the sympathetic NS (high arousal) and parasympathetic NS (low arousal) (see also fight, flight, freeze, shame and regulation).

biopsychosocial

integrating biological, psychological and social aspects.

boundaries

personal limits by which an individual defines himself, experiences himself as separate from others and acquires self-agency.

brain stem

developmentally the 'oldest' part of the brain, which regulates temperature, respiration and heart rate (and basically defines whether we are alive!).

Brocha's area

area of the left hemisphere of neo-cortex of human brain closely associated with verbal symbolism and speech.

C

cerebral cortex (neo-cortex)

most recently evolved part of human brain. Allows conscious decision making, social communication and symbolic transformations.

cognitive

conscious thinking processes; take place in the cerebral cortex of the human brain.

coherent narrative

explicit memories that are accessed, recalled and interpreted by an individual in a consistent, organised manner (see also Adult Attachment Interview).

comorbidity

co-existence of symptomatology, suggesting more than one discrete diagnosis.

Conduct Disorder

(descriptive) diagnosis frequently given to children and adolescents demonstrating serious aggressive or destructive behaviours (often along-side ADHD or ODD). Does not refer to aetiology of the individual's difficulties but current literature tends to make significant links with experiences of dysfunctional parenting.

Connors Questionnaire

well-known behavioural checklist for children.

containment

provision of acknowledgement, reassurance and security, usually by parent or other trusted adult. Can be physical or affective.

cortisol/corticosteroids

hormones secreted from HPA axis that prepare individual to manage stress, including immune system response. In immature youngsters, or in excess, can lead to destruction of neurons and neural pathways (see also synaptic pruning) and to auto-immune disease.

critical periods

periods of maximum growth and development in childhood, during which relatively small adversities can pose serious developmental challenges.

D

development

process of moving from the total dependence of a newborn towards the independence of adulthood. Implies growth and change at physical, emotional, psychological, intellectual and spiritual levels.

developmental reparenting

structured parenting programme, derived from attachment and developmental principles, allowing opportunities for healthier attachment experiences and encouraging neural rewiring.

discrete behavioural states

term introduced by Putnam (1997) to denote highly charged and disparate behavioural states in dissociative individuals.

dismissing

corresponds to avoidant attachment pattern in children. Associated with avoidance of intimacy and/or affect and devaluation of early relationships.

disorganised attachment

pattern of attachment most commonly found in maltreated children and correlated with adult psychiatric disorders (see also attachment – insecure).

dissociation

lack of appropriate connections between senses, feelings, knowledge, behaviours, memories or areas of the nervous system, leading to weakened ability to make sense of self or others, behave consistently and learn from new experiences. Early trauma inhibits developmental integration (not 'joined-up'); later trauma can cause dissociative splits ('blown apart') (see also BASK).

dissociative disorders

dissociative responses, including dissociated sensations, feelings, thoughts and behaviours in childhood are included in diagnoses such as PTSD, Dissociative Identity Disorder (DID) and Dissociative Disorder Not Otherwise Specified (DDNOS). Dissociative processes may also occur in other disorders such as Conduct Disorder (CD) and Oppositional Defiant Disorder (ODD), and eating disorders such as anorexia nervosa. In adulthood they feature prominently in Borderline and Anti-Social Personality Disorders (BPD and APD).

dissociative response

adaptive, protective response to being overwhelmed by amount or content of incoming information. Becomes unhelpful if used too much or continues when things change for the better.

dissolution

evolutionary regression to developmentally lower level of functioning (see also polyvagal theory).

distorted

skewed, 'out of true', disorganised: as in distorted perceptions deriving from disorganised early experiences.

distress

literally dis-stress: unhealthy or uncomfortable levels of stress.

dyadic

relating to the reciprocal relationship interactions between caregiver and infant.

dysfunctional

sub-optimal or unhealthy functioning.

dyslexia

difficulties with reading, writing, spelling and understanding symbols. Neurologically-based disorder.

dyspraxia

often described as 'clumsiness': difficulty with co-ordination, involving the planning, and carrying out, of movement tasks, both small and large. Neurologically based.

dysregulation

lack of basic regulatory capacities, e.g. for arousal, affect.

E

ego state

often used synonymously with behavioural states or states of mind. If not integrated, ego states form the basis for continuing dissociative states.

empathy

sharing, getting in tune with another's feelings, thoughts, needs.

evidence-based practice

social work practice based on research evidence.

experience-dependent

Neural pathways, and hence internal working models, are organised in the developing child according to experience and tend to be self-reinforcing.

explicit memory

verbal memory processes, available for (verbal) recall and contributing to personal narrative. Includes narrative and autobiographical memory.

F

facilitated contact

therapeutic, mediated contact between adopted child and birth family members developed by Family Futures.

family cradling

'in arms' nurturing by caregivers to provide comfort, security and improved opportunities for closeness and communication through physical closeness and state-dependent experiences. Embodies the principles of developmental reparenting.

feeling states

compartmentalised ways of feeling, set in an individual's experience. See also ego states; behavioural states; states of mind.

fight or flight response

mammalian survival mechanism in event of apparent threat – either to stand ground and defend, or run away. Involves sympathetic high arousal of autonomic nervous system.

flashbacks

intense, anxiety producing images from the past which can intrude without warning into present awareness. Can be visual, auditory, olfactory or body-based.

freeze response

most primitive (reptilian) survival mechanism in response to threat; 'feigning death'. Very low arousal state, mediated by parasympathetic nervous system.

functional

offering an organism some advantage for survival.

G

good baby experiences

the reciprocal, synchronistic, nurturing caregiving that good enough parents provide for their infants. In traumatised children this term is used to denote attachment and developmentally-based reparenting experiences.

good enough

parents do not need to (cannot) be perfect. As long as they get it 'right enough' the child will thrive. Perfection would not provide child with opportunities to tolerate frustration or learn from mistakes.

H

helpless-versus-hostile diathesis

Lyons-Ruth *et al.* (1999) propose that disorganised attachments lead to helpless or hostile caregiving, resulting in helpless or hostile attachment disorganisation in offspring.

hemisphere

the human brain is divided into two halves, or hemispheres, that are roughly symmetrical. Important asymmetries exist (see below).

hemispheric asymmetry

In humans, parts of the right hemisphere mature earlier than the left, mediated by reciprocal attachment interactions (Schore 1994, 2002).

hippocampus

'seahorse' shaped process in limbic system of left and right hemispheres. Highly implicated in storage of explicit memories.

holding

containing, providing security and comfort for a baby or small child – a physical or emotional 'safety net'.

holding therapy

therapy which employs physical holding by skilled psychotherapists, in conjunction with other therapeutic approaches, to bring about effective healing.

holding time

first used by Martha Welch (1988), to describe time deliberately and regularly set aside, for the child with the parent. Involves physically holding the child in close, face-to-face, and allowing free expression of feelings in order to increase closeness in the relationship.

HPA axis

hypothalamic-pituitary-adrenal system that mediates immune response. Implicated in auto-immune disorders.

hyperactive

extremely 'busy', over-active, 'on the go', non-stop. Hyperactivity is one of the core diagnostic symptoms of ADHD.

hypermnesia

Very intense traumatic memories that become 'burned into' memory and tend to 'flood' back into consciousness uninvited.

hypersensitive

greater sensitivity and responses to experience than 'normally' expected. Often sensitised by earlier trauma, including in the womb and at birth.

hypervigilant

unable to relax, watchfulness for fear-producing events or stimuli, due to continuing internal arousal following traumatic experience.

hyposensitive

less than 'normally expected' ability to respond to sensory or motor stimuli (see also hypersensitive).

I

identificatory processes

psychoanalytic term denoting various ways in which individuals may disown, or take in, aspects of themselves or others (see also adhesive, introjective and projective identification).

infantile amnesia

tendency for individuals to lack verbal recall for events during the first three or four years of life. Does not take into account somato-sensory, sensori-affective and behavioural memories.

implicit memory

memory stored without words. Involves non-verbal or pre-verbal, somato-sensory or automatic memories, with right-hemispheric dominance.

impulsivity/impulsiveness

tendency to react without thinking of consequences. One of the core symptoms described in ADHD.

integration

weaving together of elements into a coherent whole. In developmental terms, the bringing together of behavioural or ego states to create an holistic sense of self across relationships, time and space (see also discrete behavioural states).

intelligent information system

term drawn from quantum physics to describe the recursive, reciprocal interactions of the body-mind system.

interactive repair

(Schore 1994). Denotes caregiving capacity to 'mend' temporary breaks in the reciprocal attachment relationship, such as after brief separation. Healing for traumatised children through developmental reparenting requires a profound understanding of this process (Hughes 2002).

internal working model

inner 'road maps' that an individual builds up about the world and about himself from his experiences (Bowlby 1979). Once established they are resistant to change, since subsequent perceptions are 'selected' to fit what is expected. May exist as 'parallel', or multiple, dissociated 'segregated systems' (Bowlby 1979).

introjective identification

primitive psychological process in which an individual takes in and identifies with qualities of another individual.

L

left brain

In most people this hemisphere of the brain controls the right side of the body. Predominantly rational, logical and language orientated.

limbic system

important part of the mid-brain (or mammalian brain), controlling, amongst other things, emotion, motivation and memory functions.

looked after

current term for children who are being cared for by local authorities, either in foster or residential care.

M

mentalising capacities

human capacity for mature consideration and reflection, associated with the orbito-frontal cortex.

metacognition

see above. 'Thinking about thinking'; capacity to read and reflect on others' thoughts, feelings, intentions and behaviours.

mid-brain

younger than the brain stem in evolutionary terms. Incorporates the limbic system and is responsible for functions such as body rhythms, emotion, motivation, sexuality and fight or flight.

mindblindness

term introduced by Baron-Cohen (1999) to denote poor mindreading capacities (see below), particularly in autistic children.

mindreading

developmental process by which a child learns to acknowledge, consider and take account of others' cognitive and behavioural states.

mirroring

responding and reflecting back to the child aspects of his expressions, movements, feelings.

modelling

demonstrating through example. An infant learns initially through observing and responding to parental models.

modulate

bring into balance, regulate arousal somato-sensory or affective.

modulate neurophysiological arousal

self-regulatory capacity to lower and raise levels of response in the nervous system, within comfortable limits, acquired initially through co-regulation with primary caregiver.

mother figure

single most important person in a very young child's life. In our society it is still usually the mother. Whatever the gender, this is the person who provides the caregiving that is essential to an infant's survival and well being.

multiple working models

Traumatised children retain multiple inner 'road maps' of the world that are not 'joined-up'. Their internal representations remain in dissociated (segregated) systems, leading to disorganised behaviour patterns.

myelinated

consolidation of neural pathways with protective, myelin sheath forming around nerve cell core. Enhances conduction of information.

N

neo-cortex

see cerebral cortex.

neural networks/circuits

complex linkages, or connections, between cells (neurons) in the brain and nervous system, which become organised around individual experience.

neural pathways

neural networks (internal 'road maps') that become selectively reinforced through repeated use. Initially adaptive, may become maladaptive in changed circumstances.

neurobiology

study of the biological structure and function of the brain and nervous system.

neurohormones

internal biochemical secretions that enable transmission of information within the brain and nervous system.

neuroimmunological/neuroendocrinological conditions

auto-immune system disorders in which the body fails to distinguish between self and non-self (e.g. lupus, rheumatoid arthritis) or imbalance of hormone secretions occurs, e.g. hyperthyroidism (see also auto-immune disorders).

neurological connections
> links between individual nerve cells and specific areas of the brain/nervous system that are experience-dependent, that is, laid down and reinforced through repeated use. Lack of use leads to neural pruning.

neurological organisation
> developmental organisation of connections within the nervous system. Organisation is experience-dependent and correlates with attachment organisation (Spangler and Grossman 1999).

neurological system
> made up of central nervous system, autonomic nervous system and structures of the brain.

neurophysiology
> study of functions of brain and nervous system.

neuropeptide
> informational substances or 'molecules of emotion' (Pert 1999) that transport information to receptor sites within the body-mind system.

neurotransmitter
> biochemical substances that transmit nerve impulses from neuron to neuron, e.g. serotonin, adrenaline.

O

oppositional defiant
> 'challenging behaviour' characterised by stubborn non-co-operation. Frequently understandable as part of a dissociative reaction.

orbito-(pre)frontal cortex (OFC)
> area of the 'association cortex' forming vital connections between the (emotional, reactive) mid-brain/limbic system and higher thought processes of the human neo-cortex. Right OFC matures earlier than left (Schore 2001a, 2002).

oxytocin
> hormone secreted in abundance immediately *post-partum*: the 'altruistic hormone' (Panksepp 1998) that facilitates nurturing caregiving.

P

Parasympathetic nervous system (PNS)

Part of the autonomic system responsible for decreasing arousal. Porges (1998) proposes two alternative routes: via the 'smart' ventral vagus complex (VVC) or the Dorsal Vagus Complex (DVC) (see figure 4.4 on p.87)

perceptions

reception, interpretation and organisation of incoming sensory information (from external and internal sources).

phylogenetic

relating to species evolution from earlier organisms. Individual development (ontogeny) is said to recapitulate phylogeny during foetal development.

physiology

study of how the body works.

PNI (psychoneuroimmunology)

multidisciplinary research exploring how psychological function affects immunological (including endocrinological) function. Involves neuropeptides (molecules of emotion).

polyvagal theory

Porges (1998) identifies three levels of stress response involving neural pathways of the vagus nerve system in humans.

post traumatic stress reaction

complex pattern of physiological and psychological/emotional responses to overwhelming or chronic stress. See also PTSD.

preoccupied

adult attachment classification (see AAI) characterised by emotional over-involvement or passivity in relationships.

primal wound

denotes the intense, original pain of early separation from the birth mother in relinquished infants (Verrier 1993).

primary caregiver

child's main source of physical and emotional security, the main attachment figure.

primary attachment relationship

mother-infant relationship. When good enough, provides essential synchronic attunement and co-regulation.

projective identification

strong, primitive psychological process of disowning parts of the self and 'pushing' them into others. Caregivers and therapists need to be able to recognise these projections in order to empathise and communicate with the child effectively.

psychic

of the mind, soul or spirit (in contrast to 'of the body', or somatic).

psychological containment

Winnicott (1971) proposed that for a young child to develop a sense of security, he needs to experience being emotionally held by the parenting figure. In that way he also learns to manage his own feelings and emotions.

psychological trauma

(long-term) effects on behaviour, feeling and thinking of overwhelming experiences.

PTSD (post traumatic stress disorder)

first identified in adults with distressing symptoms following a single-incident trauma. Concept now includes children and young people and recognises the cumulative effects of repeated (chronic) traumatic experiences. Includes three categories of disturbance: a) intrusive – repetitive thoughts and play, dissociative flashbacks, nightmares and somatic complaints; b) constriction or numbing – avoidance of painful reminders or thoughts and numbing of feeling; c) persistently altered levels of arousal and hypersensitivity to minor triggers.

Q

quiet alert

behavioural state in which infant is well regulated (through co-regulation with primary caregiver) and optimal learning can occur (Klaus 1998; Perry 1999).

R

recapitulation

process of going through essential, developmental sequence again to effect change and healing.

reflecting back

acting as a mirror to another's actions/feelings.

reflective function (RF)

capacity to consider experiences, explore emotions and anticipate others' responses and feelings. Involves healthy development and functioning of the orbito-frontal cortex.

reframing

re-interpreting affect, thoughts, behaviours: providing a more positive, insightful interpretation.

regression

going back to 'earlier' developmental patterns of behaviour. Often occurs under stress. Can be therapeutic if it allows completion of unfinished developmental tasks and opportunities for new learning in safe context.

regulation

modulation of physiological, somato-sensory, affective and behavioural responses. Self-regulation is acquired through good enough co-regulatory experiences with the mother.

reparenting

see developmental reparenting.

representation

structure or framework to 'map' internal patterns of belief, thought or behaviour, derived from earliest relationship interactions.

resilience

> inner durability and flexibility, allowing an individual to adapt and survive: often at some personal cost (especially in developmentally immature individuals).

resistant

> child attachment classification (insecure) denoted by reduced exploration and play, distress and inability to gain comfort from caregiver on reunion.

resolution (i)

> stage of relative calm (after an emotional storm), e.g. after family cradling or 'holding time'. Usually involves gaining greater understanding, insight or self-control.

resolution (ii)

> capacity to achieve internal congruency, integrating all aspects of self.

rewiring

> Brain cells that 'fire together wire together'. With the right developmental approach, experience and use-dependent neural networks can be reorganised to form newer, healthier connections (neural circuits).

right brain

> in most humans this hemisphere controls the left side of the body. Its functions are holistic: predominantly affect-based, intuitive and responsive to perceived patterns. Develops earlier than left brain: hemispheric asymmetry associated with 'right brain to right brain' communications (Schore 2001a) between parent and infant, influencing attachment behaviour and representations.

S

safe holding

> elective holding to provide additional nurturing, security, comfort and opportunities for closeness and communication. See also 'family cradling'.

SATS

> national, standardised attainment tests taken by children at 7, 11 and 14 years.

segregated systems

term introduced by Bowlby (1979) to make sense of chaotic internal working models of maltreated children.

selective attention

ability to pick out important, striking or frightening aspects of the surroundings and focus on them to the exclusion of less important information. Adaptive.

selective development

evolutionary tendency for some characteristics or features to persist over others during development. Normally adaptive but trauma and use-dependent phenomena may lead to the persistence of potentially maladaptive functions.

self

Awareness of self is experience-dependent, hence the sense of self may be fluid and responsive to present as well as past experiences. Early experience carries most weight, since it involves organisation of neural pathways and therefore profoundly influences future perceptions and interpretations.

self-regulation

ability to monitor and maintain, within comfortable limits, feelings, emotions, body functions and behavioural responses. Acquired through initial co-regulation with primary caregiver.

sense of self

see above; derived in major part from reciprocal and mirroring experiences within the attachment relationship.

sensori-affective

relating to bodily sensations and emotional states.

sensori-motor

perceptions and responses of the senses and/or of movement.

sensory defensiveness

under- or over-reactivity/sensitivity. Can be present in any or all of the sensory modalities, including movement.

sensory integration

> acquired, developmental ability (Ayres 1994) to recognise, modulate and interpret sensory stimuli (internal and external). See also sensory defensiveness, above.

shame

> feeling bad about who one is – as opposed to guilt: feeling bad about what one does. In small doses it brings about healthy change (shame socialisation). In excess it becomes toxic, affecting self-respect, self-worth, self-esteem. Involves parasympathetic nervous system and very low arousal.

shame-rage

> high-arousal response to defend against helpless, hopelessness of shame (Schore 1994).

shame reaction

> overwhelming, low-arousal, physiological state underpinning characteristic behaviours: including cast-down body, gaze aversion, flushing and trembling.

shame socialisation

> developmentally said to begin in infant's second year (Schore 1994), as he begins to explore his environment. Good enough caregivers momentarily withdraw vitalising positive regard. The infant experiences this as an attachment break that must be repaired immediately, to revitalise the child and reinforce reciprocal attachments (see also interactive repair).

shut down

> behavioural – see switching off. Physiological stress response involving parasympathetic autonomic nervous system and very low arousal (see also shame and freeze).

somatic

> relating to the body.

somato-sensory

> relating to body sensations, both internal and external.

state dependent

early and traumatic experiences are laid down as state-dependent, somato-sensory and sensori-affective memories that may not be accessible to verbal recall. Healing requires the laying down of newer, more appropriate state-dependent sequences that are accessible across state transitions, relationships, time and space (see also discrete behavioural states).

states of mind

Infants learn, through healthy parent-infant relationships, to make smooth transitions from one state of mind to another and to 'mindread', or make sense of and predict, others' thoughts, feelings and behaviours. Dysfunctional caregiving leads to unintegrated states of mind and body.

state transition

see making transitions and state dependent (above).

strange situation

situation contrived experimentally (Ainsworth *et al.* 1978) to test infant attachment patterns through observation of behaviour on separation and reunion. Subsequently developed and extended to school age children.

switching off/out

A child who feels threatened, afraid or ashamed may respond by distancing himself emotionally from his surroundings temporarily, through dissociation. This can become habitual, preventing the child from benefiting from comfort and security and interfering with learning.

Sympathetic nervous system (SNS)

part of the autonomic nervous system responsible for increasing arousal.

synaptic pruning

process whereby redundant nerve cells and their connections decay as part of normal developmental process. Can also occur as a result of traumatic experience and the excess secretion of stress hormones such as cortisol.

synchronic attunement

harmonising effect seen between parent and infant, which enables an infant to alter his body rhythms and internal responses to match the parent's (co-regulation) and hence learn to self-regulate his own. Hence: 'get in synch with'; 'tune in and turn on'.

symbolic transformation

> process whereby somato-sensory and affective knowledge can become conscious, through verbal representation and storage.

T

time in

> period of time set aside for parent and child to be together, involving quiet reflective communications. Effective with traumatised children, since it provides essential opportunities for co-regulation and interactive repair.

time out

> period of time spent alone as part of family discipline. Can trigger or perpetuate feelings of abandonment in traumatised children.

transitions (making)

> capacity to move from one affective, behavioural, arousal or ego state to another with control and ease. Self-regulatory function derived from initial co-regulation with caregiver.

transitional object

> tangible 'something' representing the security and comfort of the caregiver, available to the child at times of separation.

trauma

> literally: a wound. Normally taken to mean an overwhelming experience, that does not allow the individual to return to a 'normal', comfortable state of being. There are demonstrable neurobiological changes associated with feelings of powerlessness, lack of control, panic or numbing. Developmentally, the earlier the trauma, the greater its adverse impact.

trigger

> Once a traumatic response pattern is established, a much smaller stimulus can repeatedly set off the same level of response. Initially adaptive; involves experience-dependent neural pathways.

U

unresolved

> used with reference to trauma or loss to describe adults whose cognitive or behavioural representations remain disorganised, lacking coherence.

W

withdrawal

going into oneself, disconnecting (dissociating) from people and/or surroundings. Once adaptive (protective) but interferes with ability to relate and learn in new, safer environment.

References

Ainsworth, M., Blehar, M., Waters, E. and Wall, S. (1978) *Patterns of Attachment: A Psychological Study of the Strange Situation.* Hillsdale, NJ: Erlbaum.

Aldridge-Morris, R. (1991) *Multiple Personality.* Hove and London: Lawrence Erlbaum Associates.

Alvarez, A. (1992) *Live Company: Psychoanalytic Psychotherapy with Autistic, Borderline, Deprived and Abused Children.* London: Routledge.

Amen, D. (2002) *Healing the Hardware of the Soul.* New York and London: The Free Press.

Archer, C. (1999a) *First Steps in Parenting the Child Who Hurts: Tiddlers and Toddlers.* London: Jessica Kingsley Publishers.

Archer, C. (1999b) *Next Steps in Parenting the Child Who Hurts: Tykes and Teens.* London: Jessica Kingsley Publishers.

Archer, C. (1999c) 'Re-parenting the traumatised child: A developmental process'. *Young Minds Magazine 42*, 19–20.

Archer, C. (2000a) *Making Sense of Attachment in Adoptive and Foster Families.* Northamptonshire: Adoption UK.

Archer, C. (2000b) 'From the other side of the mirror: A worm's eye view of family therapy'. *Context 52*, 14–16.

Archer, C. and Swanton, P. (2000) 'Adoption: Changes in the light of experience'. In K. White (ed) *The Changing Face of Child Care.* London: NCCVCO.

Archer, C. (2001a) 'Thinking toddler'. *Adoption Today 97*, 14–16.

Archer, C. (2001b) 'The hidden fragility of the adopted child'. In R. Gordon and E. Harran (eds) *Fragile: Handle with Care.* Leicester: NSPCC.

Archer, C. (2002) 'Education for adoptive parenting'. In M. Nolan (ed) *Education and Support for Parenting.* London: Bailliere Tindall.

Attachment and Bonding Center of Ohio, Dr Gregory Keck, 12608 State Road, Cleveland, OH.

Audit Commission (1994) *Seen But Not Heard.* London: HMSO.

Ayres, A.J. (1994) *Sensory Integration and the Child.* Los Angeles, CA: Western Psychological Services.

BAAF (1996) *Planning for Permanence Practice Note 33.* London: BAAF.

Balbernie, R. (1999) 'Infant mental health'. *Young Minds Magazine 39*, 17–18.

Balbernie, R. (2001) 'Circuits and circumstance: The neurobiological consequences of early relationship experiences and how they shape later behaviour'. *Journal of Child Psychotherapy 27*, 3, 237–255.

Barker, P. (1993) *Regeneration*. London: Penguin.

Barker, P. (1995) *The Eye in the Door*. London: Penguin.

Barker, P. (1996) *The Ghost Road*. London: Penguin.

Baron-Cohen, S. (1999) *Mindblindness – An Essay in Autism and Theory of Mind*. London: A Bradford Book (The MIT Press).

Bates, B. and Dozier, M. (2000) *The Importance of Maternal State of Mind Regarding Attachment and Infant Age at Placement to Foster Mothers' Representations of their Foster Infants*. Newark, DE: University of Delaware.

Beechbrook Services for Children, Cleveland, OH.

Begley, S. (1997) 'How to build a baby's brain'. *Newsweek (special edition) Spring/Summer*, 28–32.

Bentley, E. (1999) *Bentley on Brecht*. New York and London: Applause Books.

Bentley, E. (2000) 'Are Stanislavsky and Brecht commensurable?' In C. Martin and H. Bial (eds) *Brecht Sourcebook*. London and New York: Routledge.

Bentovim, A. and Bingley-Miller, L. (2001) *Family Assessment*. Brighton: Pavilion Publishing Ltd.

Bernhardt, P. (1992) *Somatic Approaches to Traumatic Shock: A Review of the Work of the Bodynamic Institute and Peter Levine*. Albany, CA: Bodynamic Institute.

Bick, E. (1968) 'The experience of the skin in early object relations'. *International Journal of Psycho-Analysis 49*, 484–486.

Boal, A. (2001) *Games for Actors and Non-Actors*. London and New York: Routledge.

Borysenko, J. and Borysenko, M. (1994) *The Power of the Mind to Heal*. Carson, CA: Hay House Inc.

Boston, M. and Szur, R. (1983) *Psychotherapy with Severely Deprived Children*. London: Karnac Books.

Bowlby, J. (1969) *Attachment* (Volume I of *Attachment and Loss*). London: Hogarth Press.

Bowlby, J. (1973) *Separation: Anxiety and Anger* (Volume II of *Attachment and Loss*). London: Hogarth Press.

Bowlby, J. (1979) *The Making and Breaking of Affectional Bonds*. London: Tavistock Publications.

Bowlby, J. (1980) *Loss: Sadness and Depression.* (Volume III of *Attachment and Loss*). London: Hogarth Press.

Bowlby, J. (1988) *A Secure Base*. London: Routledge.

Bradshaw-Tauvon, K. (1998) 'Principles of psychodrama'. In M. Karp, P. Holmes and K. Bradshaw-Tauvon (eds) *The Handbook of Psychodrama*. London: Brunner-Routledge.

Braun, B. (1984) 'Towards a theory of multiple personality and other dissociative phenomena'. In B. Braun (ed) *Symposium on Multiple Personalities*. Psychiatric Clinics of North America, 7, p.171.

Braun, B. (1988) 'The BASK (behavior, affect, sensation, knowledge) model of dissociation'. *Dissociation 1*, 1, 4–23.

Brazelton, T. (1992) *Touchpoints: Your Child's Emotional and Behavioural Development.* Reading, MA: Addison-Wesley Publishing.

Bremner, J., Randall, P., Scott, T., Bronen, R., Seibyl, J., Southwick, S., Delaney, R., McCarthy G., Charney, D. and Innis, R. (1995) 'MRI-based measurement of hippocampal volume in combat-related post-traumatic stress disorder'. *American Journal of Psychiatry 152*, 973–981.

Bridge Child Care Consultancy (1991) *Patterns and Outcomes in Child Placement.* London: HMSO.

Briere, J. (1996) 'A self-trauma model of treating adult survivors of severe child abuse'. In J. Briere, L. Berliner, J. Bulkley, C. Jenny, T. Reid (eds) *The APSAC Handbook of Child Maltreatment.* London: Sage Publications.

Britton, R. (1981) 'Re-enactment as an unwitting professional response to family dynamics'. In S. Box (ed) *Psychotherapy with Families*. London: Routledge and Kegan Paul Ltd.

Brodzinsky, D. (1990) 'A stress and coping model of adoption adjustment'. In D. Brodzinsky and M. Schechter (eds) *The Psychology of Adoption*. New York: Oxford University Press.

Brodzinsky, D., Brodzinsky, A. and Smith, D. (1998) *Children's Adjustment to Adoption.* London: Sage.

Brook, P. (1975) Preface to J. Grotowski, *Towards a Poor Theatre.* London: Methuen and Co. Ltd.

Buckwalter, K. and Schneider, M. (2002) 'Why Theraplay works'. *Connections, May*, 4–6.

Burnell, A. and Briggs, A. (1995) 'The next generation of post placement and post adoption services: A complementary contract approach'. *Adoption and Fostering 19*, 3, 6–11.

Byng-Hall, J. (2002) 'Telling one's own story: From farmer to family therapist' and 'My story: Why I became a family therapist'. In J. Hills (ed) *Rescripting Family Experiences – The Therapeutic Influence of John Byng-Hall.* London: Whurr Publishers.

Cabinet Office (2000) *Prime Minister's Review of Adoption.* London: HMSO.

Cairns, K. (1999) *Surviving Paedophilia.* Stoke on Trent: Trentham Books Ltd.

Carlson, V., Cicchetti, D., Barnett, D. and Braunwald, K. (1989) 'Finding order in disorganization'. In D. Cicchetti and V. Carlson (eds) *Child Maltreatment: Theory and Research on the Causes and Consequences of Child Abuse and Neglect.* New York: Cambridge University Press.

Carnicke, S. (2000) 'Stanislavsky's system: Pathways for an actor'. In A. Hodge (ed) *Twentieth Century Actor Training*. London and New York: Routledge.

Carter, R. (2000) *Mapping the Mind*. London: Orion Books Ltd.

Carvel, J. (2002) 'NHS may fund parenting lessons'. Report in *The Guardian*. London: 24 August 2002.

Catherwood, D. (1993) 'The robustness of infant haptic memory: Testing its capacity to withstand delay and haptic interference'. *Child Development 64*, 702–710.

Chamberlain, D. (1987) 'The cognitive newborn: A scientific update'. *British Journal of Psychotherapy 4*, 30–71.

The Children Act (1989) London: HMSO.

Clarke, A.M. and Clarke A.D.B. (2000) *Early Experience and the Life Path*. London: Jessica Kingsley Publishers.

Cline, F. (1992) *Hope for High Risk and Rage Filled Children*. Evergreen, CO: EC Publications.

Clinton, H. (1997) *It Takes A Village and Other Lessons Children Teach Us*. London: Pocket Books.

Cornwell, J. (1983) 'Crisis and survival in infancy'. *Journal of Child Psychotherapy 9*, 1, 25–33.

Cornwell, J. (1985) 'The survival functions of primitive omnipotence'. *International Journal of Psychoanalysis 66*, 4, 481–489.

Cowan, P. and Cowan, C. (1991) 'Becoming a family: Marriage, parenting and child development'. In P. Cowan and C. Heatherington (eds) *Family Transitions*. London: LEA.

Cox, M. and Theilgaard, A. (1987) *Mutative Metaphors in Psychotherapy*. London: Tavistock.

Crank, M., Morrall, P., O'Hanlon, L. and Wilkins, H. (2002) *Briefing to House of Lords on Adoption Support*. England: After Adoption, Adoption Forum and Adoption UK.

Crittenden, P. (1995) *Coding Manual: Classification of Quality of Attachment for Pre-School Aged Children*. Miami, FL: Family Relations Institute.

Dawkins, R. (1995) *River Out of Eden*. London: Phoenix (Orion Books Ltd).

De Casper, A. and Fifer, W. (1980) 'Of human bonding: Newborns prefer their mothers' voices'. *Science 208*, 1174–1176.

Delaney, R. (1991) *Fostering Changes: Treating Attachment Disordered Foster Children*. Fort Collins, CO: WJC.

Delaney, R. and Kunstal, F. (1993) *Troubled Transplants: Unconventional Strategies for Helping Disturbed Foster and Adopted Children*. University of South Maine, ME: Edmund S. Muskie.

Dennett, D. (1987) *The Intentional Stance*. Massachusetts: MIT Press.

Department of Health (1998a) *Adoption – Achieving the Right Balance*. LAC(98)20. London: DoH.

Department of Health (1998b) *Quality Protects Programme: Transforming Children's Services*. LAC (98) 28. London: DoH.

Department of Health (2000) *Adoption, a New Approach*. A White Paper. London: HMSO.

Department of Health (2001) *National Adoption Standards for England*. London: DoH.

Dozier, M., Stovall, K.C., Albus, K. and Bates, B. (2001) 'Attachment for infants in foster care: The role of caregiver state of mind'. *Child Development 72*, 5, 1467–1477.

Drell, M., Siegel, C. and Gaensbauer T. (1993) 'Post-traumatic stress disorder'. In C. Zeanah (ed) *Handbook of Infant Mental Health*. New York: Guilford Press.

Egeland, B., Jacobvitz, D. and Sroufe, L.A. (1988) 'Breaking the cycle of abuse'. *Child Development 59*, 1080–1088.

Fahlberg, V. (ed) (1990) *Residential Treatment: A Tapestry of Many Therapies*. Indianapolis, IN: Perspective Press.

Family Futures Consortium (2000) *Sink or Swim? Finding A Family – A New Approach*. London: Family Futures.

Fearnley, S. and Howe, D. (1999) 'Disorders of attachment and attachment therapy'. *Adoption and Fostering 23*, 2, 19–30.

Federici, R. (1998) *Help for the Hopeless Child: A Guide for Families*. Alexandria, VA: Federici and Associates.

Ferber, R. (1985) *Solve Your Family's Sleep Problems: The Complete Practical Guide for Parents*. London: Dorling Kindersley.

Field, T., Grizzle, N., Scafidi, F. and Abrams, S. (1996) 'Massage therapy for infants of depressed mothers'. *Infant Behavior and Development 19*, 107–112.

Fisk, N. (2000) 'Does a foetus feel pain?' E. Burns *The Times*. London: 28 March 2000.

Fonagy, P. (1999a) *The Male Perpetrator: The Role of Trauma and Failures of Mentalization in Aggression Against Women – An Attachment Theory Perspective*. London: 6th Annual Bowlby Conference.

Fonagy, P. (1999b) *Pathological Attachments and Therapeutic Action*. Presentation to the Developmental and Psychoanalytic Discussion Group. Washington, DC: American Psychoanalytic Association Meeting.

Fonagy, P. (2001) *Attachment Theory and Psychoanalysis*. London: Other Press.

Fonagy, P. (2002) 'Multiple voices versus meta-cognition: An attachment theory perspective'. In V. Sinason (ed) *Attachment, Trauma and Multiplicity*. Hove: Brunner-Routledge.

Fonagy, P. and Target, M. (1997) 'Attachment and reflective function: Their role in self-organization'. *Development and Psychopathology 9*, 679–700.

Fratter, J. (1996) *Adoption with Contact: Implications for Policy and Practice*. London: BAAF.

Fratter, J., Rowe, J., Sapsford, D. and Thoburn, J. (1991) *Permanent Family Placement*. London: BAAF.

Frazier-Yzaguirre, C. (2000) Epilogue. In D. Pelzer *A Man Named Dave*. London: Orion.

Freeman, J. (2002) 'Grand plans'. *Guardian Society* 30 January 2002. London: *The Guardian*.

French, W. and Tate, A. (1998) 'Educational management'. In J. Breen and B. Jacobs (eds) *Inpatient Psychiatry*. London: Routledge.

Freud, S. (1899) 'Screen memories'. In J. Strachey (ed and trans) *The Standard Edition of the Complete Psychological Works of Sigmund Freud 3*. New York: Norton.

Freud, S. (1913) 'On beginning the treatment (further recommendations on the technique of psycho-analysis)' *Standard Edition 12*. London: Hogarth Press.

Furedi, F. (2002) *Paranoid Parenting: Why Ignoring the Experts May Be Best for You*. London: Alan Lane (Penguin).

Garvey, C. (1986) 'Play'. In J. Bruner, M. Cole and B. Lloyd (eds) *The Developing Child*. Glasgow: Fontana Paperbacks.

George, C. and Solomon, J. (1998) *Attachment Disorganization at Age Six: Differences in Doll Play Between Punitive and Caregiving Children*. Paper presented at International Society for the Study of Behavioural Development, Bern, Switzerland, July 1998.

George, C., Kaplan, N. and Main, M. (1985) *The Adult Attachment Interview* (unpublished manuscript). Berkeley, CA: University of California.

Gersie, A. (1991) *Storymaking in Bereavement – Dragons Fight in the Meadow*. London: Jessica Kingsley Publishers.

Gersie, A. and King, N. (1990) *Storymaking in Education and Therapy*. London: Jessica Kingsley Publishers.

Gesch, B. (2002) University of Oxford, Department of Physiology. Report by J. Meikle, in *The Guardian* 26 June 2002.

Glaser, D. (2000) 'Child abuse and neglect and the brain – A review'. *Journal of Child Psychology and Psychiatry 41*, 1, 97–116.

Glaser, D. and Balbernie, R. (2001) 'Early experience, attachment and the brain'. In R. Gordon and E. Harran (eds) *Fragile: Handle with Care*. Leicester: NSPCC.

Goddard, S. (1996) *A Teacher's Window Into the Child's Mind*. Eugene, OR: Fern Ridge Press.

Goldin-Meadow, S. (2000) 'Beyond words: The importance of gesture to researchers and learners'. *Child Development 71*, 231–239.

Gordon, C. (1999) 'A parenting programme for parents of children with disturbed attachment patterns'. *Adoption and Fostering 23*, 4, 49–56.

Goulding, R. and Schwartz, R. (1995) *The Mosaic Mind: Empowering the Tormented Selves of Child Abuse Survivors*. New York and London: WW Norton and Company.

Greenfield, S. (1997) *The Human Brain*. London: Phoenix (Orion Books Ltd).

Grossman, K.E., Grossman, K. and Schwan, A. (1986) 'Capturing the wider view of attachment: A reanalysis of Ainsworth's strange situation'. In C. Izard and P. Read (eds) *Measuring Emotions in Infants and Children*. New York: Cambridge University Press.

Hage, D. (1995) 'Therapeutic Parenting Parts I & II'. In C. McKelvey (ed) *Give Them Roots, Then Let Them Fly: Understanding Attachment Therapy*. Evergreen, CO: The Attachment Center at Evergreen Inc.

Hart, A. and Thomas, H. (2000) 'Controversial attachment: The indirect treatment of fostered and adopted children via Parent Co-Therapy'. In A. Hart and H. Thomas (eds) *Attachment and Human Development*. Online @ Taylor and Francis Ltd.

Healy, A. (1992) *A Survey of Research Regarding the Need for a Post Adoption Service Over the Period 1988–1992*. Lewes: East Sussex Social Services.

Herbert, M. (1996) *Post-traumatic Stress Disorder in Children*. London: The British Psychological Society.

Hilgard, E. (1977) *Divided Consciousness: Multiple Controls in Human Thought and Action*. New York: Wiley.

Hodges, J., Steele, M., Hillman, S., Henderson, K. and Neil, M. (2000) 'Effects of abuse on attachment representations: Narrative assessments of abused children'. *Journal of Child Psychotherapy 26*, 3, 433–455.

Holden, R. (1993) *Laughter is the Best Medicine*. London: Thorsons.

Holmes, J. (2001) *The Search for a Secure Base: Attachment theory and psychotherapy*. Hove: Brunner Routledge.

Home Office (1999) *Report of an Inquiry by Sir William Macpherson*. London: TSO.

House of Commons (2001) *Adoption and Children Bill Explanatory Notes*. London: Parliament.

Howe, D. (1990) 'The Post Adoption Centre: The first three years'. *Adoption and Fostering 14*, 1.

Howe, D. (1996) *Adopters on Adoption*. London: BAAF.

Howe, D. (1998) *Patterns of Adoption*. Oxford and London: Blackwell Science.

Howe, D., Brandon, M., Hinings D., and Schofield, G. (1999) *Attachment Theory, Child Maltreatment and Family Support*. London: Macmillan Press.

Howes, N. (1997) *Understanding Early Trauma: The Implications for Adoption*. Lecture given at PPIAS and Keys Attachment Centre Conference, London.

Hughes, D. (1997) *Facilitating Developmental Attachment: The Road to Emotional Recovery and Behavioral Change in Foster and Adopted Children*. New York: Jason Aronson.

Hughes, D. (1998) *Building the Bonds of Attachment: Awakening Love in Deeply Troubled Children*. Northvale, NJ: Jason Aronson Inc.

Hughes, D. (2002) 'The psychological treatment of children with PTSD and attachment disorganization: Integrative dyadic psychotherapy'. Submitted to *American Journal of Orthopsychiatry*, February 2002.

Humphrey, N. (1984) *Consciousness Regained*. Oxford: Oxford University Press.

Hunter, M. (2001) *Psychotherapy with Young People in Care*. Hove: Brunner Routledge.

IPF (2001) *Personal Social Services Statistics 2000–01 Estimates*. London: CIPFA.

Irving, K. (1997) Personal communication. London: Parents for Children.

Ivaldi, G. (2000) *Surveying Adoption: A Comprehensive Analysis of Local Authority Adoption 1998–1999 (England)*. London: BAAF.

Jackson, S. (2001) 'The education of children in care'. In S. Jackson (ed) *Nobody Ever Told Us School Mattered*. London: BAAF.

Jaffe, J., Beebe, B., Feldstein, S., Crown, C. and Jasnow, M. (2001) 'Rhythms of dialogue in infancy, coordinated timing in development'. *Monographs of the Society for Research in Child Development 66*, 2.

James, B. (1989) *Treating Traumatized Children*. New York: The Free Press.

Janus, L. (1997) *Echoes from the Womb*. New York: Jason Aronson.

Jennings, S. (1987) 'Dramatherapy and groups'. In S. Jennings (ed) *Dramatherapy Theory and Practice for Teachers and Clinicians*. Cambridge, MA: Brookline Books.

Jernberg, A. (1990) 'Attachment enhancing for adopted children'. In P. Grabe (ed) *Adoption Resources for Mental Health Professionals*. USA: Transaction Publishers.

Johnson, R. (2001) *Grounds for Optimism with Personality Disorders* (Annual Conference Proceedings). York: James Nayler Foundation Publications.

Johnson, R. (2002a) Editorial Letter. *The James Nayler Foundation Newsletter, May*, 1–2.

Johnson, R. (2002b) *Emotional Health*. York: James Nayler Foundation Publications.

Karr-Morse, R. and Wiley, M. (1997) *Ghosts from the Nursery*. New York: The Atlantic Monthly Press.

Keck, G. and Kupecky, R. (1995) *Adopting the Hurt Child*. Colorado Springs, CO: Pinon Press.

Keck, G. and Kupecky, R. (2002) *Parenting the Hurt Child*. Colorado Springs, CO: Pinon Press.

Kennedy, R. and Magagna, J. (1981) 'The aftermath of murder'. In S. Box, B. Copely, J. Magagna and E. Moustaki (eds) *Psychotherapy with Families*. London: Routledge and Kegan Paul Ltd.

Kent, L., Laidlaw, J. and Brockington, I. (1997) 'Fetal abuse'. *Child Abuse and Neglect 21*, 181–186.

Klaus, M. (1998) *Amazing Talents of the Newborn – A Video Guide for Health Care Professionals and Parents*. Johnson and Johnson Pediatric Institute Ltd.

Klaus, M. and Kennell, J. (1976) *Bonding: The Beginnings of Parent-Infant Attachment*. New York: Plume, New American Library.

Knapp, M., Scott, S., and Davies, J. (1999) 'The cost of anti-social behaviour in younger children'. *Clinical Child Psychology and Psychiatry 4,* 457–473.

Krystal, H. (1988) *Integration and Self-Healing: Affect-trauma-alexithymia.* Hillsdale, NJ: The Analytic Press.

Ladnier, R. and Massanari, A. (2000) 'Treating ADHD as attachment deficit hyperactivity disorder'. In T. Levy (ed) *Handbook of Attachment Interventions.* San Diego, CA: Academic Press.

Landy, J. (1986) *Drama Therapy – Concepts and Practices.* Springfield, IL: Charles C. Thomas Publishers.

Larkin, P. (1996) 'This be the verse'. In G. Rhys Jones (ed) *The Nation's Favourite Poems.* London: BBC Worldwide Ltd.

Ledoux, J. (1999) *The Emotional Brain.* London: Phoenix, Orion Books Ltd.

Ledoux, J., Romanski, L. and Xagoraris, A. (1991) 'Indelibility of subcortical emotional memories'. *Journal of Cognitive Neuroscience 1,* 238–243.

Leunig, M. (1990a) *A Common Prayer.* London: Collins Dove (Harper Collins).

Leunig, M. (1990b) *The Prayer Tree.* London: Collins Dove (Harper Collins).

Levine, P. (1997) *Waking the Tiger, Healing Trauma.* Berkeley, CA: North Atlantic Books.

Levine, P. (1999) *Waking the Tiger – Integrating Trauma Treatment with Body-Oriented Psychotherapies.* Boston, MA: Boston University School of Medicine Annual Psychological Trauma Conference, in cooperation with The Trauma Center, Arbour Health System.

Levy, T. and Orlans, M. (1998) *Attachment, Trauma and Healing.* Washington, DC: Child Welfare League of America Inc.

Levy, T. and Orlans, M. (2000) 'Attachment disorder and the adoptive family'. In T. Levy (ed) *Handbook of Attachment Interventions.* San Diego, CA: Academic Press.

Liotti, G. (1995) 'Disorganized/disorientated attachment in the psychotherapy of dissociative disorder'. In S. Goldberg, R. Muir and J. Kerr (eds) *Attachment Theory: Social, Developmental and Clinical Perspectives.* Hillsdale, NJ: Analytic Press.

Liotti, G. (1999) 'Disorganization of attachment as a model for understanding dissociative psychopathology'. In J. Solomon and C. George (eds) *Attachment Disorganization.* New York: Guilford Press.

Lowe, N., Murch, M., Borkowski, M., Weaver, A., Beckford, V. and Thomas, C. (1999) *Supporting Adoption: Reframing the Approach.* London: BAAF.

Ludington-Hoe, S. and Golant, S. (1993) *Kangaroo Care: The Best You Can Do to Help Your Preterm Infant.* New York and London: Bantam Books.

Lyons-Ruth, K. and Zeanah, C. (1993) 'The family context of infant mental health: Affective development in the primary caregiving relationship'. In C. Zeanah (ed) *Handbook of Infant Mental Health.* New York: Guilford Press.

Lyons-Ruth, K., Bronfman, E. and Atwood, G. (1999) 'A relationship diathesis model of hostile-helpless states of mind: Expressions in mother-infant interaction'. In J. Solomon and C. George (eds) *Attachment Disorganization*. New York: Guilford Press.

MacFarlane, J. (1975) 'Olfaction in the development of social preference in the human newborn'. In M. Hofer (ed) *Foundation Symposium: Parent-Infant Interaction*. Amsterdam: Elsevier.

McCaskill, C. (1986) 'Post adoption support'. In P. Wedge and J. Thoburn (eds) *Finding Families for 'Hard-to-Place' Children: Evidence from Research*. London: BAAF.

McEwen, B. (2000) *Stress, Sex and the Hippocampus: From Serendipity to Clinical Relevance*. Boston, MA: Boston University School of Medicine Annual Psychological Trauma Conference in cooperation with The Trauma Center, Arbour Health System.

Magagna, J. (2002a) 'Three years of infant observation with Mrs. Bick'. In A. Briggs (ed) *Surviving Space: Festscrift for Esther Bick*. London: Karnac Books.

Magagna, J. (2002b) 'Families and child psychotherapy: A Kleinian perspective'. In J. Mills (ed) *Rescripting Family Experiences – The Therapeutic Influence of John Byng-Hall*. London: Whurr Publishers.

Magagna, J. and Black, D. (1985) 'Changing roles for men and women: Implications for marital therapy'. In W. Dryden (ed) *Marital Therapy in Great Britain (Vol. 1)*. London: Harper and Row.

Main, M. (1991) 'Metacognitive knowledge, metacognitive monitoring, and singular (coherent) versus multiple (incoherent) models of attachment'. In C.M. Parkes, J. Stevenson-Hinde and P. Marris (eds) *Attachment Across the Life Cycle*. London: Routledge.

Main, M. and Cassidy, J. (1988) 'Categories of response to reunion with the parent at age 6: Predictable from infant attachment classifications and stable over a 1-month period'. *Developmental Psychology 24*, 415–426.

Main, M. and Hesse, E. (1990) 'Parents' unresolved traumatic experiences are related to infant disorganized status: Is frightened and/or frightening parental behavior the linking mechanism?' In M. Greenberg, D. Cicchetti and E. Cummings (eds) *Attachment in the Pre-School Years*. Chicago: University of Chicago Press.

Main, M. and Solomon, J. (1990) 'Procedures for identifying infants as disorganized/disoriented during the Ainsworth Strange Situation'. In M. Greenberg, D. Cicchetti and E. Cummings (eds) *Attachment in the Pre-School Years*. Chicago: University of Chicago Press.

Marshall, L. (2001) *The Body Speaks – Performance and Expression*. London: Methuen and Co Ltd.

Maughan, B. and Yule, W. (1994) 'Reading and other learning disabilities'. In M. Rutter, E. Taylor and L. Hersov (eds) *Child and Adolescent Psychiatry, Modern Approaches*, 3rd edn. Oxford: Blackwell Scientific.

Miller, A. (1988) *The Drama of Being a Child*. London: Virago Press.

Mitchell, J. (2000) *Mad Men and Medusas: Reclaiming Hysteria.* New York: Basic Books.

Mollon, P. (1996) *Multiple Selves, Multiple Voices – Working with Trauma, Violation and Dissociation.* Chichester: John Wiley.

Mollon, P. (1998) *Remembering Trauma – A Psychotherapist's Guide to Memory and Illusion.* Chichester: John Wiley.

Monck, E. (2001) 'Work in progress: Concurrent planning in the adoption of children under eight years'. *Adoption and Fostering 25,* 1, 67–68.

Montagu, A. (1986) *Touching: The Human Significance of the Skin.* 3rd edn. New York and London: Harper and Row.

Moreno, J. (1980) *Psychodrama (Vol. I).* 6th edn. (first published 1946). New York: Beacon House.

Murray Parkes, C. (1997) 'Normal and abnormal responses to stress: A developmental approach'. In D. Black, M. Newman, J. Harris-Hendriks and G. Mezey (eds) *Psychological Trauma.* London: Gaskell (RCP).

Nelson, K. (1988) 'The ontogeny of memory for real events'. In U. Neisser (ed) *Remembering Reconsidered: Ecological and Traditional Approaches to the Study of Memory.* New York: Cambridge University Press.

Nicely, P., Tamis-LeMonda, C. and Bornstein, M. (2000) 'Mother's attuned responses to infant affect expressivity promote earlier achievement of language milestones'. *Infant Behavior and Development 22,* 557–568.

O'Connor T., Rutter, M. and the English and Romania Adoptees Study Team (2000) 'Attachment disorder behavior following early severe deprivation: Extension and longitudinal follow-up'. *Journal of the American Academy of Child and Adolescent Psychiatry 39,* 703–712.

Ogden, P. and Minton, K. (2000) 'Sensorimotor psychotherapy:One method for processing traumatic memory'. *Traumatology 6,* 3, article 3 (electronic journal).

Panksepp, J. (1998) *Affective Neuroscience.* New York: Oxford University Press.

Panksepp, J. (2000) *How the Brain Comes to Make Maps of the World by Integrating Emotion and Cognition: Implications for Treatment.* Boston, MA: Boston University School of Medicine, Annual Psychological Trauma Conference, in co-operation with The Trauma Center, Arbour Health System.

Panksepp, J. (2001) 'The long-term psychobiological consequences of infant emotions: Prescriptions for the twenty-first century'. *Infant Mental Health Journal 22,* 132–173.

Parker, R. and the Advisory Group (1999) *Adoption Now: Messages from Research.* Chichester: John Wiley and Sons Ltd.

Parnell, L. (1999) *EMDR in the Treatment of Adults Abused as Children.* New York: Norton.

Pennebaker, J. (1997) *Opening Up: The Healing Power of Expressing.* New York: Guilford Press.

Perry, B. (1993a) 'Medicine and psychotherapy. Neuro-development and the neuro-physiology of trauma (1): Conceptual considerations for clinical work with maltreated children'. *The Advisor, American Professional Society on the Abuse of Children* 6, 1, 13–18.

Perry, B. (1993b) 'Neuro-development and the neuro-physiology of trauma II: Clinical work along the alarm-fear-terror continuum'. *The Advisor, Journal of the American Professional Society on the Abuse of Children* 6, 2, 1–12.

Perry, B. (1994) 'Neurobiological sequelae of childhood trauma: PTSD in children'. In M. Murburg (ed) *Catecholamine Function in Post-traumatic Stress Disorder: Emerging Concepts.* Washington, DC and London: American Psychiatric Press Inc.

Perry, B. (1995) *Principles of Working with Traumatized Children.* Houston, TX: CIVITAS Child Trauma Programs.

Perry, B. (1996) *Clonidine Decreases Symptoms of Physiological Hyperarousal in Traumatized Children.* Houston, TX: CIVITAS Child Trauma Programs.

Perry, B. (1999) 'The memories of states: How the brain stores and retrieves traumatic experience'. In J. Goodwin and R. Attias (eds) *Splintered Reflections, Images of the Body in Trauma.* New York: Basic Books.

Perry, B., Pollard, R., Blakely, T., Baker, W. and Vigilante, D. (1995) 'Childhood trauma, the neurobiology of adaptation, and "use-dependent" development of the brain: How states become traits'. *Journal of Infant Mental Health 16,* 4, 271–291.

Perry, B. and Marcellus, J. (1997) 'The impact of abuse and neglect on the developing brain'. *Colleagues for Children, Missouri Chapter of the National Committee to Prevent Child Abuse 7,* 1–4.

Pert, C. (1999) *Molecules of Emotion, The Science of Mind-Body Medicine.* New York: Touchstone.

Pesso, A. and Boyden-Pesso, D. (1969) *Movement in Psychotherapy.* New York: New York Press.

PIU (2000) *The Prime Minister's Review of Adoption.* London: Cabinet Office.

Porges, S. (1997) 'Emotion: An evolutionary bi-product of the neural regulation of the autonomic nervous system'. In C. Carter, B. Kirkpatrick and I. Lederhendler (eds) *The Integrative Neurobiology of Affiliation. Annals of the New York Academy of Sciences 807,* 62–77.

Porges, S. (1998) 'Love and the evolution of the autonomic nervous system: The polyvagal theory of intimacy'. *Psychoneuroendocrinology 23,* 837–861.

Portwood, M. (1999) *Developmental Dyspraxia.* (2nd edn.) London: David Fulton Publishers.

Prime Minister's Review (2000) London: HMSO.

Putnam, F. (1997) *Dissociation in Children and Adolescents: A Developmental Perspective.* New York: Guilford Press.

Quality Protects Programme (1998) *Quality Protects Programme: Transforming Children's Services*. London: DoH.

Randolph, E. (1994) *Children Who Shock and Surprise*. Kittredge, CO: RFR Publications.

Riesenberg-Malcolm, R. (1999) *On Bearing Unbearable States of Mind*. London: Routledge.

Roberts, M. (2000) *Horse Sense for People*. London: Harper Collins Publishers.

Robertson, I. (2000) *Mind Sculpture: Your Brain's Untapped Potential*. New York: Fromm.

Ross, C. (1997) *Dissociative Identity Disorder*. New York: John Wiley.

Sapolsky, R., Hideo, E., Rebert, C. and Finch, C. (1990) 'Hippocampal damage associated with prolonged glucocorticoid exposure in primates'. *Journal of Neuroscience 10*, 2897–2902.

Sawbridge, P. (1988) 'The Post Adoption Centre: What are the users teaching us?' *Adoption and Fostering 12*, 1.

Scher, A. and Verrall, C. (1988) *100+ Ideas for Drama*. London: Heinemann Educational Books.

Schore, A. (1994) *Affect Regulation and the Origin of the Self*. Hillsdale, NJ: Lawrence Erlbaum Associates.

Schore, A. (1998) *Affect Regulation: A Fundamental Process of Psychobiological Development, Brain Organisation and Psychotherapy*. London: Tavistock 'Baby Brains' Conference.

Schore, A. (2001a) 'Effects of a secure attachment on right brain development, affect regulation, and infant mental health'. *Infant Mental Health Journal 22*, 7–67.

Schore, A. (2001b) 'The effects of early relational trauma on right brain development, affect regulation, and infant mental health'. *Infant Mental Health Journal 22*, 201–269.

Schore, A. (2002) 'Dysregulation of the right brain: A fundamental mechanism of traumatic attachment and the psychpathogenesis of Posttraumatic Stress Disorder.' *Autsralian and New Zealand Journal of Psychiatry 36*, 9–30.

Schoutrop, M., Lange, A., Brosschat, J. and Everaerd, W. (1997) 'Overcoming traumatic events by means of writing assignments'. In A. Vingerhoets, F. van Bussel and J. Boelhouwer (eds) *The (Non)Expression of Emotions in Health and Disease*. Tilburg, Netherlands: Tilburg University Press.

Schwarz, E. and Perry, B. (1994) 'The post traumatic response in children and adolescents'. *Journal of the Psychiatric Clinics of North America 17*, 2, 311–326.

Sellick, C. and Thoburn, J. (1996) *What Works In Family Placement?* Barkingside: Barnados.

Shakespeare, W. (1963) *Macbeth*. London: Signet Classics.

Sherborne, V. (2001) *Developmental Movement for Children*. London: Worth.

Shirar, L. (1996) *Dissociative Children – Bridging the Inner and Outer Worlds*. New York: WW Norton & Company Inc.

Siegel, D. (1997) 'Memory and trauma'. In D. Black, M. Newman, J. Harris-Hendriks and G. Mezey (eds) *Psychological Trauma, A Developmental Approach*. London: Gaskell (RCP).

Siegel, D. (1999) *The Developing Mind. Toward a Neurobiology of Interpersonal Experience*. New York: Guilford Press.

Silberg, J. (2002a) *Games to Play with Toddlers*. Beltsville, MD: Gryphon House Inc.

Silberg, J. (2002b) *Brain Games*. Beltsville, MD: Gryphon House Inc.

Sinason, V. (1988) 'Smiling, swallowing, sickening and stupefying. The effect of abuse on the child'. *Psychoanalytic Psychotherapy 3*, 2, 97–111.

Sinason, V. (1992) *Mental Handicap and the Human Condition*. London: Free Association Books.

Smith, S.C. and Pennells, M. (1995) *Interventions with Bereaved Children*. London: Jessica Kingsley Publishers.

Solomon, J. and George, C. (1999a) 'The etiology of attachment disorganization'. In J. Solomon and C. George (eds) *Attachment Disorganization*. New York: Guilford Press.

Solomon, J. and George, C. (1999b) 'The place of disorganization in attachment theory: Linking classic observations with contemporary findings'. In J. Solomon and C. George (eds) *Attachment Disorganization*. New York: Guilford Press.

Southgate, J. (1996) *An Attachment Perspective on Dissociation and Multiplicity*. York: The Centre for Attachment-based Psychoanalytic Psychotherapy.

Southgate, J. (2002) 'A theoretical framework for understanding multiplicity and dissociation'. In V. Sinason (ed) *Attachment, Trauma and Multiplicity*. Hove: Brunner-Routledge.

Spangler, G. and Grossman, K. (1999) 'Individual and physiological correlates of attachment disorganization in infancy'. In J. Solomon and C. George (eds) *Attachment Disorganization*. New York: Guilford Press.

SSI (1996) *For the Children's Sake Part 1: An Inspection of Local Authority Adoption Services*. London: DoH.

SSI (1997) *For the Children's Sake Part 2: An Inspection of Local Authority Post-Placement and Post-Adoption Services*. London: DoH.

SSI (2000a) *Adopting Changes. Survey of Inspection of Local Councils' Adoption Services*. London: DoH.

SSI (2000b) *Excellence Not Excuses. Inspection of Services For Ethnic Minority Children and Families*. London: DoH.

Stanislawski, C. (1981) *An Actor Prepares*. London: Eyre Methuen Ltd.

Stanislawski, C. (1985) *My Life in Art*. London: Eyre Methuen Ltd.

Steele, M., Hodges, J., Kaniuk, J., Henderson, K., Hillman, S. and Bennett, P. (1999) 'The use of story stem narratives in assessing the inner world of the child:

Implications for adoptive placements'. In *Assessment, Preparation and Support: Implications from Research*. London: BAAF.

Steele, M., Kaniuk, J., Hodges, J., Haworth, C. and Huss, S. (1999) 'The use of the Adult Attachment Interview: Implications for assessment in adoption and foster care'. In *Assessment, Preparation and Support: Implications from Research*. London: BAAF.

Steinberg, L. (2002) Presentation to National Family and Parenting Institute Conference, England. Reported in *The Times* (*T2 Lifestyle* 4–5) 16 April 2002.

Stern, D. (1985) *The Interpersonal World of the Infant*. New York: Basic Books.

Stovall, K.C. and Dozier, M. (2000) 'The development of attachment in new relationships: Single subject analyses for 10 foster infants'. *Development and Psychopathology 12*, 133–156.

Target, M. and Fonagy, P. (1996) 'Playing with reality II: The development of psychic reality from a theoretical perspective'. *International Journal of Psycho-analysis 77*, 459–479.

Terr, L. (1991) 'Childhood traumas: An outline and overview'. *American Journal of Psychiatry 148*, 10–20.

Teti, D. (1999) 'Conceptualization of disorganization in the pre-school years: An integration'. In J. Solomon and C. George (eds) *Attachment Disorganization*. New York: Guilford Press.

Thoburn, J. and Sellick, C. (1997) *What Works in Family Placement*. Barkingside: Barnardo's.

Thoburn, J. (1991) 'Evaluating placements and survey findings.' In J. Fratter, J. Rowe, D. Sapsford and J. Thornburn (eds) *Permanent Family Placement*. Barkingside (London): Barnardo's.

Thomas, N. (2000) 'Parenting children with attachment disorders'. In T. Levy (ed) *A Handbook of Attachment Interventions*. San Diego, CA: Academic Press.

Treacher, A. (2001) 'Narrative and fantasy in adoption: Towards a different theoretical understanding'. In A. Treacher and I. Katz (eds) *The Dynamics of Adoption*. London: Jessica Kingsley Publishers.

Trevarthen, C. (1979) 'Communication and cooperation in early infancy: A description of primary intersubjectivity'. In M. Bullowa (ed) *Before Speech*. London and Cambridge: Cambridge University Press.

Trevarthen, C. (2001) 'Intrinsic motives for companionship in understanding: Their origin, development, and significance for infant mental health'. *Infant Mental Health Journal 22*, 95–131.

Tustin, F. (1990) *The Protective Shell in Children and Adults*. London: Karnac Books.

Tyrrell, C. and Dozier, M. (1999) 'Foster parents' understanding of children's problematic attachment strategies: The need for therapeutic responsiveness'. *Adoption Quarterly 2*, 4, 49–64.

van der Kolk, B. (1994) 'The body keeps the score: Memory and the evolving psychobiology of post-traumatic stress'. *Harvard Review of Psychiatry Jan–Feb,* 253–265.

van der Kolk, B. (1996a) 'The body keeps the score'. In B. van der Kolk, A. McFarlane and L. Weisaeth (eds) *Traumatic Stress: The Effects of Overwhelming Experience on Mind, Body and Society.* New York: The Guilford Press.

van der Kolk, B. (1996b) 'Trauma and memory'. In B. van der Kolk, A. McFarlane and L. Weisaeth (eds) *Traumatic Stress: The Effects of Overwhelming Experience on Mind, Body and Society.* New York: The Guilford Press.

van der Kolk, B. (1996d) 'The complexity of adaptation to trauma: Self-regulation, stimulus discrimination and characterological development.' In B. van der Kolk, A. McFarlane and L. Weisaeth (eds) *Traumatic Stress: The Effects of Overwhelming Experience on Mind, Body and Society.* New York: The Guilford Press.

van der Kolk, B. (1999) *PTSD Master Class.* London: Mole Conferences.

van der Kolk, B. (2000) *Integrating Basic Neuroscience and Clinical Realities: A Comprehensive Treatment Approach to Complex Post-Traumatic Stress Disorder.* Boston, MA: Boston University School of Medicine, Annual Psychological Trauma Conference in co-operation with The Trauma Center, Arbour Health System.

Verny, T. and Kelly, J. (1982) *The Secret Life of the Unborn Child.* Glasgow: Collins.

Verrier, N. (1993) *The Primal Wound.* Baltimore: Gateway Press.

Waites, E. (1993) *Trauma and Survival.* New York: Norton and Co.

Waites, E. (1997) *Memory Quest.* New York: Norton and Co.

Watkins, J. and Watkins, H. (1997) *Ego States, Theory and Therapy.* New York: Norton and Co.

Watson, K. (1997) Paper given at North American Council for Adoptable Children.

Welch, M. (1988) *Holding Time.* New York and London: Simon and Schuster.

Williams, A. (1998) *Understanding the Criminal Mind.* London: Jason Aronson.

Williams, D. (1998) *Autism and Sensing: The Unlost Instinct.* London: Jessica Kingsley Publishers Ltd.

Winnicott, D. (1971) *Playing and Reality.* New York: Basic Books.

Winnicott, D. (1984) *Deprivation and Delinquency.* London: Routledge.

Contributors

Contributors were asked to provide brief details of their life experiences that they felt particularly informed their work at Family Futures.

Caroline Archer

Concealed behind the facade of 'happy families' my traumatic childhood passed unrecognised. My healing began within a stable, adult relationship. Most of my formal therapy has been body-centred and includes several complementary approaches. With my husband I am proud to have raised four adopted children from infancy to adulthood; I also acquired a degree in social sciences along the way. My children have offered me many challenges and number amongst my greatest teachers. Their tenacity, creativity and courage have been inspirational.

Adrian Briggs

Childhood experiences of social services, including a period in care, led me to social work. As a social worker I was impressed by adoptive families' courage, tenacity and optimism. Later I became painfully aware of adoptive families struggling with little help to care for children damaged by abuse and the care system. Contact with Alan Burnell then director of the Post-Adoption Centre led to the first 'complimentary' contract between a local authority and a voluntary post-adoption society to provide post-adoption services. Since Family Futures' inception I have been glad to help with organisational development including establishing a charitable arm.

Alan Burnell

Being adopted as a baby has had a profound impact on my personal and professional life. Following my degree and social work training I was privileged to work with some very inspired practitioners, who led me to believe that it is always possible to improve services for each generation of children. My commitment to adoptive families stems from my own adoptive parents, who embodied the spirit of adoption at its best, and from the adoptive families with whom I have worked over the past years.

Christine Gordon

When my birth son was 20 years old, my husband and I adopted a highly traumatised ten-year-old boy. As a social worker I believed I was prepared for the challenges he would bring. I was soon to learn otherwise. I wrote an account of these early years under a pseudonym. Joining Adoption UK opened my eyes to the impact of attachment difficulties and early trauma and gave me the hope that I could make a positive difference in my son's life. It also helped me recognise and process traumas in my own adult life. My years of supporting adoptive families have confirmed my admiration for the parents and children who struggle with similar difficulties.

Jeanne Magagna

In my first five years I had two mothers, since we lived with my Italian grandmother, who seemed to adopt me as a daughter. When, at age five, I moved with my parents and sisters to a new house it felt like entering a new family. All the processes of experiencing the past relationship with my 'nona' and adjusting to sharing my parents with my sisters was difficult. This helped me understand some of the difficulties faced by adopted and fostered children. Subsequently I found education to be a source of security and pleasure. As an adult I trained as a psychotherapist, family therapist and adult psychotherapist at the Tavistock Clinic. Their child observation seminars profoundly influenced my respect for the difficulties and joys of parenting and of being a young child. I currently work as Consultant Child and Adolescent Psychotherapist at Great Ormond Street Hospital and Ellernmede Centre for eating disorders.

Griselda Kellie-Smith

After years of trying to hide my difficulties with learning I finally felt safe enough to attempt to untie some of the knots. With massive support and encouragement from my unruly family, I finally achieved a B.Ed as a mature student, then an MA in special education in New York, when even more mature! This was followed by invaluable teaching experience in Harlem, a diploma in dyslexia teaching and qualifying as an integrative arts psychotherapist. The courage of the children and families with whom we work is heart-stopping: that courage is a vital part of what helps us all to learn. A messy mixture of challenge, children, husband, families, grandchildren, trust, therapy, supervision, fun, play, mistakes, fear, friendship and love keeps me alive and curious.

Elsie Price

Childhood memories include the pain of watching my mother struggle with, and receive blame for, my brother's behaviour problems. As a residential social worker I experienced the 'invisibility' of the carer in other professionals' eyes. My subsequent work as a placing social worker made me aware of the trauma many children have suffered and the complex support needs of adoptive and foster families. In particular it alerted me to the degree of undisclosed maltreatment, especially of sexual abuse, that children coming into care have experienced and the stresses this 'taboo subject' places on youngsters and their substitute families.

Jay Vaughan

I grew up in a theatrical family, with my own family dramas along the way. Training as a dramatherapist provided me with the opportunity to rescript some of my personal dramas and express the inspiration that the theatre had given me. Fifteen years of working with children who have been traumatised has formed the backdrop to my belief in the need for integrated services for children and families, like those at Family Futures.

Subject Index

Author Index